Best of the Field

An insight into the duties and lives of Pennsylvania's Conservation Officers.

Editing and publishing services provided by
Gerard J. Zeidler, Jr.
for the Conservation Officers of Pennsylvania Association.

Dedication

To
the Families
of Pennsylvania's Conservation
Officers

For Their Undying Support
and
Many Sacrifices.

Acknowledgements

Special thanks to:

Marlin Adams for use of his personal archival materials.

Bob Bell, former *Game News* editor, and

Lou Hoffman, *Pennsylvania Sportsman* publisher for their advice and encouragement.

Cheryl Bodan, Game Commission librarian, for her invaluable assistance.

Guy Bowersox, Jeff Bridi and Brian Burger, Waterways Conservation Officers, for their help incorporating a few last-minute changes into this book.

Lantz Hoffman, Game Commission Information and Education Director, for his support and guidance.

Bob Mitchell, editor of *PA Game News*, and

Betsy Maughan for their answers and advice.

Brian Reed, **Michelle Watts** and **Drew Weiser** for their willingness to lend a hand when it counted most. Only you would show up at a "proofreading party!"

Bernard Schmader, Wildlife Conservation Officer and President of COPA, for the opportunity to take this project and make it work.

Nick Rosato for his artistic contributions to this publication and its promotion. What would a book of *Field Notes* be without Nick's cartoons?

Jack Weaver, PGC Regional I&E Supervisor, for the benefit of his publishing experience.

Gerard Zeidler, Sr., PGC Regional I&E Supervisor (and my dad!) for countless introductions necessary for the research and all other aspects of this book (to say nothing of the motivation he offered).

And many thanks to **all** members of COPA for their innumerable gifts to everyone who enjoys the natural resources of Pennsylvania! Without your dedication to the highest standards in conservation, Pennsylvania would be just another state.

SEND IT IN

If you have a bit of news, send it in;
Or a joke that will amuse, send it in;
A story that is true, an incident that's new;
We want to hear from you, send it in;
Never mind the style,
If the news is worth the while,
It may help or cause a smile,
Send it in!

- from the November 1929 *Monthly Service Bulletin*,
predecessor to *Pennsylvania Game News*.

Introduction

Few are fortunate enough to have the opportunity to work outdoors, and even fewer work specifically with fish and wildlife. The majority of us who love to hunt and fish, camp and boat, or just be outdoors for any reason, must be satisfied to gaze wistfully out the window - if we're lucky enough to have one - and count the days, hours and minutes until we can head for the state's woods, fields and streams.

Pennsylvania is blessed with an abundance of natural resources, and its conservation officers routinely encounter more of nature and wildlife in a single year than most of us do in an entire lifetime. For the conservation officer, his or her main office is the woods; out there among the trees; somewhere on the lakes and rivers; or on the back-country roads of this huge commonwealth.

Most of what you find on these pages has already been written, but it's doubtful there's a sportsman or conservation officer anywhere who won't thoroughly enjoy *Best of the Field*. Thoughtfully compiled from over a half-century of "Field Notes" or "Notes From the Stream," because there - on a few well-edited pages - we can perhaps connect with what it must be like to be a real, honest-to-goodness conservation officer working in the great outdoors.

Best of the Field conjures up a lot of wonderful memories for those of us who have worked in wildlife law enforcement, but it gives all outdoorspeople a closer look at hunting and fishing, and the ever-growing conservation movement in our great state. Some struggles and problems our officers were confronted with fifty years ago still remain; lots of what we thought we knew about wildlife and nature has changed, too.

When it comes to telling it like it was - and the way it is - *Best of the Field* is as good as it gets. We hope you'll enjoy reading this book, over and over, as much as we have.

Lantz A. Hoffman, Director
Bureau of Information and Education
Pennsylvania Game Commission

Foreword

As early as 1929 in the PA Game Commission and 1931 in the PA Fish Commission, there were regular monthly publications pertaining to Pennsylvania hunting, fishing and conservation. These two magazines, *Pennsylvania Game News* and *Pennsylvania Angler,* saw many changes over the years, as the emphasis of their sponsoring agencies evolved.

Since being first introduced as a regular monthly section, "Field Notes" have steadily grown in popularity in *Game News,* occupying several pages each month. The equivalent article in *Angler,* "Stream Notes", however, has been somewhat cyclic in its appearance, with years of high popularity as well as periods of little editorial notice. Fish Commission personnel are currently making an effort to increase the number of notes submitted to their editors, with hopes of stimulating the sporadically appearing "Stream Notes" into a full-blown monthly piece.

Despite the constancy of "Field Notes" and the irregularity of "Stream Notes", a common thread ties them together. Conservation efforts on the part of the Fish and Game Commissions have often addressed the same topics, and the notes quite frequently reflected this common focus. Many times, notes refer to the cooperation of the Fish Warden and the Game Protector on a patrol or other project.

In the spirit of this combined effort for the benefit of the public, the Conservation Officers of Pennsylvania Association (COPA) formed in 1993 from members of the PA Fish and Boat Commission and the PA Game Commission. COPA's members are now proud to present to you this collection of their own observations and experiences as a part of their field-work. Just as they offer the highest quality service in the capacity of Conservation Officers, now they offer to you the **Best Of The Field.** Enjoy!

Gerard J Zeidler Jr.

Chapter 1
1929-1939

During the early years of *Pennsylvania Angler* and *Pennsylvania Game News,* field officers slowly developed the habit of sending notes to the editors. At that time, both Fish and Game Commissions' main focus was on vermin control. Consequently, most of the early field notes were somewhat bland, many being of a generic format that could be summarized in one short paragraph:

"While on patrol, I observed a (insert name of vermin) attempting to kill a (insert name of fish or game species). Dispatched (vermin) and examined stomach contents. Found evidence that it had preyed upon (list at least one other game species). This predator must be controlled in order to protect these valuable game species."

The subject of most reports like this was the blacksnake, with the weasel running a close second. Yet, despite all the predator-bashing and the fact that the notes from this period are less frequent than they became in later years, field officers still had many unique incidents to report.

First Row: John Ogden, Lester Ogden, R. M. Greener, W. E. McIlnay, B. M. Carnell, Floyd Bachman, C. S. Sheldon, B. F. Barnhart, H. D. Neff, B. R. Brooks, S. F. Henderson, A. L. Walker, D. R. Davis, R. J. Womelsdorf, Clifton Iman.

Second Row: C. V. Long, G. H. James, A. S. Snyder, Wilbur Williams, Rayel Hill, Nevin LeDane, H. A. Pyle, Kenneth Aley, G. M. Noll, R. C. Bailey, H. Z. Cole, N. L. Blum, Julius Ahrens, Chas. Litwhiler, Ralph Singer.

Third Row: Harold Corbin, George Cross, A. J. Lech, M. C. Jones, Clarence Shearer, L. E. Close, F. L. Ottaway, David Dahlgren, N. W. Sickles, Keith Harter, P. D. Wilcox, C. B. Baughman, L. E. Cloos, H. F. Reynolds, J. H. Banning, J. A. Schadt, Jr., C. A. Bidelspacher.

Bears 'Round The Clock

While at my desk one afternoon taking care of some much neglected paper work, I answered the telephone to hear an excited woman's voice say, "Is this you Mr. Marsh? Well, two bears have my two sons up an apple tree in the orchard. My God: what can I do? I'm here all alone?" I knew this woman's sons were about twelve and fourteen years of age, and knew they were in no danger as long as they were in the tree. I said "If you have a gun and can shoot it, just fire a couple of shots and it will scare the bears away, and I will come up as quickly as possible."

To get to this particular farm I had about five miles of rough road, very crooked, and a ten percent grade. I reached the home in about fifteen minutes and found the boys in the house, and they told me the following story:

While picking apples, they had climbed a tree to shake down the remaining apples, and while thus employed were much surprised to see a small cub waddle up under the tree and start eating apples. They had quite a time throwing apples to the bear and were still more surprised when the old bear joined the cub in the free lunch. About this time, the boys' mother discovered the situation and to her, things did not appear so funny, and resulted in the call I received.

A few days later, I had an opportunity to talk to the boys' father and asked him if the bears had been seen since. He said, "Yes, they've eaten a hell of a lot of my apples, but I don't want them disturbed."

It seems rather strange, but I had just finished writing to you and sealed the letter when I had a call from the engine repair shop at Emporium Junction, that there were two bear cubs up a tree near the shop. This is in the borough and about 500 yards from

3

my home. I went down immediately and found two nice cubs up a South Carolina Poplar and the mother about 100 feet to one side. I walked up to within 25 feet of the old bear before she walked off. I then dispersed the crowd to give the cubs a chance to join the mother bear. The cubs are in the tree while I am writing this. I am now going to seal this letter and go see how things are going.

Time: ten minutes to twelve P.M.

P.S. Time: 1:00 A.M. Got the cubs out of the tree. When I went back another crowd had collected and three young fellows, half soused, were stoning the cubs. Dispersed the crowd and sat in the house and watched mother bear come and rear up against the tree and whine. The cubs immediately came down.

-- Cecil Marsh, Emporium.

November 1929.

Black Sheep

Sometime ago I came in possession of a young grey fox about three days old. I fed him on a bottle for one day. Then a friend of mine, who has a female rat terrier with puppies about the same age as the fox, called at my home and we put the fox with the puppies. Whether or not we fooled the mother dog we do not know, but she is taking the best of care of our young fox, and he seems to enjoy it immensely.

-- Archie Smith, Schuylkill County.

June 1930.

Caught In The Act

Some few days ago while endeavoring to catch some dogs running deer on Tuscarora Mountain, I was just getting in good range of the dogs when I heard a very queer noise just across a small ravine. Very quietly I approached the spot from whence the noise came and upon coming closer, I discovered a large pole cat [skunk] dashing furiously back and forth and apparently showing fight. A few steps closer revealed that the duel was between a big mountain grouse and a pole cat mother and her family of six small black cats. My presence did not disturb either of the battlers until I closed in a few feet from the battle. I discovered that the cat had attacked a grouse sitting on eleven eggs and had succeeded in eating or breaking seven of the eggs. The remainder were being protected by the mother grouse, and I assure you it was a real battle.

During this time of battle the deer chase was still in progress and thinking the noise caused by shooting the pole cat would spoil the chase, I decided to break up the cat and grouse fight with a fair sized club which worked perfectly. I never once thought of the resistance the cat might offer until I made the first blow; then the second blow was purely by random as I was totally blind from the effect of about one pint of real perfume straight in the face. When I regained my sight my next thought was the dog which had passed close by during my time of blindness. In the course of an hour the chase came back up the mountain and to my surprise the dog was reinforced by another dog, but the reinforcement did not enjoy much of the chase as he was interrupted by an 8 M.M. I then proceeded on the chase only to travel about one mile when I heard something similar to an 8 M.M. which proved to be an interested sportsman endeavoring to put an end to the deer dogs in this community. Neither dog had any marks of identification.
-- Noah Hertzler, Deputy Game Protector, Port Royal.
June 1930.

Ignorance Is Bliss

An interesting report from Deputy Game Protector Edmund D. Groff of Worthington, Pa. reached the Game Commission recently It stated that during a recent forest fire in Armstrong County a Ruffed Grouse's nest with 11 eggs was discovered. Upon seeing that the fire would soon destroy the nest Mr. Groff removed the entire nest, wrapping it in his vest and carrying it to safety. After the fire had been extinguished, he placed the nest where it had formerly been. The next day he returned and found that the grouse was back on the nest as though nothing had happened.
June 1930.

Match This One

Alligator hunters generally trek to Florida for their sport, but Howard Carey, of Wilson Borough, bags his reptiles in the Lehigh River. Carey was rowing in the vicinity of Island Park near Easton, when he saw a four foot 'gator sunning itself on the surface of the water. With a well directed bullet from his .22 cal. rifle he put the finishing touches to the reptile. The question now is; where did the alligator come from? The place where this alligator was killed is a horseshoe shaped out of the lower end of the Island and is one of the best pickerel and bass fishing places near Easton. The popular opinion as to the origin of the alligator is that someone had it as a pet and it got away. The bottom there is all soft mud and would afford a likely place for it to hibernate during the winter.
-- Fish Warden Joel Young, Fullerton.
December 1931.

Pairs Off Trout

While stocking trout in the North Fork, I was at the truck draining water out of the cans, and the men were stationed at one hundred yard intervals on the stream. Attention was centered on one of the men. The process of stocking was slowed up to such an extent that I was called to ask them what the trouble was. They answered that they were waiting for a signal to start stocking. I then saw the leader of the group carefully remove two trout and release them. Presently, however, something seemed to block the process. "Hey Warden," one of them shouted, "better come down here. We need you. We're trying to stock these trout in pairs, and we don't know which are the males and which are the females."

-- Fish Warden Donald Zeitler, Punxsutawney.
January 1932.

Kamikaze Bunny

About three years ago I was gunning up near Gardenville, Pa., with my father and two brothers. Our dog was running a rabbit around the bottom of a hill when my youngest brother scared up another. This rabbit ran down the hill, bumping into the dog. The dog jumped and let out a yelp and the rabbit fell, but got up again and ran under the dog's stomach. The dog started after the rabbit but was so excited he did not know what to do so we lost both rabbits.

-- Russell E. Fitzgerald, Deputy Game Protector, Ardsley
May 1932.

Shoes Come Second

A McKeesport woman seeking a divorce has given 58 reasons why she and her husband should be separated. One of the reasons, alleges the applicant for a separation, is that instead of buying their baby a pair of shoes he bought a hunting license and went hunting. Married men who are hunters take notice-buy the baby a pair of shoes first.
June 1932.

One Of Those Days

A few days ago, while fishing in the high and swift waters of Lick Run, Clinton Co., I hooked on to a nice trout. While trying to land said trout, I lost my balance, and in righting myself, my line got fastened to my deputy badge. After loosening my badge to unfasten line, I did, what I mean, lose my balance right. I got out O.K. after which I retrieved my rod and line, but as far as the trout and badge are concerned, they are still somewhere in Lick Run. May I have another badge?
--G. J. Rathgeber, Deputy Protector, Lock Haven.
June 1932.

Grouse Headwork

William Taylor, an assistant superintendent of Cook Forest, Clarion County, and his helpers on a road building job found two grouse nests in fairly close proximity. One of them was ten yards to one side of the road under the uplifted roots of a maple tree, the other on the opposite side under the end of a log, both in plain view.

The bird under the maple stood for the road construction work without flinching, but after several days the bird under the log decided to move.

Mr. Taylor observed her walking away from the nest with a peculiar hunched-up shuffling gait. She went to a point about twenty yards away, then returned, sat upon her old nest, shuffled her wings, and again moved off in the same peculiar manner to the nest site.

After watching this performance for more than an hour, and the visits to the old nest stopped, an examination showed that all the eggs were gone from under the log and that they were snugly reposing in the new location.

This observer believes the eggs were tucked up under the wings, a few at a trip, and moved. Who said grouse aren't smart?

August 1932.

Went For Reinforcements

The story is being told that on a certain farm the wild pheasants developed the habit of coming into the barn yard and feeding with the domestic poultry. One morning an old gander attacked the only pheasant present at the time and succeeded in thoroughly licking him.

The pheasant cock beat a retreat across fields with bloody head and bedraggled tail feathers - that is, the few tail feathers left after the battle. But, much to the surprise of the farmer, the next morning Mr. Defeated Pheasant of the preceding day came marching back to the barnyard followed by five other cock pheasants. On the yard the leader marched around the gander flapping his wings, stamping his feet, and in every way challenging the gander to try it again. Mr. Gander rashly accepted the challenge, whereupon the five reinforcements joined their leader and proceeded to give the gander the thrashing of his life, and apparently would have been killed if the owner had not rescued him.

August 1933.

9

Whose Fault Is It, Anyway?

Game Protector Leslie H. Wood says that W. Fischler, of Wellsboro, has a good case against the Game Commission or the Fish Commission or both. He hung his fish basket on the back porch and when he went to get it a few days later a wren flew out of it. He opened the cover and there was the nest with five eggs.

He says jokingly, of course, that since Wrens are protected birds, he dare not disturb the nest, therefore either the Game Commission will have to get him a new basket or the Fish Commission refund the money he spent for a license.

In the meantime the wren is sitting on five eggs in perfect safety, as Mr. Fischler has nailed the basket fast so no one can take it down and disturb the bird.
August 1933.

Trout Got Away, Snake Didn't

While draining a dam on Coldstream with Game Protector Elmer Pillings, I saw a big watersnake catch a 14-inch trout within a few feet me. When we approached the breast of the dam, we saw the watersnake which measured about two feet, slide into the water. A moment later, we saw a commotion under one of the willows fringing the stream. Pillings reached into the water and dragged the snake out by its tail. It was clinging like a bulldog to a big trout, refusing to relinquish its prey until completely out of the water. The audacity of this particular snake was amazing.
Special Fish Warden T.R. Griffith, Phillipsburg.
February 1934.

No Respect

Deputy Tom Hoffman reports a deer having jumped against the side of his car at night, knocking itself semi-conscious. When Mr. Hoffman got out and touched the animal with his foot it bounded off into a field. He wished to determine the extent of the injury to the deer and turned his flashlight on it. The deer immediately jumped and struck him, almost knocking him to the ground, and then ran off, apparently no worse off than Mr. Hoffman, who was somewhat bruised up.
-- Refuge Keeper Isaac Baumgardner.
January 1935.

Of Bucks and Antlers

Game Protector Clarence Moss, Wyoming County, reports the following incidents during the past deer season: A party of deer hunters found eleven different antlers in one day while driving.

A chap named Zurcheski shot at a buck and knocked him down. The buck fell but got up and disappeared in the brush. In falling the animal lost both antlers. which the hunter picked up. Zurcheski followed the deer trail for a couple of hours and then lost his way. Darkness being near at hand, he spent the night in an old barn. It was a very cold night and the next morning a Game Protector found him with his trophy dangling from his belt. After an hour at one of the Game Commission's cabins the hunter was fed, warmed and put on the right path.

Deputy Smith, of Alderson, while on a stand watching for deer spotted a nice buck coming leisurely toward him. The animal had but one antler, a nice five pointer.

Waiting to get a better shot Smith let the deer come closer. Soon it passed behind a small clump of hemlock trees. The hunter waited for a good five minutes and then out stepped a doe. Smith had been on that stand for over an hour but he had not seen any does about. After the doe had passed out of sight Smith got suspicious, went down to the clump of trees, and sure enough there lay the five point antler.

A hunter reported to have shot a 27 point (both antlers), 140 lb. buck near Loyalville, Luzerne County, during the past season. The deer was in very poor condition and had in its ear a steel tag with a date twenty years old.

Weston Ruff, of Noxen, shot a buck in Monroe Township, Wyoming County, that had six points to each antler but weighed only eighty pounds
April 1935.

Some Lifeguard

It is a well-known fact that squirrels migrate, according to food and other conditions, but whether they actually swim streams has no doubt been the subject of many a lively debate among sportsmen at the old camp fire. This question was conclusively answered for me recently when I had the following interesting experience:

On Saturday afternoon, August 24, 1935, while fishing, I was standing in the middle of the Conodoguinet Creek near Hogestown, Cumberland County. An occasional splash in various directions attracted my attention as the fish leaped in feeding. Suddenly a small animal appeared to my right, swimming rapidly on the surface of the water. I recognized it at once as a red squirrel, its head and bright brown back plainly visible on top of the water. All four feet were paddling rapidly as he swam directly across the current toward the left bank He was making good progress, holding his head well above the water.

As he approached me, he growled and chattered angrily, but never altered his course nor slowed his pace. He swam right under my rod, not five feet away from my hand, evidently recognizing me with confidence as a member of the "Bureau of Protection."

I watched as he swam through the deeper water, around four feet at places. When he reached the bank, he scampered up quickly, shook himself thoroughly, chattered some more, and disappeared among the heavy foliage.
-- Chas. M.. Stambaugh, Head Game Protection Clerk.
October 1935.

Fighting Fire With Fire

Citizens of Abington, Pa., struck upon a good plan to rid the community of skunks when they routed seven of the animals by the use of tear gas.
May 1936.

Why Do They Do It?

On the first day of the bass season, we conducted a car search on Pine Creek. Two fellows came down and when I looked at their creels, I thought "here is a story for the *Angler*." They each had three black bass from 16 to 19 inches in length, five that ran from 12 to 15 inches and several nice rock bass apiece. But in the bottom of the basket of each fisherman was a black bass measuring less than 8 inches in length which spoiled the story. I prosecuted both of them with pleasure.
-- Fish Warden C. A. Bidelspacher, Williamsport.
January 1937.

Communication Gap

A Game Warden approached a party of five deer hunters in the Poconos who were gathered around a fire. After establishing his identity he asked to see their licenses. They seemed to be in order, so he asked "Who is the captain?" A big lad piped out "Me Capitan, Mister, me Capitan." The Warden then asked "Where is your roster?" To which, the captain replied "Me no got rozzter, Mister, me got sedan."
-- Richard H. Lentz
February 1938.

Sometimes You Get Lucky

On December 21 at 8 P. M. I delivered a report to Deputy Game Protector J. R. McLure, New Castle. I was only in his home about seven minutes but when I came out some one had stolen a chest out of my car in which I kept my .38 pistol, handcuffs, blackjack, field glasses, Kodak [camera], shells, field receipt book, etc. The car was locked. I found the crooks' tracks in the snow and followed them up through a field and out onto another street where one of them fell and lost his driver's license. I called the police and we started looking for the one who lost the license. About 1:00 A. M. we chased them out the Eastbrook Road and caught them. They did not have the stuff with them but after some persuasion they took me where they had hidden the things they were keeping to sell. They threw the chest and contents they didn't want into the Shenango River about a mile above the harbor. The river was high, the chest wooden (and floated) so I kissed it good-bye. Thursday, the 30th, I got a call from Fred Green who lives about a mile below the Harbor, saying that his son found my chest in their field where the river had washed it. Of course everything was ruined and a couple of envelopes with material in had been washed away. By strange coincidence the boy who found the chest was a young lad only 14 years old who I saw shoot at a ringneck hen the past season. I gave him quite a little talk at the time but did not prosecute on account of his age and because his father's and uncle's land is always open to hunting. They say "Cast your bread upon the waters and it shall return after many days," only this was a chest.

-- Frank L. Coen, Game Protector, Lawrence County.
March 1938.

Rescue

While working at Douglasville, H. L. Moyer, of Leesport, observed a crow suddenly alight on the ground. When Corvus took off he had a small rabbit in his claws. Mr. Moyer succeeded in causing the crow to drop the rabbit by throwing sticks and stones. After the crow disappeared the old mother rabbit arrived and took charge of her young one.

August 1938.

Just Ducks Her Head

I recently heard of an interesting case of a ringneck hen nesting between the rails of a trolley track. A car passes this point about every 20 minutes, but the hen never moves from the nest and the car passes directly over her. I checked on this information and found it to be correct. The nest was located a short distance out of Quakertown between the rails of the Lehigh Valley Transit Co.

-- E. W. Flexer, Traveling Game Protector, Bucks County.

August 1938.

Rough Day For This Deer

William E. Johnson, Sunbury, was motoring near Weikert recently when he encountered a six-foot blacksnake coiled around a young buck deer.

Halting his car, Johnson battled the snake until it released the buck, which was lying apparently dead along the road. The snake finally crawled into the woods.

Johnson picked up what he believed was the carcass of the young deer, placed it in his car and started toward Sunbury to report to Game Protector Bruce Yeager. As he proceeded along the highway the animal suddenly revived and created furor in the rear of Johnson's car. It was with difficulty that he succeeded in keeping the deer from battering out the windows of the car until he arrived at the home of Yeager, who assisted in overpowering and removing the deer from the car.

August 1938.

Aid and Litter Team

On June 24, 1938 while bicycling on Route No. 522, one half mile south of Fort Littleton in Fulton County, Messrs. Ralph McCoy and Gilbert Colledge both of Fort Littleton saw four half grown skunks in the side ditch of the road. One was apparently injured. Two of the others would squeeze in from each side of the injured one and lift it clear from the ground. The fourth one pushed from the rear with its head and in this manner the procession proceeded up the bank and out of sight to a place of safety. Another example of nature's methods of aiding one of her kind when in distress.

-- William Lane, Traveling Game Protector.

September 1938.

Glutton

On Sunday, September 18, while patrolling for pre-season squirrel shooters I came upon a very peculiar feast. A small garter snake had succeeded in catching a large toad and was starting the difficult task of devouring it. The snake was about eighteen inches long and the diameter of the body was no greater than the size of a man's forefinger. However, the snake managed to stretch and enlarge the front part of its body to a much greater size. Very slowly the toad was devoured. After one hour of very strenuous work the snake had succeeded in getting the toad swallowed until nothing could be seen but the mouth and eyes. At this point, I interfered by striking the snake over the back. With little persuasion it gave up its meal and the still alive and much puzzled toad hopped away.

-- Refuge Keeper Raymond M. Sickles, Fayette County.
November 1938.

Headgear

I went to the home of Mr. Bailer on November 20 to interview him concerning a deer reported seen in that vicinity with a wire cylinder covering its head. The wire cylinder, approximately 9 inches in diameter and 14 inches long, was evidently forced over the deer's head when it attempted to browse on flower plants encircled by the cylinder. Spikes about three inches long helped to make it secure. This deer was reported seen for approximately two weeks, and seemed to be getting along fairly well as the cylinder, open at both ends was forced back in line with the nostrils.

-- Refuge Keeper Gilbert Bowman, Lackawanna County.
January 1939.

Jackpot

While training my bird dog on Farm Game Refuge No. 1, he came to a point. Upon investigation I found that he had pointed a black snake about five and one half feet long, which was swallowing a quail. After killing the snake I cut it open to find a rabbit about two-thirds grown. Can any of the readers tell me what my dog scented - snake, quail or rabbit?

-- Newton McDowell, Deputy Game Protector, Chester County.
April 1939.

Now That's Service

Too many deer left on Game Lands 12 and 36. They are eating pine seedlings as fast as they are planted. In fact one WPA crew was planting Bank Pine and in looking behind them saw deer following and eating the seedlings as they were planted.
--Refuge Keeper Walter Zellers, Bradford County.
June 1939

Reward

A very interesting incident was observed on May 1. While on weekend leave, I stopped in to visit old friends at the Honesdale Sub-Station of Motor Police. Two of the Officers just arrived, after apprehending a car load of gypsies, charged with theft. In searching the auto used by the gypsies, they discovered a live grouse, apparently unharmed, except that its wings and feet were securely tied. The bird was brought in the Station, untied and placed in a box. Apparently as though in gratitude for being thus relieved of its shackles, the bird promptly laid an egg. The Motor Police called Game Protector Maynard Miller, Wayne County, and grouse and gypsies were turned over to him for further action.
-- Division Game Supervisor Rollin Heffelfinger, Div. G, Westmoreland County.
July 1939.

18

Disturbing The Peace

I investigated a report of wildcats bothering a fisherman from Crawford County while on the Farnsworth Creek and found that the hideous sounds heard were caused by two amorous porcupines. No wildcats or their tracks have been seen in this section since 1927.

--Refuge Keeper John Hopkins, Warren County.

July 1939.

Unstuck

Last week a farmer reported the following to me:

While plowing he noticed something peculiar in the adjoining field. Upon investigation he found a groundhog with a tin can, one about the size of a medium soup can, forced over part of its head and covering its eyes. It would move forward slowly until it touched something then back around and start in another direction. With some difficulty the farmer was able to remove the can by cutting off the lid which had been forced inside. By the impression left on its head he thought the can had been on for several days. He was unable to tell what had originally been in the can.

-- Game Protector John S. Shuler, Armstrong County.

July 1939.

Tough Ruff

Refuge Keeper Fuller Coffin, Erie and Crawford County, reports that a WPA worker, while assisting on the construction of a fire lane on Game Lands No. 101 Erie County was half scared to death by repeated attacks of a mother grouse. He was grubbing the lane when the grouse flew out of the brush straight at his face. It made several such attacks then settled in the lane and tried to coax him away from the spot. Other workers came up and upon looking around discovered the young birds.
August 1939.

Next, The English Channel

On Sunday, May 7, 1939, Mr. Howard Jones, Philipsburg, and James Tuba, Brisbin, were enjoying a boat ride on Black Moshannon dam when they noticed a woodchuck that apparently was trying to swim across the dam and became exhausted. The first thing it came to was their boat whereupon it promptly climbed aboard, sat on the front end, and accompanied them to shore. This incident was witnessed by Mr. Cletus Kephart, Hardware merchant of Philipsburg, who told it to me.
-- Elmer J. Turner, Game Protector, Centre County.
August 1939.

It's Not Polite To Play With Your Food

While visiting Refuge No 508, supervised by George W. Koehler, the other day he told me about a pet chipmunk that would swing on an ear of corn in his back yard. The corn was fastened just high enough that the little fellow had to reach on its legs for it, and after he had eaten as high as possible he would crawl up to the top, and work downward. In the latter operation, however, he would sometimes forget to hold on with one of his front feet,and in his greediness try to stuff both pouches at the same time, consequently he would fall to the ground head first. Then he would get mad and jump at the cob and hang on, swinging back and forth like a child at play.

-- Leo A. Luttringer, Editor, PA Game News.
August 1939.

Bad Bruin

A 400-pound black bear operating in the vicinity of Little Bear Creek and Red Ridge Creek, 15 miles northeast of Williamsport, was reported recently to be terrorizing early summer campers of that locality.

Local game protectors received three complaints since May 28 of attacks the bear has made upon cottagers. In every case the animal was interrupted while raiding cabin refrigerators.

Guy Wheeland, Williamsport, camping near the mouth of Little Bear Creek, was the first to sight the large animal. It drank four quarts of milk and stole a four-pound beef steak after tearing out an ice box he had buried in the ground.

On Memorial Day, it threatened Russel Woolever, tearing off a screen door in its attempt to rush him.

Sunday morning, its activities at the cabin of Police Captain Joseph M. Schumucker, Williamsport, aroused that officer and his family. The captain surprised the animal at the refrigerator, fired a revolver at it and was then chased by the bear. He escaped only by darting into the cabin door.
August 1939.

Crossing Guard

Recently while coming over Tussey Mountain from Pine Grove Mills, toward McAlevys Fort, Vernon J. Dietz, of Huntingdon, encountered a wild turkey hen leading her flock of 10 young across the highway. The way was blocked for some time by obliging motorists who stopped to watch the proceedings. The hen stood in the middle of the road and clucked her offspring across one at a time. As each small bird passed the mother she gave it a nudge toward safety with her wing. After all were safely over she followed and the motorists proceeded on their way:

-- Wm. J. Davis, Division Game Supervisor, Huntingdon.
September 1939.

Chapter 2
1940-1949

During the years surrounding World War II, *Game News* and *Angler* reflected the patriotism and sense of national unity sportsmen displayed by willingly contributing empty shells to scrap drives, raw furs to be made into gloves for servicemen overseas, conserving fuel by carpooling to the field, and by increasing conservation efforts to ensure that their colleagues would have something valuable waiting for them when they returned.

The frequency of Field Note and Stream Note publication increased, and both magazines began to establish solid identities. Although many articles and photoessays still urged sportsmen to control the population of vermin, fewer of the notes printed regarded the issue, as the years passed. By the mid-forties, regular monthly columns featured more and more notes from Game Protectors and Fish Wardens. Because of the quantity of submissions, the editors of *Game News* and *Angler* could afford to be somewhat more selective with the notes they would publish. As a result, the notes increased in quality and in the level of interest to the readers.

Smart One

Game in Somerset County is apparently getting educated, at least to the point of being able to read. While patrolling in Addison Township last week I saw a grey squirrel sitting on a large oak tree about three feet below a sign reading, "No Hunting Allowed."

-- Game Protector Nicholas Ruha, Somerset County.
January 1940.

Teaching Him The Ropes

Recently Mr. Ralph I. Buffet, of Berwyn, Chester County, was out crow hunting with his .22 rifle, which is equipped with a four power telescope sight. He saw a young crow in a tree, but there were so many leaves that he could not see it clearly enough to shoot. While he was watching it an old crow came along and, cawing furiously, circled the young crow. The youngster flew only a few feet, and lit on a dead branch in full view. Mr. Buffet moved his rifle and was sighting on the young bird which he saw clearly through his telescope sight. The old crow flew over toward the young one and, just before it reached it, folded its wings and dove into the youngster, knocking it off of the branch. Then, still cawing furiously, it fluttered right in back of the young one until it had herded it safely away from the vicinity of Mr. Buffet. The hunter was so interested in the performance that he did not shoot.

-- Wilbur KIapp Jr., Deputy Game Protector, Chester County.
September 1940.

Lost Their Map
On Friday evening, August 30, 1940, while working on Game Lands No. 97, near the Black Valley Church, I noticed large numbers of nighthawks flying about; evidently, they were migrating. The peculiar thing was that the birds were flying northward. At any time, at least 50 birds could be seen darting about, all flying in a northerly direction. A few nights later any number of birds could be seen flying around, but they seemed to be flying nowhere in particular.
-- Albert R. Bachman, Game Protector, Bedford County.
November 1940.

Happy Anniversary
On July 4, 1939, I discovered a robin caught in a neighbor's garden. It was caught in a wire put up for peas to grow on. When I went to release it I found it was banded, so I sent the bird in to Washington. When I got an answer I was told that the robin was banded in the same place five years before, and in the same month in which I found it.
-- Donald Gomer, Lititz.
November 1940.

Clowning Around

There is a certain bear around one of my refuges that persists in tearing down the boards and metal signs. If he feels so inclined, he may follow along a wire and destroy as many as twelve in twenty-four hours. I have often heard the bear called "the clown of the woods", and while this may seem funny to the bear, it certainly does not to me.
-- John A. Hopkins, Game Protector, Warren County.
January 1941.

Finicky Eater

While coming to work one morning one of the men on project work in Huntingdon County saw two rabbits sitting along the road, seemingly sick or hurt. On going by them he found that they had been hit by a car. He was able to pick both up, but one died a few minutes later. The other one was taken home and nursed back to good condition. This rabbit now is comparatively tame, and has developed a taste for milk and bread. If apple parings are placed before it with bread and milk, it will always eat the bread and milk, and not touch the apples.
-- Ross G. Metz, Land Management Protector, Huntingdon County.
March 1941.

Split Personality

I observed a ringneck pheasant floating on the water like an old Mallard duck. While releasing pheasants near the inlet of Edinboro Lake, one of the birds walked out of the crate, followed the creek bank to a low plank bridge and jumped into a quiet pool of water under it. It then proceeded to sit there, floating lazily about on the water, thinking it was hiding from us.

-- F.H. Coffin, Game Protector, Erie County.
July 1941.

Learned the Hard Way

Sometimes it doesn't pay to be too "cocky". The ringneck that has been living on Overbrook Road in Dallas Township, found that out recently. It seems the baker truck that passed every morning made him very angry and he was wont to expel his pent up wrath by trying to puncture the tires with his bill and chasing the truck down the road about a quarter of a mile every morning for the past couple of months. The other day he was in fine form. He pecked and ran with more gusto than ever. The baker truck was making him awfully mad. Then he took to wing, made a circle from the rear of the truck, and flew right into the windshield. Result: a broken glass and a broken neck.

-- Samuel K. Weigel, Game Protector, Luzerne County.
October 1941.

Vandal Bruin

Some time ago, a black bear entered the Refuge, clawed up a few signs and scratched up a few trees, then dismantled the driver's seat on a bulldozer and chewed off the pressure hose.

-- George Koehler, Game Protector, Lycoming County.
November 1941.

Magic Lure?

In December one day about noon, while on routine patrol in the vicinity of Laurel Summit, Westmoreland County, my attention was attracted by shooting. I started in the direction of the shots and soon met a hunter leaving the woods. Upon my inquiry about the shooting, he stated that "some fool was shooting at a mark."

I hurried in the direction of voices I heard. As I climbed a hill toward a group I could now see, I stopped in amazement and began to wonder if my eyes were deceiving me. There was a group of five hunters with a doe standing docilely among them; two of the group had their arms around its neck. A short distance away was a small fawn, not quite as tame as its mother, and another hunter trying to get closer to it. This hunter had a rock in his hand and was taking the stance of a baseball pitcher about to put a "Dizzy Dean" third strike across the plate. He appeared to be so intent in his endeavor that I really think he meant to kill the fawn. I called to him not to injure the animal unless he was prepared to pay a hundred dollar fine. He immediately dropped the rock and started to walk away. I went up to him and questioned him about his actions and checked his license certificate.

We then went back to join the other men. They were seated on a fallen log, the deer nosing at their backs and at their pockets. I asked them to tell me the secret of being able to find deer in the woods that would eat out of their hands. They said the deer had just wandered up to them; they couldn't explain their presence nor could they understand it. They were as puzzled as I was. They got quite a kick out of it, and had and had taken two rolls of pictures. One fellow explained that he had fed them his entire lunch.

The question of who was guilty of the "shooting at random" was soon settled. The fellow who tried to "throw a strike" at the fawn was the guilty person. He was hunting alone and not a member of the party of five. He had been trying to cut an upper limb from a dead tree with a 12 gauge pumpkin ball, never realizing the danger that existed with the woods so full of hunters. Needless to say he paid for his carelessness.

Later in the day, I learned the source of the tame deer. They had escaped from a roadside menagerie nearby early in the fall.

--Robert D. Parlaman, Game Protector, District G-11.
April 1942.

Happy In High Water

On the morning of May 23, 1942, I was advised that flood conditions had hit Hawley, Honesdale, and towns between.

Several people on Milford bridge informed us that a body was coming down on a log; it turned out to be a large beaver riding down the flooded river, unconcernedly oiling himself or, as one bystander put it, "washing his face."

-- John H. Lohmann, District Game Protector, Pike County.
July 1942.

Mother Knew Best

We had a forest fire on the west side of the Pine Creek Gorge, about one-half mile north of Refuge No. 516-B. This is a very good bear section and while Fire Wardens C. Butler and Bert Davis were trying to get back on top of the rim from Pine Creek by way of Four Mile Run, they saw an old bear and one cub coming down to the stream just ahead of them. The bear looked at the wardens and then waded across the water, about two feet deep, after starting the cub across a hemlock tree about 5 inches in diameter that had fallen across the stream. The cub walked out on the tree to where the limbs started to branch out and stopped there. The mother came back across the stream and started the cub out on the leaning tree again, but each time for three times the cub would go to the branches and stop there. The fourth time the mother came to the middle of the stream, she reached up her full length and got the cub by the neck, gave him a good shaking, carried him to the bank away from the fire, gave him a good hard cuff and went up the steep mountain to Colton Point.

Each time the old bear crossed the stream, she would look at the wardens, snarl and snap her teeth. These men stood about 100 feet downstream from the bears and it took about 15 minutes for the animals to get across.

-- Game Protector Hugh E. Baker, Division C, District 2.
August 1942.

Big Mistake

Jim Williams, of Matamoras, foreman of the Rockland Light and Power Company, observed a Red-shouldered Hawk alight on the 11,000 volt line and reach over to a cross arm to wipe his bill. Result: A flash of light, a fried hawk, and the high line out for ten minutes, or until the hawk was thoroughly fried and dropped off the line.

-- Game Protector John Lohmann, District No.7, Division B.

October 1942.

Murphy's Fish & Game Law

On the evening of September 15, Deputy Peter Zikowsky was fishing plugs from the shores of Brady's Lake. After a futile three hours of fishing without a strike, Mr. Zikowsky was on the verge of giving up for the day. On the final cast his plug became detached from the line and fell some forty yards offshore. It was a Surf-Oreno, costing $1.25, riding the ripples of the chilly waters. Being a new and rather successful plug, "Pete" decided to undress and rescue it. Wading into the cold water up to his neck he was soon within a few yards of it when a good sized bass broke water and disappeared with one dollar and twenty-five cents worth of timber. Neither bass nor plug was seen again.

-- Game Protector Paul L. Failor, Division B.

December 1942.

Moved In

While traveling through Great Bend Township, Susquehanna County, I was told by a farmer that some funny type of a little duck had taken up quarters with his flock of tame ducks. He also asked me to look at the duck and possibly identify it for him.

Investigation proved it to be a mature male wood duck apparently in good health. When approaching the flock it made no effort to escape other than walk away with the tame ducks. During the day, it would spend its time on the pond with the other ducks. At night, it would return to the buildings with the flock.

-- Game Protector H. F. Hoffman, District 4, Division B.

March 1943.

Knew Karate?

While trapping rabbits for restocking, I caught a rabbit and a small white weasel in one of the box traps. The rabbit had evidently killed the weasel, and the rabbit seemed unhurt. The same thing happened to one of my agents by the name of Kroft, except both the rabbit and the weasel were alive.

-- Game Protector Frank E. Crouse, District 10, Division E.
April 1943.

Houdini

We had a funny one happen with a skunk in a box trap. An agent found the skunk when he checked the traps early in the morning. He left it there and called me to help get it out of the trap. We arrived there about noon. To our surprise the trap was empty. There were no other footprints around the trap, and the trap had not been moved by any other person. We are positive there was a skunk in the trap. Yet the trap was empty, the door open and on the wire, and the treadle ready to spring the door shut.

-- Game Protector Clair W. Dinger, District 2, Division F.
April 1943.

Unexpected Guest

I had a peculiar complaint this week. A school teacher living away from her home except weekends found, upon her return, that a ringneck hen had flown through a large window without injury and by the evidence had spent the entire week roosting on her davenport. She or her father asked $10.00 for window repair and damage.
-- Vern A. VanOrder, District 1, Division F.
July 1943.

Sbould've Known Better

Heard a report of a family on the east side of the city who, when they found a skunk in their cellar, closed all the exits and put their dog after said skunk. The last report I heard still had them living with the neighbors.
-- Game Protector Clair W. Dinger, District 2, Division F.
August 1943.

Sounds Like Antlers, Anyway

My five year old son, Billy, after seeing a young fawn and thinking it was the cutest thing, said "Dad, how old will it be before it has anchors on its head?"
-- Game Protector W. T. Campbell, District 10, Division F.
August 1943.

32

The Bravery of Being Out of Range

While conducting a car check station in French Creek Township during the deer season I was listening to a group of nimrods bemoaning their luck, when suddenly a buck deer bounded across the highway barely missing being hit by a car and ran into a fence. Picking itself up, it leisurely walked across a large field, stopping now and again to look back at the surprised nimrods as if defying them to shoot because he was in a refuge and had the protection of six Game Protectors.

-- W. T. Campbell, Game Protector, District 10, Division F.
February 1944.

Still Don't Believe In Fate?

On January 1, 1944, a young trapper living in Springfield Township, Fayette County, met with an unusual experience. A fresh snow having fallen he decided to set out to do some prospecting on trapping. Eventually he came to a mink track which led him to a large rock, under which he found several holes. He immediately began to set some traps around the rock. By the time he had completed setting his traps, and came around to where he had set the first one, he was very much surprised to find Mr. Mink in it. After securing a stick, he hit it over the head and put it in his hunting coat, resetting his trap again. He then proceeded on his way. Having gone but a short distance, he realized the mink had come to life again. By the time he had gotten his coat off, the animal had found a hole and jumped out, running in the direction from whence it came. By the time the lad got back to the rock, Mr. Mink had gotten himself caught in the same trap again. This time the trapper made sure it was dead before he put it in his hunting coat.

-- Game Protector Lester Sheaffer, District G-14.
March 1944.

Was He Carrying An Easter Basket?

I received a call from a lady in Clark's Summit who was quite excited and I don't blame her. She reported seeing a purple squirrel in her yard and she fed it some peanuts and claims that two or three other friends saw the same thing at that time. She told me that the squirrel was all purple and that the tail was beautiful. Since purple is worn very freely at this time, she is of the opinion that the squirrel is modeling that color for this spring. I asked her what brand she was taking, and she informed me that the only thing she was drinking was hard water from the faucet in her home. I informed her that I had heard of pink elephants, etc. but never heard of purple squirrels and advised her that I would try and trap it some day in the future and put it on display to clear up any doubt that people might have regarding the story. It looks to me that due to the scarcity of rabbits people are resorting to Easter Squirrels instead of Easter Bunnies.

-- Game Protector Francis E. Jenkins, District B-5.
May 1944.

Take Off

During the evening of April 10 and for approximately a week or ten days thereafter, I had the opportunity of watching several woodcock go through their seasonal singing flights. These woodcock would raise in flight as near vertically as possible to a great height and then start descending almost straight down in a sharp zig-zagging flight. At the same time chattering and singing all the way, always alighting on approximately the same spot. I watched them make a dozen of these flights in about as many minutes and they kept up this exhausting pace even after it had become totally dark. They made a flight on the average of every minute and one half during the time I watched them.
-- Howard Hoffman, L.M.O., Susquehanna County.
July 1944.

Buzz Cut

On May 10 while checking over damage done by a forest fire to State Game Lands No. 119 in Luzerne County, I came upon two deer feeding upon what little browse was left. One of them was a large doe, the other was a last year's fawn. At first glance I thought the larger one had been to a barber shop recently because she looked as if someone had used clippers or shears to cut out large spots of hair, making her look like a spotted cow. While holding the animal's attention I was able to get close enough to see that she was a victim of the recent forest fire, and what I thought was a poor haircut turned out to be a very close singe in spots. Otherwise she was in good shape.
-- Game Protector Peter A. Zikowsky, Minooka.
August 1944.

Enemy Invasion

While the Allies were getting ready for an invasion of the French coast we had an invasion in the upper end of Northumberland County of a BEAR.

Mr. Bruin not only invaded our county but proceeded to declare war upon an apiary owned by The Merrill Bee and Honey Company of Muncy totally destroying 21 of 45 hives.

During my more than twenty years as a Game Protector in charge of Northumberland and Montour Counties this was the first bear to have been seen in either of the two counties. Mr. Harvey Merrill, Manager of the Bee and Honey Company, stated that to his knowledge he never knew of bear to have been in that part of Northumberland County until last summer when an old female and two cubs were sighted in the same vicinity on May 29. A son of Mr. Merrill's while on watch at the apiary shot at the animal when it came back for additional honey on the 30th.

Now comes Mr. Thomas Hoffmam, a farmer of Point T. S., Northumberland County, who resides along Montour Ridge about three miles north of Northumberland, with a report that a bear skinned one of the large apple trees in his orchard. While this animal has not been sighted, all the evidence points to bear damage.

Twenty years ago we had no deer in Northumberland County; nor beavers - in fact only a limited amount of small game. Today we have one of the best small game counties in the State, with a large number of deer and beavers and now even a few bears. I will let you know when we have our first Elk for then we will have about everything.

-- Game Protector Bruce P. Yeager, Northumberland County.

August 1944.

Had the Right Idea

Bobby Bishop, of Ebenezer, Lebanon County, went bass fishing midnight July 1 and quit fishing at 6 a.m. so he could be at a certain farm at the opening of the groundhog season. He got to his place at 7 a.m., and sat at a bush waiting for Mr. Hog to show up. At 5:45 p.m. the farmers son saw him sitting there and ran for his father thinking he was shot. The farmer found the lad. He had slept in a hot sun from 7 a.m. until 6 p.m., thus ending the first day of the groundhog season.

-- Game Protector Raymond Holtzapple, Mt. Gretna.

October 1944.

Half a Dozen Skunk Tails, Plus One

I had an unusual experience with a family of skunks this past month. About ten thirty on the evening of September 5, I received a call from the Warren police department. Officers Munn and Outrie had received a call from the Warren General Hospital that a litter of small skunks were sleeping on the table in the basement of the nurses home, and would they please do something about it. Officers Munn and Outrie proceeded to the scene and, accompanied by a half dozen nurses, attempted to scoop the animals into a cardboard box. Well, they made one pass at the little family, and things happened! The Officers beat a hasty retreat, changed their clothes, and put in a call for me.

Like a conquering hero I proceeded to the Hospital with my trusty rabbit traps and some spoiled woodchuck for bait (some of my fox-trapping equipment) and in the morning I had two of the little fellows. The next morning I removed three more and completed the chore.

The next morning I received a call from the Hospital that the mother skunk had fallen into the cellar window and would I please come and get her, too. I think I can claim the world's record for a quick catch on this skunk. I baited the trap with spoiled woodchuck, tied a rope around the trap and dropped it down to where the skunk was marooned. The trap had hardly settled until Old Mother Skunk stepped into it and got a free ride to the country.

But all is not joy. I also had a very sad experience with a skunk- none of the above, but a skunk just the same. We were working traffic checks on out-of-state cars. I picked up a skunk in a box trap and rather than make an extra trip to the woods with it, I took it along with me when I took up my station on the State line. Deputy Reynolds was with me and as we arrived at our station I told him we had a skunk to release. We both went around to the rear of the car to release it and I pulled up the trunk door.

You can imagine my surprise to see that little skunk sitting there outside of the box trap. I was rather taken back and to top it off I dropped the trunk door. Well, it seems that the skunk was tired of sitting back there and when the door come open he figured on getting out. He started to move out and the trunk door started down about the same time. You know what happened without my telling it. Mr. Skunk got himself killed. The old door smacked him right on the head.

It can be said that Deputy Reynolds and Game Protector Norris spent the rest of the night a considerable distance from the car. For anyone who finds himself in the same fix, there is an oil called Oil of Cassia, which will kill all unpleasant odors instantly.
-- Game Protector George C. Norris, North Warren.
December 1944.

Tenacious
On Saturday, March 24, while Jack Crist and local sportsmen were on a fox hunt near Caledonia, Crist's dog cornered a fox in its den among the rocks and in maneuvering around, fell down a crevice. Crist and his sportsmen worked until late Saturday night, Sunday and Monday all day and night, and part of Tuesday with drills, bars and wedges. All this time the dog was fed weiners off a long, pointed stick thrust through a narrow crack. On Tuesday when the dog was liberated he seemed none the worse for his experience and started looking for another fox.
-- Game Protector John I. Hendricks, Chambersburg.
May 1945.

Row, Row, Row Your Boat
A sixty year old Washington Boro resident was fined $45 and costs for fishing without a licence and fishing with an outline following a hearing with Alderman Wetzel of Lancaster. Prosecution was brought by State Fish Warden Robert Greener who testified he pursued the violator in a rowboat for an hour before apprehending him on an island in the Susquehanna River.
September 1945.

Kinda Tastes Like Walnuts

Game food must be even less abundant than I believed. The Fish Warden reports seeing a gray squirrel cross the road at Baker's Run with a snake in its mouth and I don't think it natural for a squirrel to be carnivorous. When I told the Fish Warden I would sooner believe it was a snake with a squirrel in its mouth, he was very indignant about my doubting his veracity.

-- Game Protector Vern A. VanOrder, Renovo.
November 1945.

Some Never Learn

Fish Warden Sheldon and I trapped foxes together this month. We put out our first traps on the fifth and had our first fox the next morning. By the end of the month we had pelted 97 foxes. Besides these, we had 17 stolen and 12 that pulled the stakes and escaped. The weather was very unfavorable for fox trapping as we had so much rainfall that it was impossible to make a set in this low flat country without carrying along some sand. In fact it got so wet that when we dug the bait hole, water would immediately fill it. Stakes seemed to be quite firm when driven, but as soon as a fox was caught and the stake was worked by the fox, the water filled the hole and the stake pulled out very easily. Last year we had no trouble of this kind, but we learned that every trapping season is not the same. Raccoon hunters and duck hunters accounted for some of the foxes that were stolen, but this is a well populated community and a fox in a trap is seldom passed up by anyone it seems.

One of the unusual experiences of a trapper happened to me this month. On one trip I had trapped a red fox and William Grimm, from the Research Department, was putting the *coup de grace* to it while I was resetting the trap. We thought the fox was finished and Bill was watching me when the fox grabbed Bill's foot. Bill jumped straight into the air in surprise and pain. The fox took off down through the woods with me after it. I almost had him several times and was still only a couple feet behind him when I decided I did not want him so badly after all.

Later I caught the same fox. This time he was caught by the left foot and the right one was infected around the mark of the first trap. He was very light in weight and evidently had not fed very much with the bad leg, but it was gratifying to know that I could fool the same fox twice. I did not let him go to see if I could catch him the third time.

-- Game Protector Raymond M. Sickles, Linesville.
December 1945.

Smarter Than The Average Beaver

The beavers I have been trying to trap in the Fayetteville section have been throwing my live traps quite regularly, no doubt with the limbs they take to repair the hole in the dam where I place the traps. This being the case I tore a large amount of the three breasts out, with the hope that the beavers will soon get discouraged and leave.

-- Game Protector John I. Hendricks, Chambersburg.
December 1945.

Cross-Training

In Westmoreland County during this duck season it was interesting and a bit amusing to note the number of fishermen-hunters at the various dams and reservoirs over the county. Wearing both the fish button and game license tag, many hunters fished with a shotgun nearby, in case ducks would fly within range. Some of the nimrod-anglers had both ducks and fish, too!

-- Game Protector R D. Reed, Latrobe.

December 1945.

False I.D.?

While checking over the hunting license applications at one of the agents in Greene County, I was asked if false teeth would be an identification. I was so surprised I thought it must be a joke but this was the story. A boy just discharged from the Army made application to buy a license and was requested to give something for identification. Driver's license? No. Tax receipt? No. Social Security card? No. Bank book? No. He simply had no identification. Finally in desperation the ex-soldier said, "Wait a minute." He reached in his mouth and pulled out a set of false teeth, made while he was in the Army, and on them were printed his name and dog-tag number . I don't think, after that, there would be any doubt in anyone's mind that he was one and the same fellow.

-- Game Protector John Blair, Waynesburg.

January 1946.

Another Houdini

Last week I was patrolling in Washington Township near Advance when I saw two men about a mile away on top of a big hill. I could see that they had guns, but couldn't tell what they were doing. I parked the car and worked my way up to them. When I got to where they were I found that they were digging out a gray fox, so I waited until they dug it out. They took the fox from the hole alive and remarked that they would like to take it home alive. I told them that if they tied its mouth shut and its legs together that they could take it alive. We all looked for some strings, and none of us having any, I took the rawhide laces from my boots, tied its mouth shut, its legs together, laid it on the ground and covered it with one of the men's coat. It lay there for about two minutes when all of a sudden it took out from under the coat like a shot and all of us after it. I took a shot at it and missed, and as far as we know it is still going. We never did get it. Now there is a fox loose in Washington Township that owes me a pair of boot laces.
-- Game Protector Bruce W. Catherman, Indiana.
February 1946.

Wanted To Be A Mechanic

I had a funny experience the other day. A Boy Scout gave me a rabbit he had trapped and, as it was late in the evening, I put it on the back seat of my car in a pasteboard box. The next day when I reached for the box, I discovered that the animal had managed to get out. I could find him nowhere. I used the car all that day and the next morning when I went to get in the car I saw the rabbit scrambling around on the floor by the front seat. I got in the car and watched to see where he went. He managed to climb on top of the heater. I then drove into the country to release him. By that time, he had crawled along the defroster hose and finally got himself lodged in back of the dashboard. After a little sweating and maneuvering I finally managed to extricate him and released him, little worse for the wear.
-- Game Protector Clyde E. Laubauch, Clearfield.
March 1946.

Sounds Like A Fish Story

One trapper reported that one morning he approached one of his traps and found a big beaver sitting on the ice, caught in his trap. He quickly secured a stout club and advanced on the beaver. He was still out of reach of the beaver when it dived through the hole in the ice and disappeared. He quickly grabbed the wire and gave it an extra good heave, about the same time that beaver gave another desperate lunge. When the tug of war was over the trapper had no need of his club. The beaver had pulled out of his trap and was gone.

-- Game Protector Clair W. Dinger, Albion.

April 1946.

Service, Please!

While hunting crows one day with two other sportsmen, a peculiar thing happened. A crow was wounded slightly in one wing, enough to bring it to the ground. We immediately retrieved the bird with the idea of making a live "caller" out of it. Our examination of the bird revealed it would make a good one, so we tied its feet together and placed it under a small grapevine entanglement while we continued with our hunt.

A few minutes later one of the hunters heard our potential "call" give a few peculiar squawks but thought nothing of it. A half hour later we returned to pick up our crow and depart. We found a few black feathers, but no other sign, even though we gave the surrounding area a thorough search. A strong suspicion was forming in my mind, but no, it couldn't be that.

Next day one of the group returned to the same area. Within a few yards of where our crow disappeared, a large Gray Fox jumped out of the grapevine and ran. I don't know if that fox got our crow or not, but somehow I have a feeling he was waiting there, hoping another good meal of crow would be coming his way.

-- Game Protector Clair W. Dinger. Albion.
June 1946.

New Woodchuck Call

While on patrol in Bensinger Township one evening recently I witnessed a novel method of chuck hunting. I heard a rifle shot and upon investigation found two boys hunting on a mown field. Both had rifles, but one of them carried his on a sling over his shoulder while he marched beside his companion playing "You Are My Sunshine" on a harmonica. The companion carried a rifle at the ready and blazed away at the woodchucks which sat up to listen to the music. I heard six shots fired but found no chucks when I checked the boys. I gathered that the mouth organist was more proficient than the rifleman.

-- Game Protector L. B. Rosenkrans, Wilcox.
October 1946.

Not Exactly Eager

I learned something that to me was new about beavers. A beaver came into a small lake this Spring and kept damming up the outlet and flooding pasture land. I couldn't locate any house but did locate the beaver sleeping on the bank. Several times I scared him off the bank from different spots and concluded that he was sleeping in the brush rather than build a house or tunnel into a bank.

-- Game Protector Joseph L. Budd, Hamlin.

October 1946.

Traveled Incognito

I suppose we have all heard some very tall hunting and fishing stories but the one which appeared in the Connellsville Courier last month relative to a Black Bear prowling the streets of Connellsville tops them all. I had all kinds of reports and calls from the residents of that city as to what could be done about its presence there. The City Police reported seeing it one morning between three and four o'clock. After a complete investigation was made it was found that what was supposed to be a bear was a large black Chow dog prowling the district.

-- Game Protector Lester E. Shaffer, Uniontown.

October 1946.

Caught Napping

I had a very peculiar experience the other evening - one that makes the shivers run up and down my spine although I am confident I was at no time in any danger. I was lying on a blanket in the late evening listening for shooting in a specially bad section of the district, when I thought I heard approaching footsteps. Upon cautiously investigating by turning my head slowly, I saw an old bear and a cub directly approaching me. They were a short distance apart when they passed one to either side of and not more than fifteen feet from me. When they got past about fifteen or twenty feet, and when I was beginning to breathe a little stronger, they really poured on the coal and were gone almost instantly from a standing start. They will get my money for being the fastest on the get away of any wild animals.

-- Game Protector Vern A. VanOrder, Renovo.
November 1946.

Too Predictable

S. S. Malone, Mt. Lebanon, called at my office to probate a fox pelt for bounty. The regular habits of this fox spelled his doom. Mr. Malone saw Mr. Fox cross an open field about 10:00 a.m. several days in succession before he decided to try to shoot him. On his first try he took a .22 rifle and hid it in a cornfield near Reynard's place of crossing. Promptly at 10:00 a.m. B'rer Reynard crossed the field, but was too fast for a try with the rifle. The next day, Mr. Malone hid in the corn patch armed with a .300 Savage, and just a couple of minutes before 10:00 a.m. the fox started across the open field. One shot was sufficient to kill it.

-- Game Protector Elmer D. Simpson, Cambridge Springs.
November 1946.

Deadeye

A Red Lion hunter, Kenneth KIinefelter, answers to the name "Kilroy" since several unusual hunting shots. Hunting rabbits in Lancaster County, Ken killed two rabbits with one shot. After the first pair fell, one of his buddies remarked that he wouldn't repeat that feat in another fifty years. The same day, he repeated the act, killing four rabbits with two shells. Later in the season, Ken was hunting squirrels in York County and scored another double.

-- Game Protector Daniel H. Fackler, Windsor.
January 1947.

Slightly Territorial

The Bower brothers of Blain R. D., report a ringneck pheasant cock which follows their Caterpillar tractor all over the fields, pecking at it.

-- Game Protector Harold E. Russell, Blain, Perry County.

January 1947.

Small World

On March 9 while hunting foxes with a party of friends we killed a female gray fox running ahead of our hounds in Robeson Township about two miles south of Birdsboro. Upon picking the animal up we found a collar on it with a name plate inscribed "Leo Swisher, R D. 2, Coatesville." Curious to know more about this fox and how it came to be wearing the collar, I wrote to Mr. Swisher, and received a reply as follows:

"I received your letter about catching a gray fox with my name on the collar. I was surprised that it went that far. I have a pack of fox hounds and I catch the fox by chasing them in a hole and then I dig them out. Well, this time I caught the gray fox and I tied it in a large box with one of my collars and name plate, and during the night it broke the chain and chewed the wire on top of the box and got away. This happened last winter (1945-46) about the middle of the season. I caught it about 2 miles from my home. I do not know how it traveled way up there. It is about 25 or 30 miles from where I live to Birdsboro. I live near Wagontown, but the address is Coatesville.

-- Luther W. Benson, Birdsboro.

April 1947.

Felt Right At Home

I have had numerous complaints of skunks invading homes. In one case when children had left the cellar door open I found a nice black skunk had made a comfortable nest in a basket of soiled laundry. The basket was taken out into the country and the laundry was carefully removed. Friend skunk ambled away to find himself a new nest.

-- Game Protector Donald E. Miller, Titusville.

May 1947.

Homecoming

An unusual crow story has come to my attention. About two years ago a family living a few miles west of Albion managed to secure two young crows from a nest. The two birds thrived and soon became very tame and easily handled. They were not confined, but remained close to their foster home. Last summer one of them died. The other crow continued on as usual. He would take short flights about the neighborhood but always returned for the evening meal and his favorite roosting site. Last Fall when the crows were leaving this part of the State for their annual flight to a warmer climate this particular crow went along with his brothers. He was given up by his owners as lost. About the middle of the month the family was much surprised to hear a crow calling on the back porch. They investigated and found a crow sitting there. The lady of the house walked out and picked it up. While their crow had no identifying marks to separate it from the others it was very apparent that the bird was theirs. After being away for nearly four months he remembered where his feeding spot was located and his favorite roosting site Needless to say he was given a royal welcome, befitting one who has traveled afar. If nothing else this incident again proves that crows are pretty smart and know when they have a good home.

-- Game Protector Clair W. Dinger, Albion.

May 1947.

Killer Mole

Mr. George Acker, Supervisor, Newport Borough, reported the following incident which happened while digging a trench for a sewer line on Fifth Street, Newport:
One day while digging this six foot deep trench, his laborers noticed a ground mole moving about. No attempt was made to molest it at this particular time. The following morning Mr. Acker and his men saw a rabbit sitting still in this ditch. Further examination revealed a ground mole perched on the rabbit's back and chewing at its ear. One of the men jumped into the ditch and removed and killed the mole. The rabbit immediately ran up to the end of the ditch, a distance of about 75 feet, and in one attempt scaled a perpendicular wall of seven feet.
-- Game Protector Joseph S. Checklinski, Huntingdon.
May 1947.

Only Wanted Some Attention

Charley Wolf, a Cooperator on Farm-Game Project No. 88, related an interesting experience he had with a ringneck cockbird recently. As Charley was plowing with big tractor, a big cock bird flew out of the fence row straight toward him, trying in sink his spurs into him. The bird followed the tractor until the plowing was finished and then followed back to the barn. Charley, alighting from his tractor, was chased into the house by the irate bird. The bird continued to stay about the house and in due course found three hen birds nearby. It seems that Charley's pursuer has now lost all interest in sinking his spurs into human flesh, and has now gathered unto himself a harem.

-- Game Protector Samuel K. Weigel, Mercer.

June 1947

Ever Had The Feeling You're Being Watched?

I had quite a few inquiries last winter from people wanting to know if we had a Deputy Game Protector by the name of Kilroy. It seems that a certain trapper was setting muskrat traps before the start of the season last Fall and one morning found a note tacked on a stake near his traps. The sign read "Kilroy is watching you." I understand that all traps were gathered up in a hurry.

-- Game Protector Chester S. Siegel, Benton.

June 1947.

Four Lucky Rabbit's Feet

Deer have started to use the plots that were bulldozed for food and cover in this area. I received a report from Fire Warden Lee Neely of Knox that fire had burned over several acres of land near Knox. After the fire was out, he was going over the charred area to see what damage had been done and found a spot about four feet in diameter that had not been burned over. In this spot a rabbit had bedded down for the day. The animal had been surrounded by fire but was unhurt and in good enough condition to jump and run out when Mr. Neely came near.

-- Game Protector Levi R Whippo, Parkers Landing.
June 1947.

Adoption Service

A few days ago a Mallard hen walked into an open office door of a local service station on West 5th Street in Erie. The unusual thing about this escapade was that the hen duck had 9 very young ducklings which were not more than a few days old. This street is very heavily travelled and is in a settled part of town. The attendant looked at the ducks and then at his companion and said: "Am I seeing things or is this real?" and the companion said it was real alright. The hen became quite excited and started to fly about and it was apparent that she would soon injure herself so the door was opened and she left, leaving behind the 9 babies which were picked up by a Mrs. William Smith who lives in the same vicinity. She is caring for them and is really quite proud of her newly acquired family. This same lady has a large pond on her yard where she has numerous other wild ducks that have been coming there and nesting for several years. It is really quite a sight to see the young ducklings on this pond as they can move so much swifter than the old ducks. They literally fly over the surface of the water using their feet and their tiny wings to help them move over the water.

-- Game Protector Clifford L. Ruth, Erie.
August 1947.

Bought a Patch Kit

I have seen beaver employ almost every little trick or method in placing dams and use almost every known material on hand to hold water, but while assisting a brother officer in removing dams and beaver which had been flooding a highway recently, I noticed a new one. Near the top of the breast of one of the dams removed a big blow-out patch - the type used in auto tires was nearly placed over a hole or depression in the dam. It was certainly serving the purpose.

-- Game Protector Howard F. Hoffman, Susquehanna.
September 1947.

Not Very Wise

A Lawrenceville resident, Mr. Norman Miller, recently found his hunting combined with fishing. While plug casting for bass, Mr. Miller hooked and landed a barred owl.

It seems he was fishing from the shore of the Cowanesque River and was partially hidden by an overhanging rock. He was using a surface lure which he cast into midstream. It had been retrieved a short distance when the owl struck it. The bird become entangled with the line and soon was too wet to fly. Mr. Miller, after recovering from his surprise, was soon successful in landing this most unusual catch.
-- Game Protector James A. Osman, Tioga.
September 1947.

Fooling the Warden

Patrolling Wyoming County streams, Fish Warden Jim Underwood came upon an old-timer sitting on the running board of his car, pulling on his boots, his fishing tackle spread out before him. When Jim asked to see his fishing license, the old fellow replied indignantly: "I ain't fishing." Picking up his rod, he started down the steep trail into a deep canyon. Jim followed him still demanding the license. But all he could get out of him was "I ain't fishing." After a hike of about a mile, the old fellow stopped and tied on a fly. Stepping into the stream, he flipped his rod a couple of times, dropped the fly onto the water, then reached into his hip pocket and produced a license.

"Now I'm fishing," he explained.
January 1948.

Quick

Recently I placed a number of fox traps on State Game Lands No. 169, Cumberland County. While selecting likely looking places to set my traps, I noticed a place that looked like a fox had been loafing around. I placed a trap at this point and walked about fifty steps away to place another trap. Returning past the first trap I happened to glance in the direction of the set and found that I had already caught a very large red dog fox. All of this happened within one half hour and I know the fox had been in the trap at least fifteen minutes because he certainly had torn up the ground.
-- Game Protector George A. Bretz, Shippensburg.
February 1948.

Wanted Some Help

Joseph Lynn, a local coal operator, has a mule that has a hatred for deer. At various times, this mule has chased deer and only recently, after the animal had hauled a string of loaded cars to the tipple, it spotted a deer standing on yon hillside and promptly took off after the deer, harness and all. Mr. Lynn and his employees eventually got the mule back to the mines but as Lynn says, "I wonder what that mule would do with that deer if he ever caught it?"
-- Game Protector Frank E. Crouse, DuBois.
April 1948.

Call Him Frosty

In early February I saw one of the most bedraggled skunks anyone has ever seen. It had been sleeting all night and the roads were entirely covered with ice. As I was driving along, I noticed this skunk walking along the road. He was completely covered with ice and was dragging his tail along as if it were a sled. I got out of the car and walked towards him. He tried to escape by climbing over the banks of snow which the plows had piled up along the road but he was unsuccessful because the banks were too slippery. Several times he tried to raise his tail to bring his defensive weapon into action but it was so ice-encrusted that he couldn't get the tip of the tail into the air. I was within a few feet of him at the time so perhaps it's fortunate he wasn't able to go into action. The last I saw of him he was ambling up the road attempting at intervals to climb the banks and get into the brush.

-- Game Protector Stephen A. Kish, Pittston.
May 1948.

It's A Long Way To Texas

You never know what strange animals will turn up in your travels. The other day I found an armadillo about a mile north of Madison lying beside a dirt road. From all appearances it had just been shot. I mentioned this at a sportsmen's meeting in Madison later and they told me of an armadillo that had been killed near Rillton the previous year. I would greatly appreciate knowing from where they came and if both escaped or were liberated at the same time.

-- Game Protector Carl E. Jarrett, New Stanton.
June 1948.

WHAT THEY WON'T THINK OF NEXT

Nick Rosato

Just Watchin'

While my wife was doing the weekly family wash in the basement of our home on State Game Lands No. 216 recently, she was quite surprised in turning from her chores to find that a woodchuck had come into the basement through the outside entrance and had comfortably seated himself at a point directly behind the washing machine. From this vantage point he seemed to be observing with considerable interest and apprehension the mysteries and intricacies of our washing machine, as well as what probably appeared to him the folly of my wife's repetitious efforts in her quest for domestic cleanliness.

--Game Protector Samuel B. Shade, New Castle.
July 1948.

Tenderizing

I had an interesting little story told to me by Mr. W. E. Thompson of Albion recently. One morning he looked across the large pond at the rear of his home and saw a Great Blue Heron on the far bank. The bird was acting peculiarly and getting his binoculars, Mr. Thompson saw that the heron had a large fish which it was holding in its mouth. The bird would throw the fish as hard as possible to the water, apparently in an effort to kill it. When the fish still failed to succumb to this treatment, the heron moved a few steps and threw it several times on some sticks laying in the water. Failing in this attempt the bird took off probably with much disgust. Mr. Thompson immediately went over to the scene and got the fish. It was a large "bullhead" and was still alive. He

placed the fish in the water and after a short time it swam away about as good as ever. I am wondering if that is the way a heron will kill a fish that is too large for it to handle or, more important, if the heron used that method to break the ribs of the fish so that it would slide down the bird's long thin neck?
-- Game Protector Clair W. Dinger, Albion.
August 1948.

Wanted A Driver's License

Approaching one of the Commission's road graders parked along the Brady's Lake Road on State Game Lands No. 127 I noticed a groundhog perched majestically on the hood. I thought that he preferred this point of vantage because the early morning sun was comfortably warm atop the metal hood and I continued on my way with the appreciation that our wild animals have more than just a mere sense of reasoning. Later in the morning it was necessary to use the grader, or, rather, attempt to use it. Mr. Groundhog had made a hearty meal of the rubber insulation and the rubber tubing on the water system. It was more than the warm rays of the sun that he was seeking.
-- Game Protector Barney Thrush, Thornhurst.
August 1948.

The Masked Bandit Strikes Again

One day this month Jim Zwald, a resident of Emporium, was fishing up Salt Run. Jim knows this stream very well, and had a favorite hole that he wanted to fish with grasshoppers. The water being very clear he had to use extra precaution in approaching this spot. He crept up to the edge of the hole and tossed in the 'hopper. As quick as a flash he had a nice strike and let the trout settle down a little. When he set the hook, he knew he was holding a nice trout about nine inches so he started slowly to bring his catch toward shore while he still looked over the edge of the bank. All of a sudden his line gave a tremendous jerk and started to move very fast upward and along the edge of the stream. The next thing Jim knew his leader, hook and fish were gone. However, being an experienced fisherman he knew that something unusual had happened. He jumped to his feet and looked over the edge of the bank just in time to see a big, fat raccoon getting away with a brook trout, hook, line and everything.
-- Game Protector Norman L. Erickson.
September 1948.

55

Crooks

You can never underestimate the smartness of the crow. Last month I saw some of the black rascals doing some fancy thievery. There was a box placed along a road I was traveling on, a bread box. The owner evidently built it so that the baker could leave bread when no one was home. But he definitely did not count on the strange proceedings that met my eyes as I drove by. A flock of crows was helping themselves to the bread, tearing the wrapper open, and carrying away the loaf a slice at a time.
-- Game Protector S. Earl Carpenter, Doylestown.
October 1948.

Made Himself To Home

Checking beaver dams for traps one day while on patrol, I saw a grouse attempting to fly but unable to get off the ground. Upon closer examination I noticed its broken wing tip. Picking up the bird, I cut off the broken part of the wing; and put the fellow back on the ground which was covered with snow. The bird fluttered around but did not make any headway in the snow. Puzzled as to just what to do with it I finally just put it in the back of my hunting coat and took it home with me. I put it down on the kitchen floor and it fluttered around soon to find a hiding place in the bottom of an open cupboard. My wife said it stayed there all afternoon. We had made arrangements to go out for dinner that evening and I figured the bird would stay put. Upon returning about an hour later we found our grouse in the parlor. It had been feasting upon an African Violet that Mrs. Bill had just received a few days previously for a birthday present. The price of African Violets, I do not know, but you can just bet that I'm going to find out very shortly. I think he will have been a pretty expensive guest, but costly or not it is one way of finding out what grouse like to dine on in the winter.
Game Protector William Overtuif, Marienville.
April 1949.

IT

One week early in February I received word that a farmer in Conneaut Township wanted to see me as soon as possible. It seems that the driver of an out-of-state car had stopped near his house, got out, walked along one of his fence rows, and had placed a red, cylindrical-shaped object about three inches long and about an inch and a quarter in diameter on one of the posts. The farmer was sure the object contained poison or, worse yet, some type of explosive. Would I please come out and determine what it was? Naturally, I was interested, contacted Deputy Greenlee, and, together, we went to the farmer's house. The farmer dropped his work immediately and we proceeded to the fence row and started walking along it. As we got to the brow of a little hill, the farmer cautioned us to be careful as we were very close to IT. A little bit further on he stopped, pointed under a thornapple tree, and in a voice filled with suppressed excitement, said,

"There IT is." I looked, Deputy Greenlee looked, and we looked at each other, and found it difficult to keep a straight face. In dead seriousness we walked over and picked up a little red, wooden, broken-handled toy mallet. All the farmer could say was, "I'll be darned." This may sound like a practical joke on the Game Protector but I think not. This particular farmer was not the kind to play tricks and he was entirely too serious about the whole affair. What I do like was his practice of calling a Game Protector for help when things happen which he doesn't understand.
-- Game Protector C. W. Dinger, Albion.
May 1949.

Combat Vet
One day early in March Jim Shoup, while filling turkey feeders with corn on the West Branch of Hicks Run, found a large raccoon that had entered one of the feeders and became trapped inside. After a struggle, Shoup managed to get the animal into a burlap bag and out of the feeder. Because of the unusual appearance of the animal, he decided to bring it to me for my opinion as to how any wild creature could get to look like it did. I could tell that coon any place and any time after one look at him. Sometime previously the raccoon must have been in a tough battle that left it marked for life. One of its ears was ripped several times, its left hind foot was half gone, its face was scarred in not less than a dozen places, and its nose had part of the left nostril missing. On top of that, there was only about two inches of tail remaining. Yet, even with all these old battle scars, the animal was in very good condition and all the earmarks of its fights were very well healed. We decided to release the animal again about five miles from the feeder.

About two weeks later Fish Warden Close, Jim Shoup, and I were checking some of the feeders again and when we came to the one where the raccoon had been trapped, we were more than surprised to see our old friend scampering away from a nice feast of corn. Five miles did not seem to he much of an obstacle to this little fellow after all he must have gone through during his life and fight for survival.
--Game Protector Norman L. Erickson, Emporium.
June 1949.

Bidding The Enemy Farewell

While trapping predators on Farm Game Project No. 146, Fayette County, in early March, 1 came upon an unsual sight. As I approached a fox set, I could see a red fox caught in the trap. To my surprise, a ringneck pheasant was strutting around just outside the circle in which the fox was held. He appeared to show no fear and would cock his head to one side and look Mr. Fox over very carefully, as if to say, "Brother, you are in a lot of trouble. "I watched this go on for a few minutes, then approached the set a little closer. The pheasant, seeing me, took off in a hurry, as it apparently had more fear of me than it had of the fox. I thought afterwards that this pheasant had better be a little more careful. The next fox he looks over may not be in a trap.
--Andrew Ewart, Carmichaels.
June 1949.

Quick Response

On May 6 I erected a wren house in an apple tree in the backyard of my home but with little expectation of attracting nesting birds since I had neither seen nor heard a wren in this vicinity for the past two years. In less than 15 minutes after I had removed the ladder, however, a wren alighted on the perch in front of the opening, inspected the house from stem to stern, inside and out, and immediately began to carry twigs and bits of grass for a nest.
-- Game Protector Thomas W. Meehan, Uniontown.
August 1949.

Good Pedestrian

On May 25 I was traveling north on the Philadelphia Pike, Route 422, and saw a young rabbit run up to the edge of the highway about 5:45 p.m. This is just at the time when the highway is crowded with autos carrying persons home from work. This young rabbit evidently had a wise mother and a good memory because it stopped at the edge of the highway, took a quick look in either direction, and made a beeline for the opposite side of the road at an opportune moment. It timed its trip so as to just cross ahead of a huge trailer truck which was coming down the road.

-- Game Protector Joseph A. Leiendecker, Reading.

August 1949.

The Bunny-Hop

One evening just before dusk I witnessed two adult cottontails playing on the lawn of the Conservation School at Brockway. The singular fact was that the game was a modified form of Leapfrog played by children the world over. The rabbits crouched facing each other at a distance of about two to three feet, each eyeing the other like a gamecock. Suddenly one of little rabbits jumped into the air about six inches high. This seemed to be a sort of preparatory signal, for only a moment after alighting, the other jumped. As if propelled by the same force, bunny made a sudden lunge toward the jumper who would leap into the air, this time about twelve to eighteen inches high, to permit the lunging bunny to pass underneath. Then they squared off again and repeated the process after a few second interval of sparring and nervous feinting. This went on for about two minutes, and then they "changed sides." The entire show lasted for about five or six minutes, after which the bunnies resumed their feeding activities.

-- John E. Harney, Assistant Leader, Pittman-Robertson Project 31-R

September 1949.

Chomper

On Sunday, June 26, a car loaded with sightseers came around a bend in the road to find a large beaver parked in the center of the highway. The animal refused to budge so the driver stopped the car. As soon as the car stopped rolling, the beaver rushed up and started chewing on a front tire. Deciding that tires cost too much to use as teething rings for beaver, the owner picked up a club to give battle, only to find himself under attack. He made a hasty retreat up the road. When the beaver found that it could not catch the man, he took a bite out of a large stone (at least, tried to), made a couple of passes at a tree, and then started to work out on the other front tire of the auto. By this time the occupants of the car were convinced that the animal was suffering from rabies. A larger club was secured and after quite a battle the animal was killed. It was the next day before I picked up the carcass and by that time it was too ripe and flyblown to send away for a rabies examination. I've had a few reports of rabies in foxes but this is the first on a mad beaver.

-- Game Protector Duane E. Lettie, District B-10, Honesdale.
October 1949.

Chapter 3
1950- 1959

As America moved into the 1950's, progress was in the minds of the people. Angler and Game News saw more changes as the years passed and the editors saw the need to "modernize" the publications. Field Notes generally outnumbered Stream Notes, but many readers of the magazines looked forward to each issue and the observations of their local wardens, especially when the subject of the note was a relative or friend, and the story a real knee-slapper.

By this time, Fish Wardens and Game Protectors had begun to recognize the interest generated by the more unusual stories, and a sort of quiet competition surfaced among them to publish the most interesting accounts of their experiences. While only a few individuals had consistently generated humorous notes prior to the fifties, the majority of field officers from that time forward were enthusiastic in their efforts to "send it in."

Boys And Bears

Most of the time, when anyone wants information about the best method to hunt a certain animal, he seeks out the old timer who has been hunting for a long time with the thought that he knows the ins and outs of the game. The situation was certainly reversed in this district this past bear season, however, and it looks like the oldtimers will have to ask the youngsters' advice before going hunting. Three bears were brought into the Dupont-Avoca section and each one was bagged by a youngster. Joseph Lasota, Dupont, age 20, bagged the largest bear weighing 550 pounds; Frank Chilek, Avoca, age 19, took second place with a bear weighing 400 pounds; and Merle Renfer, Dupont, age 18, took third place with a bear weighing 200 pounds.
-- Game Protector Stephen Kish, District B-12, Moosic.
February 1950.

Squirrels Gone Nuts

While patrolling with Deputy Mawyer in the vicinity of Middle Lancaster during October, we walked into a woods owned by a Mr. Peffer. There must have been a squirrel migration going on as the woods were literally alive with grey and fox squirrels. They were feeding on acorns and were feeding within three feet of both of us. Deputy Mawyer put his hand up to one on a tree and reached within two feet of the animal. I was leaning on a fence between two oak trees approximately five feet apart; a grey squirrel ran up one of the oaks part way, jumped, and landed on my back; then jumped onto another oak tree. The squirrel ran down the tree and went on feeding on the acorns about three or four feet from where I was standing.
-- Game Protector George Miller, District F-21, Evans City.
February 1950.

Crow With An Attitude Problem

Have you ever heard of a talking crow? I have and now I have one. A woman in the vicinity of the salt road near Summerdale called in January and reported a partly tamed crow was going around drilling holes in milk bottle tops and was drinking the milk. Would I please come and get it? I did and found its wing and tail feathers were cut very short so I decided to make a cage and keep it. Now, after hearing my daughter, wife, and myself talking, the bird calls "Paul," "Barbara," and "Joe," says "hello," and laughs. Of course, just when you want to show him off, he won't even caw.

-- Game Protector Clint Ganster, Marysville.
April 1950.

Dinner Bell

I had an unusual experience on January 12. While assisting Game Protector Les Haney with filling feeding shelters in Refuge 54-B, Haney took a stick and began to hammer on the shelter. In less time that it takes to tell it, 18 deer came bounding in from all directions. They came within 10 feet of us. The reason I think this was so unusual was due to the fact that an antlerless deer season had just closed when it wouldn't have been safe for one of them to move. Not one of these deer had visible antlers.

-- Game Protector Ed Richards, Portland Mills.
April 1950.

Dedicated Scouts

Two Boy Scouts brought a dead rabbit to me in February and told me the following story: They had caught the rabbit in one of the box traps they had set on the Alliance College grounds. After removing the bunny from the trap, they put it in a cloth bag and left the bag on the bank of a small creek. while they checked another trap. The rabbit struggled in the bag and went over the bank into the water. The boys discovered its plight, removed the bag from the creek and the rabbit from the bag, and proceeded to administer artificial respiration. After working some time and obtaining no results, they brought the rabbit to me, wondering if I could revive him so they could collect their agent's fee. An examination found the rabbit to be beyond help. It would have been interesting to watch the boys administer artificial respiration to a rabbit.

-- Game Protector Elmer Simpson, Cambridge Springs.
May 1950.

Can They Swim?

During March I received a call from a woman in Topton telling me that a muskrat had fallen into her fish pond and might drown. The pond was the small backyard type, about eight feet in diameter and three feet deep. Upon arrival I found the animal asleep and very much alive. The muskrat used his head by building a nest of moss and grass on a raft of ice that was afloat in the pond.

-- Game Protector Stephen Mace, Fleetwood.

July 1950.

When the Dogs Barked Treed

LEASBURG - On the last day of June, I received a call to come to Leasburg to get a raccoon out of the top of a cherry tree. This wasn't at all unusual for coons are always getting into some mischief or other. But the tree was situated right in the midst of a beagle kennel and about 25 beagles kept voicing their feelings at the audacity of a coon that literally "treed himself."

-- Game Protector Sam Weigel, Mercer.

September 1950.

Baled Bunny

UNIONDALE - Edward J. Ridball, Uniondale, told me recently that while he was putting baled hay in his barn this summer, he heard a squealing noise coming from one of the bales. He investigated and found a rabbit in the bale. It was quickly released, apparently, none the worse for wear.

-- Game Protector John Putnam, Montrose.

October 1950.

Moose Deer

WILLIAMSPORT - One evening in July I passed a pond back in the mountains and noticed a doe standing in the water with her head under the water until only the tips of her ears were in sight. I watched her for awhile and then timed her as to the length of time her head was underwater. The best she could do was about 50 seconds. Then she would come up with a mouth full of water plant, take a breath, and go back for more.
-- Game Protector Levi Whippo, Williamsport.
November 1950.

Mother Instinct

REEDSVILLE - Mr. Jim Bonson, a farmer near Reedsville, Mifflin County, reports that while mowing a field of hay, he ran into a ringneck pheasant nest. Several of the eggs were broken. He placed the remaining good eggs in his cap and left them on the ground, intending to replace them in the nest after he had made another cut around the field. When he approached the spot again, he found the hen on the eggs in his cap.
-- Game Protector George Smith, Lewistown.
November 1950.

Wild Turkeys

JOHNSONBURG - While I was attending a Division Meeting on September 26 and 27, there occurred a humorous but nevertheless regrettable incident at Johnsonburg. My wife received a telephone call from a local resident telling her that he had captured three young wild turkeys that had been wandering around one of the hill streets of the town. He wanted to know what disposition he should make of them. She told him she would locate someone to take them off his hands and called a Deputy in Johnsonburg to contact the turkey captor. The Deputy later called back to report he had the turkeys and wanted further orders. Mrs. Van Order, realizing that all the Game Protectors were attending the Division meeting, told the Deputy he might as well take them out and release them himself. I obtained the following story from the Deputy the following day. It was after dark when he received the birds and he wasn't too familiar with turkeys, especially young turkeys. He took them some distance from town and attempted to roost them in a tree. The birds refused the invitation. The man said they didn't appear to look just right but in the dark he couldn't decide just what was wrong with them.

The next day the Deputy learned he had just released three pet Guinea Hens belonging to a local resident. I received a call from the owner on my return home and he was very splendid about it. He really had a big chuckle at the expense of the man who originally caught the "wild turkeys" and the Deputy who released them. To date the Guinea Hens have not been located or returned so when the season opened in Elk County, there may have been several hunters who got a confused look at some exotic "wild turkeys."
-- District Game Protector Vern Van Order, Wilcox.
November 1950.

What'll You Have?

TIOGA - Manager "Bucky" Watts and several patrons were enjoying an unusually warm October evening recently at the Blackwell Hotel, when they were suddenly surprised to see a yearling bear enter the open door and jump up onto the bar. After a brief look around the room he made his exit as quickly as he entered, apparently to seek his favorite brand elsewhere, much to the relief of those present.
--Game Protector James A. Osman, Tioga.
January 1951.

Doe Fever

HOPEWELL - In Blair County on the first day of the 1950 antlerless season several men from Hopewell were hunting. They had a boy with them who had never killed a deer and, seeing a legal animal, they shouted to him to kill it. He raised his gun but instead of the doe dropping as expected, the young hunter fell to the ground, a victim of "doe fever." He had completely passed out. His companions carried him part way out of the woods and had to help him walk after he regained consciousness. He was ghastly white from his experience. And the buck hunters tell us there is no thrill in killing a doe!
-- District Game Protector John Hiller, Saxton.
February 1951

Grouse Takes Wooden Nickel

On November 7, 1950, I killed two nice grouse but when I went to dress them, I found one had a piece of wood about two and a half inches long and as big around as a five-cent piece in the right side of its breast. This piece of wood must have been in the bird a long time because the wound had healed. It hadn't hurt the bird physically, because it was nice and fat. One wonders, why, in flying full speed through the timber, most grouse aren't loaded with wooden nickels!

-- Fish Warden Wilbur Williams
February 1951.

Talented Talons

ANDREAS - In response to a telephone call, I made a hurried trip to the headquarters of Deputy Game Protector Frank Baker of Andreas in late November. Upon arriving I found a hunter who had an odd but true story to tell. This fellow had been hunting and he eventually shot at and broke the legs on a rabbit. As the hunter approached, the rabbit squirmed and before either knew what was taking place, an immature Red-tailed Hawk swooped down and set his talons in the rabbit. In the few seconds that it took the hunter to reach the rabbit, the hawk was unable to unhook his talons. The hunter lifted the hawk up by the wings and brought both the bird and the bunny to Deputy Baker to prove his story. The man also had two mean gashes in his hand to prove that the rabbit was not the only one to feel the power of the bird's talons.

-- District Game Protector Billy Drasher, Tamaqua.
March 1951.

Lost Legality

TITUSVILLE - During the buck season a Titusville hunter sighted a buck which he considered to be about an eight-pointer. He had a quick shot but missed. Pursuing the animal through a small woodlot, he emerged from the brush in time to see the buck run to the far side of a distant field and crawl beneath a strand of wire to disappear into another woodlot. The hunter followed the deer to the fence and there found a pair of antlers totalling eight points. The tracks were followed a short distance but then the man had to give up the chase when the "de-horned" buck's trail crossed a number of other fresh tracks.

-- Farm-Game Area Leader, Northwest Division, Titusville.
March 1951.

Sweet-Toothed Skunk

MILLSTONE HOLLOW - Deputy Game Protector Colman Campbell of Latrobe was patrolling in Millstone Hollow, Westmoreland County, on December 5th when he noticed a well-used groundhog hole. While pausing to eat a chocolate bar, a skunk came out of the hole and approached the man without fear and more or less with the apparent intention of "getting a share." Rather than run, which Campbell knew was the wrong thing to do, the man threw a share of the treat to the skunk. The uninvited guest stopped in his tracks and ate the candy with much speed. He apparently did not relish the sweets, for after finishing, he took off for a nearby spring, drank for some time, then returned to the hole. Campbell now carries two bars of candy - one for himself and another for any unexpected guests.
-- Conservation Education Assistant Bob Parlaman, Ligonier.
April 1951.

Eager Beaver

FREELAND - John Beitel, of Freeland, holds the record for the fastest beaver catch of the 1951 season in this area. Off to a late start on the first day of the season, he arrived at Lake Olympus about noon. Not discouraged by the number of traps placed in all the good locations, he made a set in a small stream entering the lake. Just as he placed his second trap in position, he heard a loud splashing and looked up to see a beaver coming down the stream. John barely had time to jump to the bank before the beaver was fast in his trap. P. S. - He had his second beaver the next morning.
-- District Game Protector Sam McFarland, Drums.
May 1951.

Good Deed Day For Crows

BLOOMSBURG - Occasionally crows will turn in a good deed to offset their many bad ones. Recently, while dismantling safety zones on a Farm Game Project, I observed a red-tailed hawk in close pursuit of a cock ringneck pheasant. The bird made a hedge row in safety, the hawk veered off, and immediately two crows attacked him and knocked him to the ground. Apparently not much hurt, the hawk took off for upstairs and rapidly got away from there.
-- District Game Protector Mark Hagenbuch, Bloomsburg.
June 1951.

While The Hunter Is Away...

BENDERSVILLE - Harvey Quigle, a fruit grower of Bendersville, Adams County, is beginning to wonder whether it might not be better to just stay at home and let the game come to him. Last November Mr. Quigle was highly excited about the opportunity to hunt ringneck pheasants in Lancaster County. He was so excited, in fact, that he forgot to take his shotgun with him when he left home and arrived in Lancaster County to discover that his gun was still leaning against a tree in Bendersville. Just recently he had further reason to believe that all things come to him who waits. Mrs. Quigle was working in the kitchen of her home when she heard a terrific crash upstairs. She went to the barn and called her husband to investigate. He found the bedroom window smashed and the venetian blind awry. Searching for the cause of the damage, he discovered a big ringneck pheasant cock under his bed. He caught the bird and brought it downtown as proof of the story. Later he released the bird. It took off with a "whoosh," hit some utility lines, fell to the ground and then headed for other parts on foot at the speed of a greyhound, unhurt, according to witnesses.
-- Deputy Game Protector Charles W. Bretzman, Bendersville.
June 1951.

Milk Moochers

RENOVO - While inspecting crop damage claims for Farmer Proctor, his son, Todd Proctor, told me of an unusual occurrence. It seems that two fawn deer have adopted one of their milk cows as their mother. At any rate, the fawns can occasionally be seen making use of the portable milk bar provided by Farmer Proctor's cow.
-- District Game Protector Charles F. Keiper, Renovo.
August 1951.

Strange Bedfellows

MARIENVILLE - Turkey Hunters hunting in Forest County this fall will have to be on the lookout for a bantam turkey. As far as we know this turkey must have lost her own brood and as a last resort came into a farmer's back yard and adopted his bantam chick. The turkey and bantam pay a visit to the farm occasionally but the farmer cannot get the peep from its foster mother due to the turkey giving him an awful fight every time he tries.

-- Arthur T. Biondi, Allegheny National Forest.

September 1951.

No Eviction Notice

READING - George Reeser of R. D. 2, Reading, told me about a litter of beagle puppies that he is raising. Mr. Reeser noticed that the mother was removing the puppies from the kennel and he was rather curious about the procedure. Upon investigation he found that a groundhog was in the kennel. When trying to remove the animal he was severely bitten.

-- District Game Protector E. J. Turner, Centerport.

November 1951.

Greedy Bass

MONTROSE - Some time ago a Montrose business man, while fishing on Lake Montrose, caught a nice bass that after being placed in the boat regurgitated a muskrat that was about ten inches long.

-- District Game Protector James W. Clouser, Montrose.

November 1951.

High Flying Beavers

ERIE - Apparently the Erie County beavers have heard of "flying saucers" for they are out to excel not only man with his newfangled ideas but Nature as well. Long known for their engineering prowess, they have now taken to nesting in trees. While patrolling a length of a tribtitary to LeBoeuf Creek in lower Erie County on the flrst day of the recent beaver season, District Game Protector Elmer Simpson, of Union City, called my attention to a beaver house complete with food supply built in a wide crotch of a large willow tree. The house was about six feet above the ground or normal water level of a beaver dam which occupied the site. It was obvious that one of these busy animals, confronted with the need for vacating his regular dwelling by spring floods, had selected the tree rather than move outside the flood line. Not all beavers can move to a "second floor apartment" when the need arises, but this one certainly proved the exception.

--PR Western Area Leader Raymond A. Shaver, Northwest Division Office, Titusville. *December 1951.*

The Home-Lovin' Type

OIL CITY - Received a call from a Mr. Hankie on Highland Avenue, in Oil City, that he had a grouse. Upon arriving there this is the story that was related to me. This grouse came up on the back porch, and into the kitchen through a hole in the screen door. It continued on its way past the lady of the house who was ironing; on through a hallway and into the bathroom, where it hopped upon a clothes hamper. Mr. Hankie picked up the bird and called me. When released it seemed very glad to be free, and took off at full throttle.

-- District Game Protector William Shaffer, Oil City. *February 1952.*

Nice To Know

On September 5, I checked a non-resident angler from Alabama with a non-resident license fishing Deer Lake. He was very much pleased with the set-up we have in our State as to the two different Commissions for Fish and Game. He also said that he fished in three different counties and was checked in every one, commenting that our enforcement officers are really on the job.

-- Fish Warden Anthony J. Lech, Schuylkill County. *November 1952.*

Don't Count Your Turkeys

BUTLER COUNTY - Edward Young of Argentine, near State Game Lands No. 95 relates the following story: During July Mr. Young noticed a wild turkey hen with her brood of poults. Curious to know the number of poults in the brood, Mr. Young drew closer in an attempt to count them. Suddenly the angered hen flew at him, striking him on the chest and knocking him off his feet. He then got up and dismissed the idea of counting the brood, and the old turkey hen went merrily on its way.
-- District Game Protector Woodrow E. Portzline, Slippery Rock.
January 1953.

What Goes Up Must Come Down

BRUCE LAKE, Pike County - An unidentified hunter, while hunting bear and grouse in the Bruce Lake area of the Promised Land State Forest last fall, really had himself a time. He had a 30-30 rifle and was on stand under a hemlock. Suddenly he saw a grouse alight in the tree above him. Although it was a difficult shot, he raised his gun to fire. When he shot, he saw what was coming and tried to cover his head the best he could but -plunk- the grouse hit him square on the topknot. Feathers flew, the hunter roared with laughter, and several nearby hunters came running over to see what the commotion was all about. The hunter was none the worse for his experience and the grouse was then killed since the shot had only broken a wing and leg.
-- District Game Protector Albert J. Kriefski, Blooming Grove.
February 1953.

Welcome Home

HUNTINGTON COUNTY - On March 10th, while releasing ringneck hens in Shirley Township, I witnessed a sight that was new to me. We had just released several hens and three of them landed in a snow covered field about 60 yards away from the truck. All at once we noticed a large ringneck cock bird take off from a hillside about 250 yards away. It flew straight towards us and landed right in among the three hens. From then on he just strutted his stuff and ran from one hen to the other as if greeting long lost sweethearts. I feel sure spring propagation of ringnecks on that particular farm will be a great success if that beautiful cock bird retains only part of such enthusiasm.
-- District Game Protector Dean M. Lesnett, Huntingdon.
June 1953.

Refrigerated Robin

WAYNE COUNTY - Last year a robin built a nest and hatched her young on our second story window sill. She came back again this year and used the same nest and laid three eggs. She incubated the eggs during nights so cold that it froze one-fourth inch of ice and days that we had snow squalls which covered the ground. On April 30, she hatched two of the eggs.

-- District Game Protector Theodore Schafer, Honesdale.
July 1953.

Hunter Takes Steps to Success

YORK COUNTY - While attending a Field Trial this month I was told about a rabbit hunter that carried as extra equipment a step ladder. It seems he hunted in a spot with very good cover, plenty of rabbits, but it was hard to get a shot because of the dense cover. The hunter evidently decided he needed extra altitude so he carried a ladder from which he could do his shooting. It is surprising what steps some persons will take to shoot game.

-- District Game Protector Earl Geesaman, New Salem.
July 1953.

Mechanical Mother

BUCKS COUNTY - On May 29th we had two settings of quail eggs due to be hatched out by jungle fowl hens. For a day or two we had observed one of the hens did not appear too well and because of the cold and wet weather assumed she might have a cold. Both hens were checked on the morning of the 29th and all appeared to be normal, but the chicks had not hatched. I went to the Eastern Game Farm, picked up more quail eggs and some medicine for combating the cold. However, we never had the chance to use it, for when we checked that afternoon the hen was dead and the eggs cold. Two chicks had hatched out but were practically dead. These we placed under the other hen which had hatched all but two of her eggs, and they revived. The problem was what to do with the remaining eggs. Due to the fact that they were cold, it seemed hopeless, but we broke one egg and the chick was still alive. The next problem was heat. The only heat available was the car heater, so we placed the eggs in a small box and turned on the heater. That heater turned out to be a pretty good mother for it hatched out fourteen chicks, all of which are doing fine at the present time.

-- District Game Protector Edwin W. Flexer, Quakertown.
August 1953.

Checking the Line

CARBON COUNTY - On May 10 while slowly driving along a farm road I observed something up ahead of me climb up a telephone pole rather hurriedly. The object seemed to be about the size of a cat. As I neared the pole I saw that it was a groundhog.

The groundhog hung on to the back side of the pole, bear fashion, for about twenty minutes. He was then about fifteen to eighteen feet above the surface of the ground. After about twenty minutes be began to shift toward the front of the pole and casually inspect the insulators, pawing at them several times. After about ten minutes more he began to back down the pole and when about six feet from the ground he let himself drop the remaining distance. I have often observed groundhogs on small trees and fence posts but never at such a great height on a perpendicular post.

-- District Game Protector William E. Fulmer, Weissport.
August 1953.

Batting the Bull Around

MERCER COUNTY - When passing an area where white-faced cattle were pastured I noticed a red-winged blackbird repeatedly flying straight up in the air about 10 feet and then descending in the approximate area. So I took a better look and observed this male red-winged blackbird light on the back of the steer at the base of its tail and pick furiously at the animal several times before flying up in the air. It would then come down again and repeat the picking. This maneuver was repeated until the big steer was driven away from the nesting area I presume. This tiny 1 1/2 ounce bird didn't take very long to drive the 1500 pound steer away when it meant business. I couldn't tell even with the use of binoculars whether or not blood was drawn by those vicious picks of the little red-wing.

-- District Game Protector Ralph E. Flaugh, Greenville.
September 1953.

Interruption, Please

DELAWARE CO. - A Media woman, while talking to a friend over the telephone, happened to look up just in time to see a skunk come out from under the sofa. She dropped the phone and ran out into the street. It was not until after the local police, assisted by male neighbors, had driven the skunk out (luckily without leaving any odors behind) that she could be persuaded to reenter.
-- District Game Protector Daniel S. McPeek, Jr., Glen Mills.
October 1953.

TV Fan Ain't Funny

ALLEGHENY CO. - The following unusual incident was related to me by Mrs. John Nicholson, who is the wife of one of our deputies residing in Springdale.

On Sunday, July 12, while at home alone quietly sitting in the dining room watching television, Mrs. Nicholson felt something cold on her ankle and at the same time a sort of gentle scraping. Upon looking down, she was at first shocked and then alerted to action by the sight of a weasel investigating with nose and forefeet. She retreated to the kitchen in a hurry, regained composure and seized the wastebasket. In the mean time, the weasel retired to the living room, peeking at her from behind a chair as she watched from the kitchen -then ensued a merry go-around as she and the weasel went around from living room to dining room to kitchen; she having regained courage, trying to put the wastebasket over the critter. It proved too elusive, however, and continued to avoid her but never retreated too far and continued to peek from behind whatever object sheltered it at the moment. Mrs. Nicholson had wanted to capture the weasel to prove to her husband that the incident had occurred, but deciding 'this was impossible and not wanting to remain in the house alone with it until he returned from work, she propped the kitchen door open with the broom and succeeded in chasing it out on the porch. After she had closed the door, it still arrogantly peeked in at her from the outside. Later it retired under the porch, she then called a neighbor to look at it. It continued to peek from the latticework under the porch at intervals, but of course when her husband returned from work, not a trace of it could be found, nor has it been seen since. The Nicholsons had heard gnawing in the basement the night before and thinking it was a rat had set several traps that morning. The day before, the basement door had been left open several hours, Mr. Weasel must have gotten in at that time. Usually shy but sometimes bold, this member of the species decidedly exhibited the latter attribute.
-- District Game Protector C. R. Kinley, New Kensington.
November 1953.

76

Watch Dog

ALLEGHENY COUNTY - There are many odd things that happen while hunting, trapping or running dogs, but this is the most unusual one in my book. In October, Charles Sabo of Pittsburgh was running his beagle "Spottie" on the Mt. Lebanon-Dormont Club grounds. Unknown to him, another fellow was trapping for fox on the archery course. Spottie got caught in the trap, and when Charles went to take him out, the dog made a pass at his wrist. Instead of biting Charles, he bit his $60.00 wristwatch. Charles got the dog out of the traps and proceeded to look for his watch which was missing from the band. In the meantime, Spottie took chase after a rabbit. Not being able to find his watch, Mr. Sabo took the dog to a local veterinarian for an examination. Sure enough, the watch was in the dog's stomach. The doctor operated on Spottie and removed the watch. From last reports Spottie is doing fine in the hospital.
-- District Game Protector F. H. Servey, Clinton.
January 1954.

Sequel To The Watch-Dog Story

ALLEGHENY COUNTY - Last October, I submitted an article that was carried in *GAME NEWS,* concerning a hunting dog named "Spottie," owned by Charles Sabo of Pittsburgh. Spottie had caught his foot in a trap and while trying to get the dog out of the trap Spottie bit his owner on the wrist and swallowed his watch. I finished the article by stating that Spottie is doing fine in the hospital. Last week the owner of the dog told me this story: He watched the doctor operate on Spottie and take the watch, still ticking, from the dog's stomach. He thought at the time his dog would never run again. He took him from the hospital the Monday before season started. With his stitches still in, the owner let him run an hour or so each day before season for exercise. On Thursday, the stitches were removed, and on the opening day of season the dog accounted for four rabbits for his owner. Mr. Sabo told me that Spottie is now a more cautious, careful and better dog than he was before.
-- District Game Protector F. H. Servey, Clinton.
June 1954.

World's Only Fishing Dog

SUSQUEHANNA COUNTY - There is a small stream running through W. R. Spencer's back yard in Thompson. Some years ago there was a ten inch trout living there which the Spencers were in the habit of feeding. They would hold bread or a worm in the water and the trout would eat from their fingers. If the fish was hiding they could call him to dinner by agitating the water with their hands. One day the family dog, a Spaniel, was drinking at the trout's customary feeding place when all of a sudden the dog jumped backward and with him came the ten inch trout. Fortunately, Mr. Spencer's father was at hand to return the fish to water. It is their opinion that because agitating water was the signal for meal time, the trout mistook the dog's lapping tongue for a choice morsel of food and had a bite. Of course, the startled dog reared back and thereby landed a ten inch trout and in so doing earned the distinction of being the world's only fishing dog.
-- District Game Protector Donald Day, Susquehanna.
July 1954.

Sneak Attack

FULTON COUNTY - I became absorbed watching red ants literally eating a garter snake alive, beside one of the large ant hills on State Game Lands 453. I was wondering how they attacked him in sufficient numbers, to stop his flight, when they answered my question for me. A reinforced patrol had slipped up my pants leg. They must have had their watches synchronized for they set their hooks at the same time.
-- District Game Protector Carl E. Jarrett, McConnellsburg.
July 1954.

Motherly Instinct

SCHUYLKILL COUNTY - I have received many calls to perform unorthodox methods of protecting wildlife; however, the most recent one topped them all. A lady called and asked me to stop in to see her that it was urgent. I stopped the same day to check the call and a very sincere and annoyed housewife asked me what I could do to help keep a robin who was setting on a nest from becoming wet. At this time, it was raining very hard. I explained to her that the robin was careful to protect her nest and that it was not necessary to take precautions to protect her. She replied that I should do something to help her, even if it was some sort of an umbrella to keep the rain off the robin and her nest. She as much as implied that since it was my duty that I should hold the umbrella if necessary. The following week the robins had left the nest.
-- District Game Protector Billy Drasher, Tamaqua.
August 1954.

Pennsylvania Boasts Only Bird With Band-Aid

LUZERNE COUNTY - On May 27th I had an unusual complaint. Mr. Ponomo called and said he wanted to see me right away concerning turkey damage. Upon investigation, I found a turkey had flown through a window in his summer home adjoining State Game Lands No. 187. If Mr. Ponomo still didn't have the turkey I wouldn't have believed it. Satin drapes, shower curtains, and bed spreads were torn to shreds. Blood was showered from walls to ceiling. After a considerable amount of work, we got things cleaned up to where it was fit to live in again. I might say the only thing our friend, the gobbler, suffered was a cut on the leg. You can see that turkey running around today with a plastic band-aid which we put on to stop the bleeding.
-- District Game Protector Norman J. Forche, Conyngham.
September 1954.

No Greater Love

CRAWFORD COUNTY - A local woman told me an experience she had a few years ago while hunting ducks with her husband. They were going into a beaver dam to hunt. Her husband was carrying the decoys and she the guns. He was in the lead crossing a beaver dam when she slipped and went into the dam, started to sink into the mud holding the guns above her head. Her husband turned and when he saw what condition she was in, he got the most sorrowful look on his face. All was well until he shouted "SAVE THE GUNS!" I believe this man to be a real sportsmen always thinking about his firearms.
-- District Game Protector John Putnam, Hydetown.
September 1954.

Crab Catcher

LAWRENCE COUNTY - An Enon Valley fisherman, Ed Heath, reported to me recently that while picking soft shelled crabs from a Lawrence County stream one night, the following incident took place. While picking the crabs and sorting them, so as not to get the hard shelled ones, he happened to look toward the bank with his flashlight, and there stood a large raccoon watching the procedure. Having a hard shelled crab in his "pitching" hand he threw the crab at the curious raccoon with some force. To his amazement, Mr. Coon caught the crab in his forepaws and took off as quickly as he had made the catch.

-- District Game Protector Calvin A. Hooper, Jr., New Castle.

October 1954.

Super Sense of Duty

WESTMORELAND COUNTY I have been called upon several times to perform duties not exactly in the line of a Game Protector. One instance, I was called by a lady who wanted me to shoot a crippled horse. Recently, I was requested by another lady to please get a large blacksnake out of her attic. However, the snake had other ideas about being removed from its nice, cozy retreat. Every time an attempt was made to remove it, it would scram down the partition. I still haven't heard whether it has finally been caught. The most recent one was from a lady near New Kensington, who requested me to please scare her four- or five year old son so that he would stay off the highway. It seems that he did not believe that there was such a thing as a policeman.

-- District Game Protector D. W. Heacox, Irwin.

November 1954.

Look Who Hitchhikes Now

WESTMORELAND COUNTY - Mr. Carns of Rector, R. D., related the following experience to Deputy Frank Baum: On August 16, 1954, while driving his pick-up to work, he heard a commotion in the back of his truck. He stopped quickly and jumped out to see what was making the noise. To his surprise there was a big buck trying to get up on his feet. He finally made it and left for parts unknown. Mr. Carns said he had picked up strange hitchhikers before, but never a deer.

-- District Game Protector Charles Hertz, Ligonier.

November 1954.

It Says Here

BERKS COUNTY - While assisting sportsmen to clean up the Propagation Area at Lake Ontelaunee, I saw a rather unusual sight. A fisherman and his small son were taking time to read the Propagation Area signs. This might not seem unusual to anyone but a Game Protector. Most of our experience seems to be with fellows like the one who stopped his car during the deer season to look at a State Game Lands sign from the road. He got back in his car without reading the sign, then drove all the way home to telephone me, asking if it was permissable to hunt where those signs were.
-- District Game Protector Samuel C. McFarland, Centreport.
December 1954.

How's That Again?

SCHUYLKILL COUNTY - Prize of the opening day was the hunter who shot a second ringneck pheasant and walked over to pick up his bird. His first bird jumped from his hunting coat pocket and ran away. Doing a quick recovery the hunter shot the first bird a second time and thus was the first bird first or was the second one first? The whole episode was witnessed by Deputy Game Protector Les Wenrich, but the hunter is unidentified.
-- District Game Protector Ralph L. Shank, Pine Grove.
January 1955.

Pheasant's Bill-of-Fare Panics Plucker

MONTGOMERY COUNTY - On November 9, 1954, my uncle John Vannes of Freeland, went hunting for a few hours in the surrounding farmland and shot his limit of cock pheasants. That evening after dinner was over, he was cleaning his pheasants in the sink, with the help of my mother-in-law. All of a sudden she screamed and put one of the birds quickly back on the tray. I went out to see what happened. I found that she was cutting open the craw on one of the birds when she saw a snake curled up in the craw. I looked and found that the snake really looked like it was still alive, but when I took it out, it naturally was dead. It was a common three stripe garter snake and it measured eleven inches long. Evidently, the bird just ate the snake, prior to its being shot, because digestion had not yet started. From now on, I guess I will have to clean my own Pheasants, because I don't believe I will ever get any more cooperation from my wife or mother-in-law.
-- District Game Protector William Shaver, Mainland.
February 1955.

81

Pipe Smoking Pheasant

VENANGO COUNTY - Recently I was stocking ringnecks in Cranberry Township, assisted by Food and Cover Foreman Earl Nunemaker. I was releasing from one side of the truck and Earl from the other when I heard some "out of the ordinary" language. I soon was to discover that Earl had just opened a crate and was leaning with his head close to the door when out came a cock bird and took Earl's pipe from his mouth. Now this should have a quick ending, conditions were such we should have found the pipe in a few minutes, but it was nowhere to be found. We finally decided that the pipe must have caught in the bird's wing and he flew off with it.
-- District Game Protector Leo E. Milford, Oil City.
February 1955.

Daniel Boone Is Back

DELAWARE COUNTY - Recently when picking up hunting license applications from issuing agents, I stopped at a small sporting goods store in Havertown. This was the first year that this store had handled hunting licenses and as usually, happens they made a few mistakes. I was going through their applications when I noticed one that didn't look right to me. I turned to the clerk in the store and asked if they always ask for identification before issuing a license. I was assured they did and then showed the clerk the application I was in doubt about. She looked it over and replied, "That's all right, I know that boy personally." The name which appeared on the application was "Daniel Boone."
-- District Game Protector Daniel McPeek, Jr., Glen Mills.
April 1955.

Hunting Accident Has Happy Ending

FOREST COUNTY - Ed Snyder related the following story to me: While rabbit hunting one day he became rather warm and sat down on a stump to rest and let his two dogs work. After sitting there a short time, he noticed that his dogs were standing in one spot. Upon investigation he found a man lying on the ground with his gun beside him and the dogs were licking his face. He said this frightened him and his first thought was that the man had been shot, so he started to run for help. On second thought he went back and called to the man who then wakened, sat up, and asked what time it was. When told the time the man said, "Holy smokes, I've been sleeping all afternoon!", and took off for home.
-- District Game Protector George W. Miller, Marienville.
April 1955.

Light Attraction

GREENE COUNTY - On November 28, while attending the Greene County League Meeting, a story was related to me by Frank Trun of Fayette County. He said that one night this fall, while fishing and reeling in a catch, a strange animal swam in behind his catch. The animal took out of the water and straight for a gasoline lantern on the bank. The animal burned his nose on the glass, jumped back into the water, swam about two circles and took off. At first Mr. Trun believed it to be a muskrat, but then was sure it was a mink.

-- District Game Protector A. J. Ziros, Carmichaels.
April 1955.

Angler Angers Ringneck

FULTON COUNTY - Fish Warden Carnell and I were patrolling Barnett's Run, south of Needmore, early in March. We saw a fisherman, Stanley Sharp of Dott, Pa., coming through a field from the stream. A cock ringneck pheasant was flying at him and flogging him. Carnell and I investigated and he told us that he was glad we came along because no one would have believed him otherwise. He was fishing along the stream when he saw five hens and a cock on the opposite bank. The cock came over and made such a nuisance of himself that it was necessary for Mr. Sharp to place his landing net over the bird so that he could continue fishing. Carnell and I played with the bird for awhile, and tried to instill some fear in him, but to no avail. Other fishermen have reported like experiences at the same fishing hole.

-- District Game Protector Carl E. Jarrett, McConnellsburg.
June 1955.

Night Owl For Television

COLUMBIA COUNTY - A great horned owl that Homer Keck got out of a nest as a fledgling on March 27, and raised by hand feeding has developed into quite a pet. The bird is allowed to go out for exercise during the day and has only failed to return on one occasion. That one time he stayed out all night, but was sitting on the back steps in the morning wanting to get in the house. Mr. Keck says the bird is very fond of television and will sit on his knee by the hour, especially if there is a boxing match on the program.

-- District Game Protector Lewis H. Estep, Berwick.
August 1955.

Too Much Heat For Groundhog

MONTGOMERY COUNTY - One very hot day last June while checking along the Little Neshaminy Creek for nesting ducks, I heard a disturbance in the high grass. Thinking it was a muskrat I waited to see what it was doing. It turned out, however, to be a half grown groundhog coming down to the water. I was really surprised when the animal jumped in the creek and swam around for at least five minutes. Finally, it climbed up the bank and waddled away. I had never seen a chuck swimming before but I guess the heat was just too much without taking the swim.

-- District Game Protector Donald L. Croft, Hatboro.
September 1955.

On The House

SCHUYLKILL COUNTY - A gray squirrel with a sweet tooth recently caused quite a commotion at the Atlas Powder Company plant in Reynolds. The company has vending machines installed for dispensing candy and, finding one of them empty, employees reported to the vending machine company. When the machine was opened, they found a gray squirrel inside. He had consumed one entire row of candy bars and was too fat to escape the way he had entered.

-- District Game Protector Billy Drasher, Tamaqua.
October 1955.

Cracking Good Competition

CARBON COUNTY - This past month brought another unusual occurrence. One, where on four different occasions squirrels bit humans. In this locality where these attacks have taken place there are many hickory nut trees and naturally squirrels are fond of such nuts. When persons pass near these trees or try to pick the nuts they must be very much afraid of the squirrels. Two persons have been treated by doctors for bites inflicted by these squirrels. One was a youngster, the other a woman. On one occasion a baby being pushed in a carriage by its mother was attacked and narrowly escaped being bit, were it not for the mother warding off the squirrel. Another woman after having picked a half bushel of nuts placed them alongside a building. Seeing a squirrel remove the nuts, she took the basket and placed it inside the building. When the squirrel returned it became very angry and had to be driven off with a clothes prop. Probably the only cause for such attacks would be the jealousy of the squirrels for the nuts.

-- District Game Protector William E. Fulmer, Lehighton.
December 1955.

Just Stringing Along

ELK COUNTY - Recently while patrolling a section of my district by foot, I stumbled over a white cord strung along the ground. Being curious, I followed the cord for about a quarter of a mile to find that it led to the highway and was tied to a small sapling there. Still not satisfying my curiosity, I followed the string in the oposite direction for approximately a half mile to find to my amazement that it was tied to the belt of a hunter slowly picking his way through the brush. Upon inquiring as to the purpose of the string, he replied that he was not familiar with that territory and used the string as a protective measure to avoid becoming lost.

-- District Game Protector Gerald Kirkpatrick, Portland Mills.

January 1956.

Rare Retriever

BEDFORD COUNTY - I stopped in the barber shop at Woodbury during the early part of duck season. It was a rainy cool day with some fog gathered along the mountains. Roy Greene the barber said, "John, I am going to tell you something that happened this morning that is hard to believe. Rev. D. I. Pepple, the local banker, another man, and a farmer and I heard a shot on the Woodbury Dam. We looked out the window and observed a man taking off his clothing and shoes and swimming out in the dam to retrieve a duck. Then he pulled his pants on and stood in the rain, bare back, gun in hand, waiting for more ducks."

-- District Game Protector John S. Dittmar, Loysburg.

January 1956.

Slippery Rock Surprise

BUTLER COUNTY - Charles Stringer, Jr., while hunting near Boyers the first day of the buck season had a rather unusual experience. He saw several deer running in the distance but due to the inclement weather could not tell the sex of the deer. So he started to run, trying to head off the deer. As he was running, he leaped to span what he thought was a large rock. To his surprise the rock turned out to be a live doe which raised as he leaped, striking him in the feet which sent him and his rifle sprawling in the snow. The doe trotted off a short distance and stood looking back at its victim lying there in the snow with an expression on her face that said the joke was on Stringer.
-- District Game Protector Woodrow E. Portzline, Slippery Rock.
February 1956.

Squatters Rights

YORK COUNTY - About three months ago, I received a call from Mr. C. Gurreri in east York and was requested to attempt to remove a rabbit from their home. The Gurreri family had moved to a new home but found that the home was occupied. Mrs. Gurreri answered her son's calls the first night in the new home and while doing so she stumbled over a rabbit in the hall. The rabbit disappeared but the following morning the violets that had been at the window had been eaten. A rabbit trap was placed in the kitchen and that evening a hungry and bewildered rabbit was caught.
-- District Game Protector Earl E. Geesaman, York.
March 1956.

Fisherman's Surprise

SUSQUEHANNA COUNTY - I guess everyone is inclined to treat fish stories lightly. It wasn't until I learned there was a witness involved that I began to take some stock in a tale being passed around by Bob Brown, a barber in Montrose. It seems Bob and a friend were fishing for pickerel through the ice on Warner's Pond when one of Bob's tip-up flags went up. As Bob began to haul in the line he realized by the struggle that he must have a fish of unusual proportions on the other end. Confident that he had the bet of a buck for the largest fish of the day in the bag, Bob called his buddy over to witness the catch. It is difficult to tell who was more surprised, Bob or a large muskrat which had a hook through the lip when pulled out. The irate rat was returned to water and with it went hopes of the days prize.
-- District Game Protector Donald C. Day, Susquehanna.
April 1956

86

Pandora's Box

SUSQUEHANNA COUNTY - Ed Rudball, owner of a rabbit farm in Clifford Township, was furnished with 40 box traps. He told me that during the month of January he caught the following in addition to his catch of rabbits: 12 grey squirrels, 27 red squirrels 2 flying squirrels 8 opossums, 1 house cat, 1 rat, 12 field mice and 1 mole.
-- District Game Protector Casimir M. Stanis, Uniondale.
March 1956.

Sense of Humor

WESTMORELAND COUNTY - The following incident was told to me by a trapper friend who wishes to remain anonymous. He had been out tending traps when he heard what he thought was someone laughing. Being interested as to who might be in the vicinity he decided to investigate, and slowly made his way toward the "voice." He had only gone a short distance when he heard the laugh again. Looking up in a tree he saw a crow perched on a limb. It had something clutched in its foot and would reach down with its bill, take hold of the object and rear back, then give out with a "ha-ha," and flap its wings. The crow's sharp eye finally caught sight of my friend and he dropped the object and flew off. Upon examination of the object, it was discovered that the crow had been snapping a rubber band. I have heard a lot about crows, but this is the first time I have heard of one with a sense of humor.
-- District Game Protector J. M. Maholtz, Mt. Pleasant.
June 1956.

Entomologist, Too!

BERKS COUNTY - It has long been an established fact that some people call a game protector for legal advice or wildlife information. The other day a woman called and described the location of her house, stating that a large grove of oak trees surrounded the building. She also stated that last year they had quite a time when the inch-worms came down from the trees onto their home. This spring they intend to have the house painted. She called to find out when the inch worms were coming this year, so that the house could be painted before the invasion.
-- Land Management Assistant Roy W. Trexler, Reading.
July 1956.

Sweet Deer

CLARION COUNTY - During my service with the Game Commission I have received many complaints of damage done by wildlife and thought that I had just about seen everything as far as deer damage was concerned, until I stopped to contact John Gammon of Elk Township. Seems as though John had tapped his maple trees this spring and was boiling down the sap to make some maple syrup. After several weeks of collecting and boiling some 75 gallons of sap, John had finished up with about four gallons of syrup. The syrup was kept outside in one large container to cool after the boiling process until one night John forgot to cover the container. The following morning the container was empty and with the tracks of half a dozen deer leading up to and away from the spot, left no doubt as to where the four gallons had gone.
-- District Game Protector Donald M. Schake, Knox.
July 1956.

Ketcha Me, Ketcha Him, Too

FRACKVILLE - A few years ago, I was travelling in the neighborhood of Frackville, near the Little Mud Run Creek. As I approached a fisherman, the old gent turned around and said, "Better watch out, maybe a Fish Warden comes."

"Why?" I said. "Does he come this way?"

"No can tell," said fisherman. "He no good. He come from Shenadoor. Him just made two Mahony City men pay fines yesterday."

"What's the matter with that?" I asked, laughing to myself.

"Why, me no got license," said the fella, speaking in broken English.

"That's fine," I answered, "I'm the warden."

"Cripes!" shouted the frightened man. "Someone pointed out wrong warden to me. Vait a minute, I got buddy. Hey Joe, come here." His buddy came from behind a bush and I was surprised to hear the first man say, "Ketcha me- ketcha him, too."
-- Fish Warden Tony Lech.
August 1956.

Squirrel Fishing

BERKS COUNTY - Deputy Ernest (Dutch) Koerner answered a call from a woman who stated that she had been chasing a squirrel around inside her house all day, had it cornered in the bathroom, and didn't know what to do next. Dutch solved her problem by going to his car and returning with a landing net with which he netted the squirrel with the skill acquired through lots of fishing.
-- District Game Protector S. C. McFarland, Centerport.
October 1956.

Hotfoot Foils Broadtails

ERIE COUNTY - Early in August I received a call from Mr. Ned Bishop of R. D. No. 1, Albion, Pa., who was having beaver trouble. Investigation revealed that Mr. Bishop's corn field was being systematically cut and cleared by the flattails of Conneaut Creek which bordered the corn field on the east end. Trapping was out of the question on this site and it seemed that a barricade of some sort was needed. I offered the suggestion that a trail of commercial fertilizer be spread across the end of the field that bordered the creek hoping that the strong smell of the stuff or the mild hotfoot resulting from placing wet feet on the fertilizer would discourage the corn-loving beavers.
-- District Game Protector William E. Lee, Albion, Pa.
November 1956.

Line of Duty

ADAMS COUNTY - Each and every month brings many unusual requests and questions to a game protector, but during September I had more than the normal number. Some of these are listed below: A call from a lady in the borough-"How should I treat a severe case of Poison Ivy?" Request for assistance-"I am soon leaving for Florida for the winter and do not know what to do with my cats, would you come and get them and dispose of them?" A gentleman in distress-"The neighbors' dog bit my Father-in-law while we were riding our motorcycles past their place. What can we do about it?" A few more-"There is a nest of Hornets in my garden and I can't get to my flowers to cut them. Can you do something about removing the Hornets?" "Will you please trap the Squirrels which are eating all of our English Walnuts and release the Squirrels again after we have gathered the Walnuts?"
-- Game Protector Paul H. Glenny, Gettysburg.
December 1956.

What? No Uranium?

WARREN COUNTY - Upon draining Chapman Dam in Warren County recently it was amusing to see the number of fishermen gathering lines snagged on rocks, logs, etc. One man told me he had collected over three hundred sinkers, spoons and plugs. Another man came up with a watch while still another spent hours searching for a pair of field glasses lost overboard last summer. The search still goes on for a rifle lost by a deer hunter who fell through the ice last Fall.

-- Fish Warden Kenneth Corey, Warren County.
January 1957.

Printer's Devil

CAMBRIA COUNTY - On November 18, I received a call from Mr. Frank Cammarate of the Patton Press Courier to remove a doe deer from the printing rooms of the local paper. She gained entrance to the building by jumping through a window of the printing establishment. I proceeded to the Courier office and by that time, Mr. Cammarate and Chief of Police Ed Donahue had herded the deer into the advertising room. On the scene at this time was Dr. John Allen Murray, a local physician of Patton. With the aid of Dr. Murray, we were able to bring the deer to the floor and with the aid of a few others, we were able to tie the hoofs of the animal. But due to its thrashing around, we were unable to move it. Dr. Murray produced some ether, which after a long tussle, subdued the deer (but did not knock it out) enough so that it could be loaded into a vehicle for release in the country. After its bonds were cut off, the deer loped away across the field, apparently none the worse for its experience.

-- District Game Protector G A. Miller, Barnesboro.
February 1957.

Come What May

GREENE COUNTY - This story was related to me by Deputy Durstine of Dawson R. D. and also witnessed by Deputies Workman, Bloom and other hunters. In the 1956 big game season, one hunter in Fayette County meant to get a shot at a buck one way or another. His equipment included a pair of binoculars, rifle, two pistols, dagger, movie camera, bow and quiver loaded with arrows. One hunter remarked, "All he needs is a fishing rod and reel and he'll be ready for anything."
-- District Game Protector Alex J. Ziros, Carmichaels.
March 1957.

Hook, Line and Hunter

WASHINGTON COUNTY - One afternoon during the past deer season, Deputy John Sworden was patrolling in the vicinity of Taylorstown when he noticed an elderly gentleman fishing at one of the favorite spots in that area. While talking with the man, he saw that he had a rifle near at hand. The weather being unseasonably warm created a problem for the gentleman but the urge to go fishing won out and the rifle was brought along just in case an unsuspecting buck might show up.
-- District Game Protector William E. Cowden, Washington.
April 1957.

Pyromaniacal Sparrow

ALLEGHENY COUNTY - If sparrows want to get the tobacco habit, it's alright with Mrs. Elizabeth Muder, but she wishes they would stop smoking in bed. One of the birds slipped under the eaves of Mrs. Muder's home at 212 Jucunda St., Pittsburgh, carrying a lighted cigarette butt and set fire to the place. Firemen estimated damage at $200.
-- District Game Protector W. J. Brion, Pittsburgh.
May 1957.

91

Here Comes Hoppy Cottontail

LEHIGH COUNTY - For the first time in my life, I saw a rabbit make a flying leap over a dog's back. A bird dog was working along the top of a very steep hillside on Game Lands No. 205, and flushed out a rabbit, which started down the hill, picking up speed as it headed towards my dog. At the last moment the rabbit noticed that he was heading straight for my dog, but due to his speed, was unable to stop or turn aside. Mr. Cottontail solved the problem by leaping high over my dog's back. My dog, startled, turned and gave chase, whereupon the rabbit headed for a lespedeza patch and escaped.
-- District Game Protector W. A. Moyer, Allentown.
June 1957.

Protection Problem

BERKS COUNTY - During April I had the experience which every Game Protector fears. While patrolling with Deputy Metz at night along the Blue Mts. I hit a deer with my car. After the crash we first examined the car and Deputy Metz straightened out most of the damage to the right fender with his hands, leaving only a few minor dents. Next we walked back to look at the deer lying on the edge of the road. The deer, a buck, seemed to have some life and we were ready to end its suffering with a pistol. Suddenly the deer lifted its head and started to shake it back and forth. We then took a closer look and could see no broken legs, only a few bare patches of skin where the hair has been scraped off. A foot, applied to the rear portion of the deer, caused it to stand up. After a few minutes of shaking its head and trying to balance on wobbly legs it seemed to be okay, but continued to look at us. Deputy Metz then gave a sharp whistle and the buck took off for the woods.

If Mr. Buck had known who hit him he would probably have a poor opinion of the Game Protectors who were supposed to be protecting him.
-- District Game Protector S. C. McFarland, Centerport.
July 1957.

Spinning Surprise

CUMBERLAND COUNTY Wayne Bard of Rt. No. 1, St. Thomas, while spinning in Cowan's Gap Lake for trout had a good strike and when he stopped the running line a grebe broke water and took to the air. At the end of the line it stopped suddenly and returned to the water. The grebe was retrieved and released apparently unhurt but the spinning reel had to be returned to the factory for repairs.
-- District Game Protector Edward W. Campbell, Ft. Loudon.
July 1957.

All's Well That Ends Well

MONTOUR COUNTY - During the past nesting season, I had a very unusual incident reported to me in the Washingtonville section. One of the Mallard hens which had taken up residence on the creek which runs through the town nested and hatched her brood within the view of many of the town residents. However, 5 of the eggs were a little late in freeing the little ducklings and the mother took her first ones and left. This was noticed by an interested townsman who upon examination found that the eggs had been picked and with his help, all 5 of the little fellows were taken from the shells but too late to leave with the old hen and their brothers and sisters, thus starting an unusual chain of events.

The orphans were taken to the home of Mr. Emerson Heffner to be cared for and were at once adopted by the old setter dog which is owned by him. The dog would lay by the box and if another dog or any other animal came near, she would chase them out of the yard.

-- District Game Protector George A. Dieffenderfer, Northumberland.
September 1957.

Monkeys Is The Craziest

MONTGOMERY COUNTY - Any Game Protector certainly gets his share of unusual complaints. But I believe the month of August had more than its share for Montgomery County. The local drug firm of Sharpe & Doehme here in the County had a mass escape of about 50 monkeys that they were using in their serum tests for polio inoculations. Within the hour and for a period of more than a week, my telephone kept ringing of monkeys, monkeys and more monkeys. They scattered out over the countryside and to this day there are still some missing. I can certainly thank the Upper Gwynedd Police force for recapturing most of the animals. Otherwise, I would be afraid that more than one hunter would give up hunting and turn to a more quiet sport if he threw up his gun to bag a squirrel in a tree and found a monkey looking down on him.

-- District Game Protector William E. Shaver, Mainland.
November 1957.

Film Record

MONROE COUNTY - Deputy D. M. Bush, East Stroudsburg R. D., was trapping for fox during September. One morning in checking his traps he found a coyote in one. He wanted to take some photographic evidence of the catch before dispatching the animal and was able to take about 3 feet of movie film. Then the camera-shy coyote gave an extra hard lunge, and pulled the trap stake out of the ground. The coyote took about three jumps, and promptly put his back feet against the trap and pushed it right off his front feet. Deputy Bush lost the coyote, but is mighty proud of the film showing his trapping ability.

-- District Game Protector John Doebling, East Stroudsburg.
December 1957.

Trap Gun

FULTON COUNTY - Fish Warden Carnell and I were checking two hunters. One carried a fine old trap gun of yesteryear, upon which I commented:

"Fine old trap gun you have."

"What the heck you mean, Crap Gun?"

"No! No! TRAP GUN."

"Cheeses Mac! You can't shoot nutting in a trap with no gun like that; blow it all to pieces."

-- District Game Protector Carl E. Jarrett, McConnellsburg.

January 1958.

Bait In A Boot

ERIE COUNTY - The weekend of January 11th and 12th saw one of the largest crowds of ice fishermen ever observed on Presque Isle Bay in Erie County. As darkness approached and the people started to leave the peninsula, the traffic was almost equal to a busy weekend in the summer. Thousands of Yellow Perch and Smelt were taken and all persons interviewed reported success.

One bait dealer at the public dock tells of a fisherman who, having forgot his minnow bucket, asked the dealer to put a dollar's worth of minnows into a hip boot. (No, he was not wearing the boot.)

-- Regional Fish Warden Supervisor S. Carlyle Sheldon.

March 1958.

94

Artificial Respiration

ERIE COUNTY - Recently Deputy Howard Gay related the following incident to me: One of the residents of this district was enroute down into one of the more famous deer counties during this past season. While traveling east on U. S. Route 6 he came upon a situation, which at first looked somewhat odd. The motorist noted that a deer had been hit by an automobile and he also noted that attempts were being made to save the deer. The deer lay helpless but soon came to after artificial respiration had been administered for a few minutes. According to the report, which we believe to be reliable, the deer was brought back to normal breathing only through the artificial respiration.
-- District Game Protector Roger J. Wolz, Albion.
July 1958.

Danger-Blasting Ahead

CHESTER COUNTY - While out patrolling on Project No. 45, checking groundhog hunters one evening I ran across a hunter who was taking no chances. On the back of his hunting jacket he had a flag - the type used on construction jobs - about two foot square- red background and in large letters "Danger-Blasting Ahead" printed on the flag.
--District Game Protector P. J. Filkosky, Parkesburg.
August 1958.

Where Do Goslings Come From?

MONTGOMERY COUNTY - During the month of May, a sportsman living in Mount Clare, William C. Blatt, Jr. was wading the Schuylkill River behind his home. In this immediate vicinity there are usually a flock of Canadian Geese which number between 60 and 80. They make this part of the river their home and also raise their young on the many small islands in the river. Mr. Blatt went up on this one island and saw a female goose lying on a nest. He walked up to her and as he got about 10 feet away she stood up and started to hiss like they do. He looked in the nest and saw that she was incubating two goose eggs and a large glass bottle. It was so interesting that Mr. Blatt took a picture of this and sent it to me. As Mr. Blatt said, "We all know that young geese come from eggs but evidently the geese themselves were not told about this."

-- District Game Protector E. W. Shaver, Mainland.

September 1958.

Bill of Fare

ROSS LEFFLER SCHOOL OF CONSERVATION - Students of the school enjoyed an order of fried rattlesnake, prepared by School Cook, Art Webb, early in August. The snake was killed by Game Protector Leo Milford while conducting us on a field trip to the Waterfowl Impoundments in the Allegheny National Forest. Suprisingly enough, all but a few of the Students tried a portion, and most found the meat somewhat agreeable, but not agreeable enough to warrant any new hunting.

-- Student Officer Edward F. Divers, West Mifflin.

November 1958.

Cast For Duck Lands Bass

BEDFORD COUNTY - On October 18, 1959, at the Shawnee Lake, a hunter shot a mallard duck. It fell into the water out of the hunter's reach. To retrieve it he went to his car and secured a casting rod and a large surface plug. On his first cast, he hooked an 18-inch largemouth bass. On several more attempts, he hooked the duck and landed it. Later, when this man was checked, he had three mallard ducks and one bass.

-- Fish Warden William E. McIlnay.

December 1958.

96

Eh?

CAMBRIA COUNTY - During the night patrol the evening of October 31, 1958, Deputy Stinson and I observed a teenager along country road carrying something under his arm. Upon stopping and talking with the youth we found it was a B. B. gun. I asked the reason for the gun. He replied protection from the wildcats that were reported around there. I asked his name, he said "Watt," but I thought he said "What?" so I asked him again, he replied "Watt." I told him to spell it; he did. WATT.

-- Game Protector James Burns, Jr., Ebensburg.
January 1959.

Dry Run

DELAWARE COUNTY - While hunting deer in archery season in Marple Township, Delaware County, George P. Buchser of Newtown Square had the good fortune to get within close range of a buck and two does. Naturally, he shot his first arrow at the buck but due to his excitement he shot a little low and the arrow passed harmlessly through the buck's legs. One doe and the buck darted away but the other doe ran a little closer and stopped facing Buchser. While keeping his eye on the doe, Buchser reached over his shoulder and pulled another arrow from his quiver. His aim this time was for the chest of the deer which was still facing him. Just as he released the arrow, the deer crouched and instead of hitting the chosen mark, the arrow hit her right between the eyes, and much to the surprise of the archer, fell to the ground not harming the deer which sped off. Upon retrieving the arrow, Buchser discovered the point was missing. When he couldn't find it on the ground, he decided to look in the quiver. Yep! That's where it was. At least he had a good story to tell.

-- Game Protector Daniel S. McPeek, Jr., Matamoras.
January 1959.

Deer Roping Champion

SOMERSET COUNTY - During the past antlerless deer season the following story was related to me by an unknown hunter. He was watching a large field with binoculars when several deer came into view at the far end of the field. Suddenly a young boy emerged from the field edge, shot at and hit one of the deer. The deer kept on going across the field with the youth in hot pursuit. At the edge of the field the wounded deer became entangled in a wire fence. When the young nimrod finally reached the deer he had expended his supply of ammunition. He stood momentarily and pondered the situation. He then took the "drag" rope from the back of his hunting coat and proceeded to truss up his quarry and tie it fast to a fence post and fill out his big game tag and tie it on the deer's ear. By this time the other hunter came over to investigate and the youngster asked him if he could borrow his rifle to finish the job he had so laboriously commenced.

-- District Game Protector Eugene Utech, Confluence.
March 1959.

Friendly Fellow

BUTLER COUNTY - Gene Isaly, a sportsman from Evans City, Butler County, asked me to drop in one day when I happened to be near there. This I did and he said he had something to show me. While sitting in the auto Gene got out and started to call, "Oscar." Soon a big male ringneck pheasant came running out and sat there. He reached down and petted it, picked up the bird and set it down. Then it followed him all around the yard. Next he tapped the hood of the auto and "Oscar" flew up and sat there. Now Gene said, "Watch this." Then he opened the door of his home and said, "Come on, Oscar," and just as big as life the bird followed him in. Gene related many other things that the bird has done, including watching television for hours on his lap. The bird came in from the wild as an adult and just took to Gene.
-- District Game Protector Paul Miller, Butler.
May 1959.

Risky Red

BLAIR COUNTY - Recently while traveling along Federal Highway 22 between Water Street and Hollidaysburg I noticed a Red Squirrel setting up in the middle of the road. I straddled him in order not to hit him, and as I passed I looked in the rearview mirror and saw that he was still sitting in the middle of the road and hadn't even stopped eating the nut which he was holding in his front paws. Guess that he was either awful hungry or just plain contemptable.
-- District Game Protector Russell Meyer, Altoona.
May 1959.

Action-Camera

WAYNE COUNTY - Mr. Forkey and Mr. Wyman of Honesdale participated in trapping beaver this season and it was their habit to carry an 8mm camera to record the unusual while on the trapline. Mr. Forkey was setting a #4 trap when it suddenly sprung, catching the handler about the largest joint of his thumb. Mr. Wyman arose to the occasion and proceeded to record this on film for posterity, much to Mr. Forkey's annoyance. Insult was added to "injury" when Mr. Wyman inquired of the now fuming Mr. Forkey as to the correct camera setting. Then he released his friend from the trap and when last seen, Mr. Forkey's thumb resembled the business end of a Louisville slugger.

-- District Game Protector Frederick Weigelt, Honesdale.

June 1959.

Rock-A-Bye Baby

ALLEGHENY COUNTY - Mel Clear, Deputy Game Protector of Pittsburgh, has many damage complaints to take care of, particularly regarding squirrels and raccoon. One of his most unusual experiences in this respect happened last month. Upon receiving a call that squirrels were invading the privacy of a home, Mel was looking about on the second floor of the residence, when he noticed a movement in the mattress of the baby's crib. Mel probed the mattress with his hand, and hastily drew back this appendage with a mama squirrel hanging on his index finger. Three babies (squirrel) were also in the mattress. The locale? Why, Squirrel Hill, of course.

-- District Game Protector Samuel Weigel, Gibsonia.

July 1959.

Mary Had A Little Fawn

MONTGOMERY COUNTY - Mary had a little deer, it followed her to church one day... The story as told to me by a resident of Huntingdon Valley happened this way. One Sunday morning as the people of Huntingdon Valley were on their way to honor the Sabbath, a very friendly deer approached from a nearby woodlot. Of the many people going to Sunday Morning Services, the deer (a yearling) chose to follow a girl by the name of Mary. It followed her directly into church and prepared to stay for the entire services. It took one hour of persuasion by means of apples, corn, lettuce and celery to remove our hero from the church. Since this usually quiet Sunday morning our friend has since returned to the. peacefulness of the wild.

-- District Game Protector Edward Sherlinski, North Wales.
August 1959.

The Cat Should Be A Deputy

WAYNE COUNTY - While patrolling Lake Wallenpaupack with Game Protectors Weigelt and Kriefski, and Fish Warden Joseph E. Bartlett, I arrested a man for fishing with too many devices. His remark to his fishing buddy was, "If that black cat hadn't crossed the road in front of us this morning, we never would have been caught and arrested."

-- Fish Warden Harlan F. Reynolds
August 1959.

Maternity Ward?

LANCASTER COUNTY - Deputy Martin Stoner told me of a very interesting occurrence that he witnessed. Deputy Stoner runs a welding shop in the Boro of Quarryville. Right across the street from his shop is a large metal building that is used for the storage of steel and other supplies. From time to time Deputy Stoner noticed a very tame rabbit fooling around this building. On the morning in particular the doors of the building were not opened at the usual time and he saw the rabbit just sitting there as if waiting for them to open the doors. Finally the fellow showed up to open the doors. The rabbit still kept sitting until he opened the door whereupon the rabbit hopped into the building and went directly behind some boards that were propped in a corner. Deputy Stoner investigated and found that the rabbit had a nest of young behind the boards. At the time of this writing the whole family is doing nicely.

-- District Game Protector J. P. Eicholtz, Strasburg.
September 1959.

100

Nothing Ventured, Nothing Gained

VENANGO COUNTY - A rabbit damage complaint this month brought to mind how little many people know about coping with a wildlife situation. A rabbit trap was given to a family to take a rabbit or two out of their garden. After some time, I stopped to pick up the trap and ask how many rabbits were taken. I was told they had caught a rabbit, but didn't have the heart to kill it. A neighbor offered to shoot it with a shotgun, but they didn't want to do this, so they just released it. I asked why they didn't take it out into the country and release it. They just never thought of that and never thought of calling me.

-- R. V. Rea, District Game Protector, Cranberry.
October 1959.

Time For Alarm

FULTON COUNTY - While on a Field investigation, Trooper Eiker froze in his tracks, saying "Don't move. Rattle Snake." The villian was promptly located, wrapped around his wrist. His little daughter had set the alarm on his Dick Tracy Wrist Alarm Watch.

-- District Game Protector Carl Jarrett, McConnellsburg.
November 1959.

Dove Spinning

COLUMBIA COUNTY - Dove hunting has become a very popular sport and is one sport that will really tax the hunters skill. Take for instance this hunter who on the first day of the season picked out a good stand over a one acre farm pond where the birds came to water. He shot down six birds in a row, but could find only two in the high weeds surrounding the pond. Becoming disgusted at the waste down over the water, and by using stones he could shove them in to shore by the action of the waves. This he did on the second day, but soon ran out of available stones. On the third day this person returned with a spinning rod and jitterbug lure. After the bird fell into the water he would pick-up the rod and cast out over the bird, retrieve until the lure caught on the bird and then bring it in. Needless to say he lost no more doves since he could easily see where they landed.

-- William E. Fulmer, Land Manager, Bloomsburg.
December 1959.

Chapter 4
1960- 1969

The sixties were a time of political and social flux across America as a new generation challenged the standards they were expected to meet. This new attitude was even observable in the woods and on the waters in Pennsylvania. Conservation officers soon began to encounter "hippies" and other interesting people in some of the strangest situations imaginable. On occasion, even the wildlife seemed to be a part of the rebellion. Yet, despite the new disregard for authority among the younger generation, a growing number of people began to take an interest in the conservation and proper, respectful use of the natural resources found in Pennsylvania.

Most of the cartoons found in this and subsequent chapters are Nick Rosato's originals, used in *PA Game News* at the time the notes were published. All illustrations for notes from Fish Commission personnel have been created by Rosato exclusively for use in this compilation, as *PA Angler* Stream Notes were infrequently illustrated.

Smoke Chuck
BERKS COUNTY - Members of the Reading Exchange Club held their annual picnic last September at the Linnette Farm, Alsace Township. As they were building a fire in the fireplace they experienced trouble in getting a draft through the chimney. They finally moved the fire out in the fireplace so there would be some draft to carry off the smoke. After the fire had burned for a considerable time, they noticed a violent eruption and a well smoked and slightly singed groundhog dash through the fire. After the groundhog made his exit, they had no more trouble with the chimney.
-- District Game Protector Joseph Leiendecker, Reading.
January 1960.

No Fooling
ALLEGHENY COUNTY - On the first day of the buck season some humorist was at play in Pine Township. A paper mache deer was erected in a clover field some 50-odd yards from the highway. It possessed a very nice set of antlers but the Allegheny County buck hunters are hard to fool. No one had taken a shot at it by noon when the owner shyly removed it.
-- District Game Protector Samuel K. Weigel, Gibsonia.
February 1960.

Bronx Cheer
WAYNE COUNTY - Although this event did not happen in Pennsylvania, it is passed along both for the humor and the lesson it may contain for Pennsylvania hunters.

Not far from our border, in New York, a successful hunter stopped for lunch after bagging his buck and was highly elated. He went into great detail relating the events of his kill to the waitress who served him. Finally, he insisted that she take a look at his prize. After viewing the deer, the waitress hesitantly told the hunter he had killed not a deer - but a goat. Our hero was adamant to the end as he quickly put on his coat, gave one and all a tolerant sneer and reached for the door. His parting shot showed his sincerity and pity for all those within earshot, "Don't tell me that isn't a deer. You people just don't know your wild animals. I've seen plenty of deer in the Bronx Zoo."
-- District Game Protector Fredrick G. Weigelt, Honesdale.
March 1960.

None the Worse

PIKE COUNTY - George Compton of Mill Rift, Pa., stopped at Deputy John Hanrahan's home one evening to advise him that a deer had just been hit by a car on the Matamoras road. John asked if he would need to take along a rifle to dispatch the deer, if it were not already dead. He was told that the deer was quite dead and to make sure, George had kicked it in the ribs.

When John and George arrived at the scene, they were quite surprised to see, not a dead deer, but a live deer standing in the middle of the road. They shouted and waved their arms at it, but it refused to move. When the deputy approached the deer, it still refused to budge. He felt its legs to see if any were broken, and then decided that the deer had to be removed from the road before being hit again. The Deputy placed his hands on the deer and attempted to push it off to the side of the road, but instead of moving, the deer actually braced itself and leaned into the Deputy. Finally it was necessary to pick up the deer bodily and carry it to the side of the road where after being placed to the ground, again refused to move. About this time Deputy Hanrahan was about out of ideas, when he thought that the deer might be blinded by the car lights. He requested George to turn off the lights and was much relieved to see the deer take off for the woods apparently unhurt by the experience.
-- District Game Protector Daniel S. McPeek, Jr., Milford.
March 1960.

Who Dat Who Say Whoo?

JUNIATA COUNTY - It was an average looking package the rural mail carrier accepted along his route and brought into the post office at Thompsontown in Juniata County. It was processed and dropped into the canvas bag to await shipping. However when Mr. Harold Haines heard noises coming from the bag he decided he had better investigate. He dumped the contents onto the floor and noticed the package the noises were coming from. It had a return address of Paul Van Horn from McAlisterville, Pa. It seems Mr. Van Horn had pole trapped a Great Horned Owl and was sending it for bounty. However, he had not quite finished the job of killing it. I imagine at least for awhile this incident broke the routine for the Post Office employees in Thompsontown.
-- District Game Protector Robert Shaffer, Mifflintown.
April 1960.

Sucker For A Trap

CLARION COUNTY - A local trapper by the name of Walter Switzer related this incident to me. He had been trapping muskrats on a small spring run for two weeks. Each morning in one certain set the trap would be sprung but there were no tracks to indicate how this happened. At last one morning the villain was caught. It was, to his surprise, a six-inch sucker.
-- District Game Protector J. Leo Badger, Knox.
May 1960.

Blast Off

FULTON COUNTY - When a story has made the rounds enough times, one at least assumes there must be a bit of truth in it. I have heard this one in Fulton County a number of times. I can never pin down names since there is a violation involved. Three men were hunting coons. Their dogs treed in a large den tree. There was one large hole at the base of the tree, with water trapped below the hole. They decided to dump their can of carbide in the water and stuff their jacket in the hole.

They smelled carbide pretty strong; so decided to stuff the jacket a bit tighter. The light they used for this operation was a carbide light. This of course was a mistake that netted them a blast that Russia may have picked up. The last man who told me this story wears a hearing aid, and hunts a three legged dog.
-- District Game Protector Carl Jarrett, McConnellsburg.
June 1960.

Full of Getup And Go

FULTON COUNTY - On the opening day of the trout season, I met a very young angler with an exceptionally fine Rainbow Trout. I asked the lad if the fish had given him a good fight. To which he replied, "Nope, he kept trying to get away the whole time."
-- District Game Protector Carl Jarrett, McConnellsburg.
July 1960.

Hitch Your Feather To A Star-ling

ADAMS COUNTY - During the past month while at SGL #169 with Officer Thrush we witnessed a real indication of thought on the part of a nest-building starling. The starling had found a tail feather from a pheasant, the feather being about 12 inches in length. The starling, being unable to fly against the wind with the feather held in its bill at right angles, first made several attempts to break the feather in half. Failing in this attempt, the starling finally took the feather, quill-end first, pointed the quill directly ahead with the head held at an angle, and allowing the full length of the feather to trail under the body, and between the legs, flew to the site of the nest. The starling gave a good imitation of a Halloween Witch on her broomstick.
-- District Game Protector Paul Glenny, Gettysburg.
August 1960.

Bucket for a Beau

CRAWFORD COUNTY - Deputy Game Protector Bob Oates reports that a goose has taken for a mate a bucket that sits on the Fish Commission hatchery where they dry their nets. The goose guards the bucket and lays its head over it when one goes near. No explanation as yet for the strange behavior.
-- District Game Protector Paul R. Miller, Butler.
September 1960.

Share and Share Alike

PHILADELPHIA COUNTY - One complaint of 1959 recently told Deputy P. Thompson of Collegeville, was that to cope with the pheasant problem this summer, he planted 12 rows of tomatoes for himself and 5 rows for the pheasants. He said, "By golly you know somethin'? It's working."
-- District Game Protector Edward F. Sherlinski, North Wales.
October 1960.

Trouble and Toil

CENTRE COUNTY - Once more it has come to my attention the trouble that a well-meaning person will place himself in to "save" a wild bird or animal from the "hardships of wildlife."

I was quite surprised in more ways than one to hear of a turkey vulture that had been picked up and raised. (When released the wingspread was over 70 inches.)

A young man crawled into a small tunnel in the rocks in a rattlesnake den to get the young "polt" to save it from being burned when the snake den was destroyed. However, instead of returning the "polt" to its home after the fire or leaving it nearby, it was taken home. Neighbors were very very happy to see the bird leave.
-- District Game Protector Charles M. Laird, Pleasant Gap.
November 1960.

Lure of the Wild

PIKE COUNTY - Deputy Jay Lutz set some fox traps near his home. One set was located near a hunting camp and when the weekend came, he noted that the people had a dog with them. He did not want to catch the dog and he also did not want to take up the set so he found some old 1 x 8 boards about 8 feet long nearby. He put both boards together covering the set trap that was buried about an inch underground in what is well known as a dirt hole set. Come Monday morning, the campers left so Jay went to put the set in working order. To his amazement, he found a nice mature gray fox in the trap. Mr. Fox could not resist the powerful and attractive scent and had pulled the boards aside, then accidentally put his foot in the wrong place.
-- District Game Protector Albert J. Kriefski, Tafton.
December 1960.

There's Always a First Timel

I apprehended a squirrel hunter before the small game season with two gray squirrels. He had them tied to his ankle with an old shoe string and was dragging them along the ground. If anyone came by he'd step on the string breaking it, walking on leaving the evidence behind. Then, he'd say he was out hunting Woodchucks. He told me this was the first time his little scheme didn't work!
-- Fish Warden Bryce Carnell, Franklin & Fulton Counties.
January 1961.

Light Diner

SOMERSET COUNTY - While parked in a remote corner of Somerset County early in the month of November watching for jacklighters, Deputy Harry Ringler and I helped an owl get a meal. It was about 11:00 p.m. when Deputy Ringler decided to get out of the car and take a look around in the adjacent fields to see if there were any deer feeding. As he walked through some high grass, he jumped a rabbit and followed it with a light as the rabbit ran through a small clearing. Out of nowhere came a Great Horned Owl and snatched the rabbit right out from the rays of Deputy Ringler's light.
-- District Game Protector Robert H. Muir, Meyersdale.
February 1961.

By Land, Sea or Sky

BERKS COUNTY - During the year, various types of hunters afford you with a good laugh. On the first morning of buck season, Land Manager Shank and I saw a new fad, which was quite amusing. One of those short hunters was walking along the Greenland Road, on Game Lands No. 210, fully equipped with Woolrich suit, gun and knife. As if this equipment was not enough to load him down for the day, he also had a pair of pole-climbers strapped to his legs. Too bad that we did not see him climb a tree with a full field pack.
-- Land Management Assistant Roy W. Trexler, Wyomissing.
March 1961.

Doctor of Ornithology

CAMBRIA COUNTY - On January 11, 1961, while making a pick-up of trapped rabbits from Agent Earl F. Graham at Connellsville, Commissioner Miller and I heard a real "deed of the day" story from the agent. He said, "I picked up a song bird at my feeding station I considered near dead, took the bird inside the house, gave it first-aid pouring half a teaspoon of water and crushed aspirin down its throat and awaited the outcome. In ten minutes the bird was on his way to again match his wits for survival." Since the great feat, Agent Graham has earned a new title from his admirers, "Dr. Earl F. Graham" by an honorary degree.
-- District Game Protector Alex J. Ziros, Connellsville.
April 1961.

Winter Wonders

BEDFORD COUNTY - Many stories were told, retold and added to during our emergency winter feeding program. Reports that twenty deer starved one place, and many other reports that were checked out were found untrue. One started in a locker room of a local plant; nine deer were found near Bedford starved. After being checked out it was found that this report was started just to worry certain individuals who were concerned about the deer herd. A farmer who related this one to me. A friend of his found 22 deer standing all in one bunch. After trying to make the deer move he approached them and found they were all starved, dead and frozen in their tracks.
-- District Came Protector W. H. Shaffer, Bedford.
May 1961.

Merry-Go-Round

CUMBERLAND COUNTY - When a dog bites a man that's not news but when a man bites a dog that's news. So goes the old story. Recently I heard a story along these same lines. A local farmer was spreading fertilizer on his field just after the thaw from the big snow when his beagle pup spotted and chased a fox which it spotted along a fence row. The dog chased the fox out of sight but not out of hearing. Suddenly the usual baying turned to cries for help. Back came the pup with a red fox in hot pursuit seeking refuge from his owner who was driving a tractor. The farmer had to get off the tractor and drive the fox away from the cowering beagle.

-- District Game Protector Eugene Utech, Carlisle.

June 1961.

Trout Up a Tree

BUTLER COUNTY - The following story was told to me by Fish Warden Clifton Iman: Clift made the statement to me that he has seen hunters hunting for deer and bear from trees. But on the opening day of trout season this year, he came across a fisherman up in a tree trying his best to get his creel limit. The crowd along the banks of the stream had forced this determined fisherman to head for higher places. With Clift's 29 years with the Game and Fish Commissions, this was the first time he had seen a person fishing from a tree.

-- District Game Protector Jay G. Swigart, Butler.

July 1961.

Fish By the Bucketful

ALLEGHENY COUNTY - While assisting Fish Warden Paulacovich stock in-season trout at North Park Lake, I was carrying a bucket of trout to the lake. A small boy ran up to me. He was equipped with rod and reel. He wanted to fish in the bucket. I told him that he would have to fish in the lake. He stated that he thought he could do better in the bucket than the lake.
-- District Game Protector G. T. Szilvasi, McKees Rocks.
August 1961.

Bald Bait Bucket

GREENE COUNTY - In June, I stopped along Ten Mile Creek to check a fisherman who had just completed seining for crayfish. As I counted the contents of his minnow pail, this honest sportsman bent over and took off a fine imported straw hat, which revealed five more crayfish and a shining head, smooth as the ivory of a pool table. How he withstood those under that hat, later years will only tell. Was he afraid of going over his limit? This wasn't the answer. He had exactly 35, and that included those five explorers. Or could he have read or heard where crayfish were the secret to restoring a youthful crop of hair?
-- District Came Protector Theodore Vesloski, Carmichaels.
September 1961.

Bad Luck Clover

LUZERNE COUNTY - This incident was reported to me by Deputy Game Protector Raymond Harned, RD. 1, Shickshinny, Pa. He came home from work one evening very tired and hungry. After eating supper he noticed a woodchuck eating in his clover field. He went into the house for his rifle and walked to the field where the chuck was eating clover. He disposed the woodchuck with one shot. The deputy walked to the scene of the killing and noticed that after death the chuck had a four-leaf clover sticking from its mouth. Therefore all four-leaf clovers are not good luck charms.
-- District Game Protector Edward R. Gdosky, Dallas.
October 1961.

A Salty Kiss

GREENE COUNTY - In early August a Carmichaels barber was telling one of his customers of his fishing pleasures the afternoon before at the mouth of Muddy Creek on the Monongahela River. He said that a very clever raccoon kept sneaking up behind him and was stealing the crayfish from his bait can. The customer remarked that he had fished there the same day, but in the early evening. The day was warm, he was well relaxed and soon fell asleep. Something touching his face awoke him. He opened his eyes, and there was a raccoon licking his cheek. This was probably the same raccoon, who just came back for a little salt to season the meal he had earlier that day.
-- District Game Protector Theodore Vesloski, Carmichaels.
November 1961.

Trick or Treat

CLINTON COUNTY - Recently an article appeared in the Lock Haven Express about a bear seen in Dunnstown, a suburb of Lock Haven. Within a few days I received a call from a woman who lived in the middle of Lock Haven who claimed that a bear had stolen her goldfish from a pond in her back yard. It took me quite a time to convince her that the culprit that had created the havoc around her fish pond had been a raccoon and not a bear.
-- District Game Protector John B. Hancock, Mill Hall.
December 1961.

What Did She Say?

FULTON COUNTY - Retired Supervisor M. E. Sherman stopped at a farm and asked the lady who answered the door if he could have permission to hunt woodchucks. She replied, "I wish you'd kill all of them! They have all the trees pecked full of holes." -- District Game Protector Carl Jarrett, McConnellsburg.
January 1962.

Rub On Luck

LACKAWANNA COUNTY - During the course of the deer season I met an old-timer in the woods and while checking his license asked him how the luck was. He answered not too good; that he had seen a number of does but no bucks. This surprised me because when I first saw him I observed that quite a bit of fresh deer hair was clinging to his woolen clothing. Another batch of deer hair was wedged between the magazine and barrel of his rifle below the front sight. With all this hair in evidence I thought that perhaps he had assisted a companion with handling a deer. When I asked him about all the deer hair clinging to his person and also the wisp which was attached to his rifle he appeared to be somewhat embarrassed. However, finally he told me the reason behind it. He had noticed where a more fortunate hunter had killed a deer and in his desire to acquire a little "luck" for himself, he had picked up some of the deer hair and had placed it on his clothing and had also stuck the wisp in his rifle. He stated that if it didn't do any good for him it certainly couldn't do any harm and he was willing to try anything.
-- District Game Protector Stephen A. Kish, Avoca.
March 1962.

Manure Treatment

TIOGA COUNTY - Ask the farmer's permission to park in his field while hunting because he can get awful close with a manure spreader if you don't. This happened twice in Tioga County this fall. One hunter had permission but the farmer didn't recognize his new car, so he got the manure treatment.

-- District Game Protector William D. Denton, Elkland.

April 1962.

TV Fans

BERKS COUNTY - While on duty at the Commission's exhibit at the State Farm Show in January, Gordon Howard, R. D. 1, Cogan Station, Pa., related the following incident: One evening, just prior to Christmas, Mr. Howard drove to the home of his mother-in-law. As he drove into the driveway, he observed several deer on the lawn and noted that they seemed engrossed in a television program which they were apparently watching through a large picture window. Mr. Howard related that the deer paid no attention to him until he got out of the automobile and walked around toward the deer. At this time, they evidently decided that the program was not interesting enough to hold their attention with a human so near and they departed. Fortunately, when departing, they went away from the house instead of through the picture window as deer have been known to do when excited.

-- Conservation Information Assistant Paul H. Glenny, Leesport.

May 1962.

No False Point

WESTMORELAND COUNTY - On March 19, 1962, Chuck Kidney, of Delmont, was working his Brittany spaniel on a nearby farm. The dog had pointed two birds. On the dog's third point, Mr. Kidney walked in to flush the bird. Suddenly about ten feet in front of the dog a red fox jumped up and took out across the field. A very surprised Mr. Kidney approached the dog to scold him. Just as he reached the dog, who was still on a point, a ring-necked pheasant flushed about five feet in front of the dog.
-- District Game Protector Philip L. Young, Apollo.
June 1962.

Happy To Help

CENTRE COUNTY - While on stream patrol during the early part of the current trout season I watched a man fishing or attempting to fish. He would make a cast, become tangled, lower his rod, then straighten out the tangled mess and cast again. I watched him repeat this several times, then offered my assistance. I discovered this fisherman was blind. Talking with him, looking over his tackle I found his casting trouble was caused by the swivel at the end of his line that kept coming through the top guide of his rod. His fishing partner then appeared, found an oversize bead which I attached to his line ahead of the swivel. When he made a cast and retrieved the line, the bead now stopped his reeling in at the tip of his rod and he knew he was ready for another cast. I wanted to see him catch a fish but he had no luck and I had to leave. He thanked me several times for my help but I just couldn't help thinking I was the one who should be thanking him for making my day a little brighter.
-- District Fish Warden Paul Antolosky.
July 1962.

Bird Attacks Cat

YORK COUNTY - A complaint was received that a resident of York County had just killed a mockingbird to protect his cat. I wondered if the whole story might be just a rumor as I could not believe that a cat would need protection from a bird. However, upon investigation, I learned from the accused that he did kill a mockingbird and that it really was to protect his cat who he claimed was afraid to come down off the porch because of the bird. The man was sure his cat was about to have a nervous breakdown. While driving home, I could picture the cat on a little couch telling the whole story to his analyst who explained the cat's trouble this way: "You must have been frightened by a feather when you were a kitten."

--District Game Protector W. A. Griffie, Dover.
August 1962.

Game Referee

JEFFERSON COUNTY - Last month as I was driving along in Oliver Township, near State Game Lands No. 31, I noticed a commotion some distance away in a hay field along the edge of the woods. I stopped the car and walked along the woods toward where this was going on. As I got closer I could see a red fox apparently jumping up and down, rolling around on the ground, and doing all sorts of acrobatic tricks. When I got within about 25 yards from the fox I could see another animal which was a full grown groundhog. I watched these animals fighting for at least ten minutes and I know they were both aware of my presence. Although I tried to referee this fight fairly, I still do not know which one won. Appearing to be disgusted with my presence, the fox went one way and the groundhog walked up on the log, shook himself, and went in his hole.
-- District Game Protector Robert Ellenberger, Punxsutawney.
September 1962.

Green Stamps Here, Too?

MONTGOMERY COUNTY - Many times upon settlement of a Game Law violation, by means of the field receipt, the violator, upon payment of his fine, will ask: "Is this tax deductible?" "How many birds will this buy for stocking?" "Does this entitle me to a free subscription to the GAME NEWS?" I thought I heard them all, until a most recent case. Upon settlement of a violation, the violator demanded $10 worth of S&H Green Stamps. He stated that food stores, car dealers, service stations, taprooms and you name it gave stamps in Philadelphia, "Why not the Game Commission?" For twenty minutes I tried explaining the reasons but none seemed to satisfy him.
-- District Game Protector E. F. Sherlinski, North Wales.
October 1962.

Watchdog for Bunny

JEFFERSON COUNTY - Recently I visited a farmer, Blair Carrier, Summerville, Pa. He said he had something he wanted to show me. He took me to where his beagle dog was tied and a few feet from the end of the chain was a small oval in the ground covered with grass and rabbit hair. Mr. Carrier said the mother had successfully raised four rabbits there. As Mr. Carrier also has cats, this rabbit apparently made her nest close to the dog for protection.
-- District Game Protector Robert Ellenberger, Punxsutawney.
November 1962.

Moving Stack

GREENE COUNTY - Hay stacked around a pole in a field is a common scene in Greene County. But it was a small moving hay stack which made me go over two fences, cross a field and climb a hill. There it was - a TRYING crow shooter, well camouflaged, pushing a small hay stack across a field on a wheelbarrow. He said he was trying to get within shotgun range of some feeding crows, which I had driven away. He also said he would try it on deer, but not in this county. Like they said in Marine boot camp years ago, "There is one in every new platoon."

-- District Game Protector Theodore Vesloski, Carmichaels.

December 1962.

Tree Thieves

BRADFORD COUNTY - Lloyd Horton, Justice of the Peace, in Windham Township, related the following story to me: A retired railroad employe from New York State recently bought a house and some property near Horton's farm. One day the gentleman from New York, quite worked up, went to see Mr. Horton about catching the thieves who were cutting down the trees on his property and hauling them away at night. When Mr. Horton went to investigate the problem, he found one tree that had been cut and only partly felled to the ground. On this tree the railroader had tacked a note which read, "DO NOT TAKE OR CUT ANY MORE OF THESE TREES, THEY ARE MY TREES AND I WANT THEM." At first glance, Mr. Horton solved the problem and explained to his neighbor that his trees were not being cut and stolen by human thieves, but by the eager beavers that were living in the stream nearby.
-- District Game Protector Donald E. Watson, Towanda.
January 1963.

Seeing Is Believing

ERIE COUNTY - Deputy Hido, while on patrol one evening during the hunting season, checked two hunters that had just finished hunting. Upon inquiring, the hunters stated disgustedly, that they had found no birds even with the use of their valuable bird dog, and that the Game Commission had probably not stocked any birds in the area. While discussing the bird problem, about 50 yards down the road from them, three cock pheasants and two hens crossed from one side to the other, in plain view, very much to the satisfaction of Officer Hido and, of course, to the surprise of the hunters.
-- Ralph Flaugh, District Game Protector, Albion, Erie County.
February 1963.

A Scarce Father

LEBANON COUNTY - During the small game and the big game seasons, a Game Protector's wife and children are fatherless, patrolling during the day and watching for jacklighters at night. On one morning early in December I had some paper work to do so I remained at home. My wife left to get my five-year-old daugher, Sandra, who attends a morning kindergarten class in Cleona. When she returned, Sandra, seeing my car, asked her mother if I was home. The answer was yes. Then, with a big smile, she exclaimed, "Good, I would like to see him."
-- District Game Protector Perry Hilbert, Cleona.
March 1963.

New Twist

INDIANA COUNTY - Fish Warden Ruddock, early in February, while patrolling, noticed a sign with big red letters stating this was a game training area. So he stopped to read it, but found that it was just an old story with a new twist. The sign read as follows: "No trespassing, GAME TRAINING AREA, hunters stay out, so that in the future, sportsmen can have the thrill of meeting game on even terms, OUR RABBITS ARE BEING TAUGHT TO SHOOT BACK, until the training program has been completed all hunters stay out at any season." I wonder what the reaction may be if there is a hunting accident on this tract of land and no offender can be found.
-- District Game Protector John A. Badger, Indiana.
April 1963.

Rabbit Outlaw Catches Self

DELAWARE COUNTY - During the recent rabbit trapping program one of my trappers "lost" several traps in one night. I went to the area in question and began searching along a highway bank for the "straying" traps. To my surprise, a car stopped on the road above me and the driver threw a bag down the bank nearly hitting me. I opened the bag and found the remains of a recently killed cottontail. The motorist was so busy watching the road to be sure no other cars were approaching that he failed to see the Game Protector he was trying to avoid. I followed the motorist home where I found the box trap used to catch the rabbit and the dressed rabbit.

--District Game Protector R. D. Feaster, Chester.

May 1963.

Dirty Dog

Former District Warden L. E. Close was helping to stock trout in the Driftwood Branch of Sinnemahoning Creek along with Game Protector Norm Erickson. Erickson's Labrador retriever was along but could hardly be called a first rate trout stocker. After the stocking was ended and all were gathered about the truck ready to leave, the group turned to look for the dog. They saw him bringing a fish out of the water in his mouth. He was warned that following the fish truck was less than ethical and the unharmed fish was returned to the water.

June 1963.

Blind Chuck

CAMERON COUNTY - On April 23, 1963, Donald Walls, a Penn State graduate student working in Cameron County on a wild turkey survey, was in the Cooks Run area when he noticed a full grown woodchuck acting in a strange manner. The chuck was first observed feeding and paid no attention to the approaching observer. When within about 15 feet of the chuck, it started to run towards its hole and dive in but missed the hole and went sprawling. On recovering its balance, it began to move about in a hesitating way and finally found the hole and went in. Walls then approached the hole to within several feet and waited. In a couple minutes out came the chuck, paid no attention to Walls, sat up in front of him, turned his head about in chuck fashion and went right back to feeding within a few feet of Walls' feet. During this close observation it was perfectly easy to see that both of the chuck's eyes were grown shut. The chuck was left unmolested and I doubt if any human will ever molest it back in that remote area of Cooks Run.

Who knows, maybe some of the tall tales we hear about the hunter shooting a blind deer and the fisherman catching his limit of blind fish are true, anyhow, we better not argue the point.

-- District Game Protector Norman L. Erickson, Emporium.

July 1963.

Dutch

PERRY COUNTY - In investigating a possible violation with Officers Utech and Moyle in Cumberland County we asked a farmer directions to the farm. The farmer replied in the following manner. "Go to the out movie, turn left, go to the first intersection turn left, go to the first ground road, turn left. If you come to a store don't pay no mind to it, but if you see it turn around - you went too far."
-- District Game Protector Jacob Sitlinger, Newport.
August 1963.

He Used Discretion

ERIE COUNTY - I ran into Gus Pulakos, of Erie, near Waterford, and he related the following: "I saw a small animal attack a rabbit on my farm near Waterford, and when I approached the animal retreated. I went up to the rabbit, saw it was still alive, and started to reach down for it. The animal, which by now I recognized as a mink, made a pass at my arm. I reached for the rabbit three times and the mink started to attack three times. Remembering about discretion being the better part of valor, I retreated and left the mink its prey."
-- District Game Protector Elmer Simpson, Union City.
September 1963.

Quite A Scene

While on a patrol of Lake Jean on the Sullivan-Potter county lines, Deputy Game Protector Roberts and I observed a boat depart from the shore only to make a wide circle and return. Occupants appeared to include a "Mom 'n Dad and two sons combination." The boat landed, Mom disembarked holding a casting rod arched not unlike a hunter's bow... she was holding the grip near the reel while the tip was bent around out of sight. As she neared us she volunteered this explanation: "He was supposed to be after fish... but he got me!" As she walked away quite embarrassed, we saw she had been caught squarely in the seat of her slacks with a large bass plug! A little piece up the road she turned and quipped. "What a scene for Candid Camera!"
-- District Fish Warden James P. Voider.
October 1963.

New Wrinkle

BLAIR COUNTY - Complaints come and go with the job of Game Protector. Some call about rabbit damage but don't want the little fellows hurt or disturbed. Squirrels in the house are a nuisance but we like to feed them nuts. How can we get a little fawn for a week to feed, and so on. But now a new wrinkle; a woman hits the bottle too much and has found that my number is a good one to call at all hours when pink elephants, leopards, snakes and deer climbing trees come before her eyes.
-- District Game Protector Paul Miller, Bellwood.
November 1963.

Beaver in the Corn

WYOMING COUNTY - On September 16, I received a somewhat unusual complaint relative to beaver damage to corn on the Hoppe Farm near Nicholson. The beavers are cutting corn and hauling it to where they are living in the bank along Tunkhannock Creek. They go a considerable distance into the field and cut a stalk of corn, after having passed dozens of stalks that are identical to the one cut. About all that is eaten is the corn off the ear; very little of the stalks are utilized. Otherwise, they are quite conservative, cutting the stalks right at ground level.
-- District Game Protector Phil Sloan, Tunkhannock.
December 1963.

Safe Another Day

MERCER COUNTY - The following was related to me by Barney Klumph, a pheasant hunter from West Middlesex. Last hunting season as he stopped at a swamp area to hunt he noticed a hunter who had two good beagle dogs barking on a rabbit track, but the dogs would take the track to a nearby gas line and would lose it. The dogs repeated the run several times; and after no results, the hunter caught his dogs and headed for the car, mumbling about his dogs. Heading down the gas line to hunt, Mr. Klumph noticed a meter box, where the rabbit seemed to disappear, so he lifted the lid very carefully and sure enough, there sat Br'er Rabbit on top of the meter about two feet off the ground. Mr. Klumph turned to yell to the hunter who was just loading his dogs, and then decided, no, this rabbit has earned his right to live another day, and closed the lid. The last he saw of it, it was still sitting high and dry on top of that gas meter.
-- District Game Protector John A. Badger, Mercer.
January 1964.

Bug Adrift

ERIE COUNTY - On Monday, November 18, Deputy Game Protector Joe Janosik and Fish Warden N. Ely accompanied me to check hunters and trappers in Waterford Township and on State Game Lands No. 109. I was checking for traps along LeBoeuf Creek in an area where a bridge is out. I could not believe my eyes when I noted a Volkswagen about half submerged in the creek. I called to Joe and Norman and we went to investigate. A gun case and a pair of shoes were on the bank near the V.W. In the car there was a camera and one shoe floating around. There was a leather belt fastened from the front bumper to a tree root to keep the car from floating farther downstream. Presently three young men appeared on the scene with towing equipment.

The owner had driven the V.W. across the stream during the dry spell when the water was low. When he and his hunting companions came to the fording spot, he attempted to drive across as usual. The water was up about two feet and the V.W. just floated down the stream until the passengers, in fright, opened the door and let the water flood the car. They abandoned ship and later anchored it to the bank. We helped them get their water-borne craft back on dry land, and requested that they refrain from litter-bugging in the future.

-- District Game Protector Elmer Simpson, Union City.

February 1964.

Skate Hunting

DELAWARE COUNTY - On December 28, 1963, at approximately 3:30 p.m. Deputy Bartholomew was patrolling near Boothwyn, on Naaman's Creek Road when he observed a young man ice skating. When Deputy Bartholomew took a second look, he saw the fellow was wearing a hunting license and carrying a shotgun. Deputy Bartholomew checked the hunting license and asked what he was doing. The fellow told him he was ice skating and hunting squirrels at the same time. Deputy Bartholomew told him that skating and hunting might prove dangerous if he was to fall. The young man said that he had considered that and the gun was unloaded. He was carrying the shotgun in one hand and a shell in the other.

-- District Game Protector R. C. Feaster, Chester.

March 1964.

Man Above

BUTLER COUNTY - The following story was related to me by a fellow sportsman, and for obvious reasons we will not use names. On the first day of antlered deer season the uncle of the person who related the story to me was hunting in Warren County. There was a heavy wet snow with the trees hanging full making the visibility very poor. It seems like the would-be buck hunter was on the stand at the foot of a tree for a couple hours watching for his buck. He heard shooting not knowing exactly where it came from until another deer hunter slipped out of the tree which he was standing under, excused himself, and proceeded to tag a nice buck which he had just shot. The hunter at the foot of the tree had neither seen the hunter up the tree nor the deer which he shot.
-- District Game Protector Jay D. Swigart, Butler.
April 1964.

Wildlife Traffic

MONTGOMERY COUNTY - On Sunday, February 2, 1964, I had an unusual day, even unusual for this area, where I have learned to expect anything. My day started in the morning when a deputy from Philadelphia brought me a red fox which he had shot at 46th and Market in the center of the city. At 1:00 p.m. I received a call from the Upper Dublin police telling me that a deer was inside an A & P store at Welsh and Twinning Roads. Arriving there I heard on the police radio that there was another deer in a bowling alley in Willow Grove. I have been here one year and so far I have had to remove deer from a bank, a grocery store and a bowling alley. Some day I hope to get a transfer where the deer aren't so friendly.
-- District Game Protector H. T. Nolf, Fort Washington.
May 1964.

129

Embarrassed

BUTLER COUNTY - Imagine the embarrassment of this Game Protector who, after engaging the help of Bob Shawgo, a local sportsman, to help dig out a den of foxes in a rocky hillside, found nothing but a sleepy groundhog at the end of a 20-foot long and 6-foot deep tunnel!

-- District Game Protector Ned Weston, West Sunbury.

June 1964.

World's Largest Coffee Pot

WAYNE COUNTY - On April 7, a trailer truck loaded with coffee sideswiped a bridge on Route 6 which crossed Shohola Creek and dumped 20 tons of coffee into the 70-foot gorge. Bystanders reported that the brook was blue with floating cans, and one was heard to say, "This should be the best place to fish the opening day, all you have to do is dip some water from the brook, heat it and add milk and sugar." Not only do we have good fishing but we have the biggest coffee pot in Pennsylvania.

-- Land Manager Wilmer R. Peoples, Hawley.

July 1964.

An Honest Mistake

WESTMORELAND COUNTY - During the time that I have been a Game Protector, I have had some very unusual calls by individuals. During the hunting season a mother called and reported her son for hunting unaccompanied as he was not yet of age to hunt alone, and wanted me to pick him up. A father reported his son for disturbing rabbit traps and wanted him reprimanded. But the one that really threw me was when a lady called and wanted me to sell her a load of manure. For a minute I wondered what the "gimmick" was, but after a brief conversation, learned it was an honest mistake.

-- District Game Protector Joseph Maholtz, Mt. Pleasant.

August 1964.

130

Nudists Find Fawn

GREENE COUNTY - The boundary line of a recently acquired Game Land in my district joins a nudist colony in a well secluded area. On June 5, I received a call from a nearby resident to pick up a fawn deer. This person informed me that some nudists had picked up the "LOST" fawn, which was all alone in the big woods. Now I often wonder how these nature lovers would take it if I found one of their "LOST" sun-tanned beauties and took her home. I know for sure how my wife would appreciate this sort of rescue.
-- District Game Protector Theodore Vesloski, Carmichaels.
September 1964.

Mountaineer Country

GREENE COUNTY - I recall a story that former Deputy Game Protector Art Boden told me. Art went on a squirrel hunting trip with his brother deep into the heart of West Virginia. Their guide was a true Snuffy Smith hillbilly who lived miles from the nearest road. Out of curiosity Art asked the guide if a Game Warden ever came around his neck of the woods. The guide answered with a slightly quickened drawl, "He DAREN'T come up here."
-- District Game Protector Theodore Vesloski, Carmichaels.
October 1964.

Good at Everything

BUTLER COUNTY - During the course of a Game Protector's activities we are called upon to perform many and varied tasks - some quite unusual ones. Recently Deputy Kenneth Thompson of Boyers came upon perhaps one of the most unusual jobs of all. During the recent Butler County Fair, my Deputies watched over the exhibit and sold GAME NEWS during my absence because I was on vacation. As Ken sat at the table selling GAME NEWS, a young lady came up and inquired of him if he worked for the Pennsylvania Game Commission, and was advised that he did. "Oh," she said, "I know you gentlemen are very reliable, would you mind watching my baby while I take a walk through the fairground?" So Ken took the only way out - he baby-sat for approximately half an hour until the lady returned, thanked him graciously, and left.
-- District Game Protector W. Ned Weston, Boyers.
November 1964.

Invisible Fish

WARREN COUNTY - Remembering the story of the Emperor's suit, at a Warren County field day, some prankster set an aquarium filled with water on a table. The sign placed on it read "Invisible Fish." This display brought 'em out in droves and it was amazing how many people got down for a better look at the water. Some people even asked where the fish were caught and what bait was used. One man said he had caught one like it and didn't know it until he got home and the cat stole it. He added he was disappointed he didn't get a chance to eat it because a friend of his said these fish were delicious.
-- District Fish Warden Kenneth O. Corey.
December 1964.

Busy Hands Are Happy Hands

WARREN COUNTY - Talk about not wasting one moment hunting and fishing... I checked a man along the river who sat on a rock with two fishing lines in the water, a shotgun across his lap and knitting a pair of sox. He told me he learned to knit while in a veterans hospital and now always knits his own sox. This guy was busier than the proverbial paperhanger.

-- District Fish Warden Kenneth G. Corey.

January 1965.

Zeroed In a Bear

CLINTON COUNTY - On the last day of the bear season I checked a nice bear killed by a young hunter from the southwestern part of the state. This lad with two companions had driven up from Washington County to hunt for bear in this area for actually only a few hours. Being curious, I asked why he had picked this particular area for his hunt. This is how he figured it: He had read about the bear kills in Clinton, Lycoming and Potter Counties, so he laid out a map and picked Renovo as the center of the kill area. When he got here he drove over a forest road until he found a spot with no other hunters. Here he started. He put his compass in his hand and he and his companions walked due north. Holding this course for about one-fourth mile, he found a log that a bear had torn open looking for grubs. "This is it, men," he stated, "there's a bear around here and he'll be back to finish his job on this log." He added, "We didn't wait very long, about 15 minutes, and here came the bear. Nothing to it. "I'm coming back next year and get another one." This was in country scoured by camp hunters for three days. I thought he was kidding, but when I looked at him he wasn't smiling, he was dead serious.

-- District Game Protector Charles Keiper, Renovo.

February 1965.

133

This Must Be the Place

POTTER COUNTY - The veracity of this yarn, as well as that of the column from which it originated, might be questioned. However, according to the Potter Puffs Column in the local newspaper, a nonresident motorist made a believer out of one of our state troopers. It seems the motorist had stopped at a "Deer Crossing" sign in hopes of observing some deer. The trooper, being curious, stopped and approached the driver and, after hearing his ideas and thoughts, explained that the signs are nothing more than warnings and that deer don't necessarily cross at that particular point at any given time, etc. Nevertheless, before the trooper had finished with his truthful explanation, eleven deer filed across the highway a short distance from the sign.
-- District Game Protector H. Richard Curfman, Coudersport.
March 1965.

Tranquilizer Needed

GREENE COUNTY - During deer season I became suspicious of a hunter's actions and followed him for over 20 miles clear out of the county. I finally got him stopped and the first thing he said was, "I'm sorry, I never should have shot, I'm glad you caught me." But something else was wrong, and I was going to find out. First it was very evident that he had "Buck Fever," and we waited for about ten minutes for him to control his trembling. His story was that he fired at what he thought was a buck. After he shot he got the "fever" and never went to check the shot out. So back to the Game Land he went, and I silently prayed that he did not shoot a man. I couldn't find a deer track and I moved over to the left of the place he showed me. Lo and behold, there lay a big 8-point buck. I then gave the novice hunter a lesson in gutting a deer and lectured him on hunting as we dragged it to his car.
-- District Game Protector Theodore Vesloski, Carmichaels.
April 1965.

Smarty Cat

LUZERNE COUNTY - On February 23, while on duty at the Philadelphia Boat and Sportsman's Show, I noticed the wildcat seemed to be getting a lot of attention. That night when we were closing the exhibit and were all behind it, there were still a few people looking at the wildcat. I peeked out and saw this one fellow had a plastic bag with a trout in it. I meowed several times and said, "I like trout." The man just looked. After I did it the second time, he left. I went out to see where he had gone and saw him hurrying back with his friends. He was excitedly telling them about the wildcat and then said with the bag outstretched toward the cat, "Do you want some trout?" The wildcat just lay there motionless. The man turned and asked me if the wildcat would talk again and I explained that he was very unpredictable and usually only talks once during a show. The last I saw this fellow, he was still talking about the talking wildcat.
-- District Game Protector Robert Nolf, Conyngham.
May 1965.

Who Said They Were Color Blind?

ELK COUNTY - During the month of March I checked on a camp in Benzinger Township and found the owner of the camp there. I found numerous feeders and an abundance of feed for the wild birds and animals. The owner of the camp showed me how well he had the wild birds and animals trained. As he would call each squirrel's name, that squirrel would come forward for a peanut. As he would call the birds' names they would fly in, land on his hand and he would give them a sunflower seed. He told me that it took him at least 4 years to get the animals in that frame of mind and that he felt the color of his jacket and hat were recognizable to the birds and animals. He related several stories about deer hunters in red coats and hats that came to his camp and commented on the crazy birds that were sitting on their shoulders and gun barrels.
-- District Game Protector Fred Servey, St. Marys.
June 1965.

No Cat Is an Island

MERCER & LAWRENCE COUNTIES - Russell Arnold, Hadley, Pa., told me that last summer he built a new farm pond above his house. On the night it was completed he closed the gates and went to bed. During the night his cat that always sleeps in the cellar started to bawl and meow, finally got the whole family awake. Upon investigation, Mr. Arnold found three feet of water in the basement and the cat floating around on a big block of wood. Thoroughly mystified, he rescued the cat. The next day he found his pond was in the same gravel bed that his basement was dug in and that the pond would build up a head, then drain into the cellar. A clay lining has since remedied this and now both Mr. Arnold and his cat are sleeping soundly and dryly.
-- District Fish Warden Richard Alplanalp.
July 1965.

Where There's A Will...

JEFFERSON COUNTY - While on patrol of North Fork of Red Bank Creek I noticed a fisherman walk to his car, lift the hood, then walk back to the creek. I saw him do this several times; each time he would make one or two casts with his spinning rod. As he came back to the car the next time, I moved in closer and watched him remove the oil dip stick and apply a few drops of oil to the reel. When I asked him about this procedure, he explained he had dropped his reel into the water and was oiling it. Most other fishermen would have given up the rest of the day for lack of a handy oil can. Just goes to prove the old adage-"Where there's a will, there's a way!"
-- District Fish Warden James Donahue.
August 1965.

High Jumper

JUNIATA COUNTY - On Monday, June 21, Carl Dressier, one of my deputies, got up at 5 a.m. to fish Caster's Hole about 2 miles north of Mifflintown on the Juniata River for bass. He had rowed his boat to a spot right out from a 50-foot ledge of high rock. He had just started to fish when a train came along farther back up over the hill. All of a sudden from the top of the high ledge leaped a nice three-point buck, it turned over twice in the air and hit the shallow water below flat on its back. This was about 25 feet from Carl. Carl rowed over, loaded it into his boat and rowed to shore and called me. We took it along with the other 3 highway-killed deer we had that morning and disposed of them. Incidentally, Carl didn't catch a bass that morning but I suggested his bucktail lure was just a little too large.
-- District Game Protector Robert Shaffer, Mifflintown.
September 1965.

Breakfast Bear

LYCOMING COUNTY - A Mr. Miller called me and stated he was having trouble with a bear and would I come and see what could be done to stop the bear. Mr. Miller has a trailer, the type that is hauled on the bed of a pickup truck. He had the trailer on the ground and was living in it until he built a cabin near the trailer. The bear came into the trailer, ripped off the screen and broke a window on one side, crawled in over the stove, took three eggs off the stove that Mr. Miller was going to have for breakfast and ate them, then went to the table where there was a bowl of stewed prunes and ate them. He also ate a bowl of strawberries, all sugared and ready for use and a cream pie which was on a shelf above the table. There was a bag of crackers on the table, he took them and jumped through another window in the end of the trailer, breaking the window. He took the crackers a short way from the trailer, ate some of them and buried the rest still in the bag.
-- District Game Protector Levi R. Whippo, Williamsport.
October 1965.

Home Sweet Home

CRAWFORD COUNTY - Butch Shaffer was having coon trouble at his refuse pit so he set a box trap. The next morning instead of a coon he had a skunk in the trap. Not wanting to cause any odor, he opened the door so the skunk could walk out. The skunk did walk out, got some more to eat, and went right back into the trap. Finally Butch just left the door of the trap off and the skunk used it as his home for two weeks, coming out at night and sleeping in the trap in the daytime. As it says in the book, you must have both food and cover to make good wildlife habitat.
-- District Game Protector John R. Miller, Meadville.
November 1965.

137

A Fox Cat?

PERRY COUNTY - Many of us own dogs trained for hunting foxes. However, I doubt that there are very many trained cats used for this pleasure. Recently such a case was brought to my attention while talking to Henry Urich, of Newport, R. D. 1. Henry was drinking coffee one morning when his wife called him to the window. Up in the field, their cat had cornered a red fox. They were looking at each other and as the fox took a step to the side so did the cat. I do not know how long this continued but long enough for Mr. Urich to get his gun and bag the fox.
-- District Game Protector J. I. Sitlinger, Newport.
December 1965.

You Don't Say

BLAIR COUNTY - The last time the little old lady (who drinks too much) called, she complained that there were four deer up in her oak tree and she was afraid they would fall. I assured her not to worry, they would fly away soon.
-- District Game Protector Paul R. Miller, Bellwood.
January 1966.

Come On Now, Fellas

FAYETTE COUNTY - I have heard of many wildlife oddities in the years with the Commission. In the small game season of 1965, Kenneth Kozel, of Connellsville, reported killing a "bald-headed cottontail rabbit," i.e., it had no ears. In the antlered deer season of 1965 an Ohio hunter reported seeing a doe deer with "two heads." What next?!
-- District Game Protector Alex J. Ziros, Connellsville.
February 1966.

138

Stool Pigeon

LAWRENCE COUNTY - Deputy Game Protector Okresic and I answered a farmer's complaint that a hunter was driving on his fields. When we arrived at the property we found the car parked in his field and the hunter's wife in the car, reading, while she waited for her husband's return. In a little while the hunter came back to the car, and because he was from out of the state we took him to a J.P. for arraignment. At the hearing he was found guilty and was ordered to pay the fine and costs. He asked the J.P. what would happen if he refused to pay and was told he would be put in the county jail. He thought about this for a bit and then wanted to know if it would be possible to put his wife in jail and let him go, for after all she was the one who was in the automobile while it was parked in the field, for he was out hunting.
-- District Fish Warden Richard Alplanalp.
March 1966.

A Long Shot

YORK COUNTY - Around the York area there is much interest in long-range shooting. Kenneth Lehman, who lives in York, Pa., was hunting turkey around noon on Saturday, November 13, 1965. He found the woods too noisy, so he scoped the hillside in Jackson Township, Perry County, and located a turkey. He raised his .257 Improved Ackley equipped with a 16-power scope, and after one shot, picked up a ten-pound turkey 400 yards away. Vern McConnell witnessed the shot as it occurred on his property. Mr. Lehman is traffic manager at York Shipley in York, Pa.
-- District Game Protector G. J. Martin.
April 1966.

Oops - Sorry!

COLUMBIA COUNTY - While on duty at the Game Commission Exhibit, Harrisburg Outdoor and Sportsmen Show, Farm Show Building, Harrisburg, I had the misfortune to make an unforgivable mistake-however, a mistake which any country boy would make. An individual with long, brown, curly hair approached me and asked to purchase the bird charts that were available. After giving this person the charts and change for $5.00, I said, "Thank you, Ma'am." This person quickly spun around and indignantly stated, "I'm a him not a her." (With the teen-agers today, both male and female, wearing long hair, trousers, and shoes with high heels, it's getting to the point where a person can't tell the bucks from the does.) One person standing by and witnessing my embarrassment came up to me and said, "That's the first time I ever saw a Warden with his mouth open and yet lost for words."
-- District Game Protector Edward F. Sherlinski, Mifflinville.
May 1966.

Those Callers Really Work

WASHINGTON COUNTY - I have heard many times of the story where a man calling fox with the electronic call had one come right up and run into him. Well, even though at the time I may have agreed with these story tellers, way down deep I couldn't see where a fox would be that dumb. On March 21, 1966, while calling for gray fox in a pine plantation, I was accompanied by some other members of the Commission when this very thing happened to me. The gray fox, trying to sneak into the call, actually brushed against my pants leg, and feeling this, I jumped and at the same time looked down into the eyes of an equally scared fox. For the next one-hundredth of a second, both the fox and I did what I was later told was the "Watusi." When it was over I had a very nice round hole approximately 3" in diameter in the ground and the same size hole through the pine tree I was standing by - but no fox!
-- District Game Protector Donald C. Madl, McDonald.
June 1966.

140

Who's in the Cookie Jar?

WAYNE COUNTY - Say, Mom, the next time you find the cookie inventory depleted, don't blame the kids right off. Virginia Lobb, of Gull Hill, Honesdale, lives adjacent to a golf course and had been subject to invasion of squirrels. However, last March, she was watching "Daktari" on TV when she heard a commotion in the console set. She knew it wasn't the crossed-eyed lion, so she investigated and out popped a chipmunk. It ran across the room and slid out the door. Miss Lobb also found its entrance hole in the wall and the record storage department was loaded with bits of cookies and cocktail nuts.

-- District Game Protector Frederick Weigelt, Galilee.
July 1966.

Well, Come In!

TIOGA COUNTY - Shortly after our two girls had left to meet the school bus, my wife heard a knock at the door. She went to the office door, but no one was there. She then checked at the front door with the same results. A few minutes later the same thing and she checked again. As we sat at the breakfast table having a cup of coffee the knock was heard again. My wife checked the office door and I the front door. She called to me to come to the office. There caught between the storm door and the inside one was a red-headed woodpecker.

-- District Game Protector Duane J. Moore, Mansfield.
August 1966.

Flying Catch

CLEARFIELD COUNTY - On the evening of June 9, while Special Fish Warden Rickard and I were shore fishing at Glendale Dam, in Prince Gallitzin State Park, we observed two mallard ducks and two common mergansers cruising off shore. The mallards came within five feet of us and began picking up tidbits of bait while the other ducks remained a short distance from shore. In the seconds that followed, the mergansers dove - line went out - pole bent and the battle began as a bird had taken the smelt I was using for bait. The bird became tangled in Warden Rickard's gear and was eased to shore where it was released. The duck swam away, ducking and shaking its head and probably wondering what kind of food that was that hit back.
-- District Game Protector Jack R. Furlong, Ramey.
September 1966.

A Night Deposit?

LAWRENCE COUNTY - Help was requested from local authorities and officers of the Lawrence Savings and Trust Company Bank recently. According to the first report the intruder was masked and considered dangerous. Entry was attempted at the rear of the bank through a rear window that was protected by heavy iron bars. Before a robbery was committed, the culprit was captured by Deputy Game Protector Thomas O'Brien and my son-in-law, Wayne Weatherby, who also heard the report. The masked bandit will no doubt spend the rest of his natural life, with other raccoons, away from the business district of New Castle.
-- District Game Protector Calvin A. Hooper, Jr., New Castle.
October 1966.

U.F.O. Again

ERIE COUNTY - During the month of August, 1 received reports of a panther in the vicinity of North East, a full-grown lion in the Waterford area, a large, strange looking bear near Franklin Center. On Presque Isle a U.F.O. landed and unloaded an 8- foot tall apelike monster that preys on the neighborhood dogs. A farmer reported missing one of his cows and it seems that a neighbor lady saw a U.F.O. hover over the cow, lower two forklike arms, pick up the cow and fly away. Maybe the U.F.O. is rearranging our animal population here on earth. I wonder where it took the cow?
-- District Game Protector Ronald L. Sutherland, Erie.
November 1966.

Licensed Pigtail

LEHIGH COUNTY - The following was related to me by two of the Deputies in the district: While on patrol the first day of dove season, the Deputies were checking hunters and among the group was a young lady. When she was asked to produce her license, she turned her back to the officers and there was the license - hanging from a long pigtail braid and in the middle of the back. Maybe she didn't want to put holes in her hunting vest.
-- District Game Protector J. R. Fagan, Allentown.
December 1966.

New Pointer

BERKS COUNTY - John Fleck, hunting ducks along the Cacoosing Creek, was unable to locate a cripple which had fallen into a pasture field. A horse in the field came over and pointed to the duck which had crawled into a clump of heavy grass.
-- District Game Protector J. A. Leiendecker, Reading.
January 1967.

Deer Smeller

BERKS COUNTY - While working at the deer checking and aging station at Clarks Ferry many interesting experiences were related to me by deer hunters. One follows: It seems that on the first morning of the season a hunter had a wounded deer but was unable to locate it due to the lack of snow. After spending about 1 1/2 hours looking for the deer, he went to his hunting headquarters and related his experiences to the lady where he was staying. Later they returned to the woods and the lady was able to find the deer for him because she could smell the deer blood and trail the deer by doing so. He brought a nice buck through the station.
--CIA R. H. Myers, Hamburg.
February 1967.

Wrong Place, Wrong Time

BUCKS & NORTHAMPTON COUNTIES - While on stream patrol one day last October, Deputy Game Protector Jack Kauffman watched two men fishing without their fishing licenses displayed. Jack checked the duo and learned they were residents of New Jersey. He asked to see their licenses, and the one man said, "I have several." He produced resident fishing liceenses from four states; New Jersey, Pennsylvania, Oklahoma and Illinois. This man had plenty of licenses, but not the right one. The second man had none at all.
-- District Fish Warden Michael Badner.
March 1967.

He Ain't Heard Nothin' Yet

LANCASTER COUNTY - While on duty at the Farm Show in Harrisburg, a gentleman came to our display and said he thought some of the stories that appear in the Field Notes of the GAME NEWS couldn't possibly happen. Had he been there five minutes sooner, he'd have heard about a hunter shooting a bear that was on a deer's back!
-- District Game Protector Henry G. Stankewich, Lancaster.
April 1967.

Real Dudes

CENTRE COUNTY - My wife received a phone call the other day and the person at the other end explained that she has been feeding scratch grain and sunflower seeds to the squirrels and birds, but would like to have a bag or two of ear corn to give the eleven turkeys she is also feeding. When asked if there were any toms in the flock she replied, "I believe so, as four of the larger birds were wearing neckties."
-- District Game Protector M. Grabany, Philipsburg.
May 1967.

First, Catch a Tiger

FOREST COUNTY - I just read in one of the new farm magazines that a foolproof repellant to keep deer away from crops is lion, tiger, or leopard manure. We could sure use a lot of it

-- District Game Protector D. W. Gross, Marienville.

June 1967.

Now He Knows

ERIE & CRAWFORD COUNTIES - While on patrol prior to the opening day of trout season, Deuty Kuntz saw two young lads fishing from a bridge on a trout stream. Deputy Kuntz stopped and asked them if they knew trout season was not in yet, when a deep voice from under the bridge said, "'Who the *@*%* wants to know?" A rather costly question.

-- Land Manager J. C. Hyde, Townville.

July 1967.

145

Broke the Camel's Back

COLUMBIA COUNTY - A local attorney told the story of a divorce case in the local courts. His client, the husband, was contesting the divorce action brought by his wife. During cross-examination of the wife, the attorney asked just what was her complaint. The wife stated that her husband did nothing but hunt and fish, hunt and fish - 9 months of fishing and 3 months of hunting every year. Then she blurted out, "The last straw was when he went out and killed two tame geese and brought them home last year." At this point the husband turned to his attorney and said. "She's really trying to give it to me, isn't she?"
-- District Game Protector E. F. Sherlinski, Mifflinville.
August 1967.

Taking Advantage

DELAWARE COUNTY - Early in May I received a call from one of the local utility companies. One of their service men had seen an injured hen pheasant near the road. He picked up the bird and put it on the back seat of the car. The caller told me the bird now seemed to be OK. I suggested that he release it, but he hesitated and said there was an additional problem. It seems the hen had laid an egg on the back seat of the car and was on it....
-- Game Protector R.C Feaster, Chester.
September 1967.

Shoulda Gone Huntin'

CLINTON COUNTY - The other day Mr. Woods Rich of Woolrich told me a strange story. While fishing in the Pine Creek area, he had hooked a nice trout of about fifteen inches. Just as he was about to land it, a large mink swam up and stole the fish from his line.
-- District Game Protector J. B. Hancock, Lock Haven.
October 1967.

Double or Nothing

BUTLER COUNTY - It is truly amazing to sit at a Wildlife Display at a County Fair and listen to the comments of one person to another concerning the various animals. I think the remark I'll remember longest is the one told to me by a woman at the Butler County Fair this year. She said that while driving one night, she ran over a bobcat which weighed 93 pounds! No amount of reminding her that a 35-40 pound cat would be huge would make her change her mind. From now on, we keep our doors locked at night!
-- District Game Protector W. N. Weston, Boyers.
November 1967.

Diaper Crowd

CAMERON COUNTY - Deputy Game Protector George Andrus checked on a fisherman who was fishing a small brook trout stream after the season's close. When conducting a search of the man's auto he came across a damp newspaper. The man told the deputy it was only a wet diaper in the paper. However, Andrus is a very thorough person so unwrapping the package commenced. It did contain a wet diaper.
-- District Fish Warden Stanley G. Hastings.
December 1967.

Display on Whose Back?

LANCASTER COUNTY - Recently I attended a Bar-B-Q at a local sportsmen's club. There I saw a gentleman that had come to my headquarters last year with quite a problem. He was having some difficulties locating a baby-sitter for his six-month-old baby. With the many unusual requests we do get, I first thought he wanted me to do the honors. But he just wanted to know if it was legal for him to carry his baby on his back Indian style and pin his hunting license on the baby when he went out hunting.
-- District Game Protector H. G. Stankewich, Lancaster.
January 1968.

Anyone Can Make a Mistake

CAMERON COUNTY - During bear season, Fish Warden Stan Hastings checked a carload of hunters on the Rich Valley Road. Stan asked them if they had any luck. One hunter eagerly proceeded to tell Stan that though he hadn't seen a bear he'd found lots of bear sign among a large formation of rocks nearby. He took a paper bag from his coat pocket, explaining that he knew his buddies would never believe him if he told them about the fresh bear sign without proof, so he had brought back some proof. The excited hunter opened the bag to show the proof. Hastings looked in the bag and smiled, then said, "Gosh, I'm afraid you made a mistake. These aren't bear signs, but porcupine." No need to say, a roar of laughter went up from the men in the car, and the last I heard a certain hunter was still digging a deep hole to crawl into.
-- District Game Protector N. L. Erickson, Emporium.
February 1968.

Violation Reporter

LUZERNE COUNTY - Special Fish Warden John Lukavitch and I had paused for a well earned cup of coffee one day after having patrolled Harveys Lake in bitter cold. As we sat sipping, an angler, recognizing my car, came into the restaurant to look for me. "I'd like to report a violation," he exclaimed, when he saw me. "Good," I said, stirred at the thought that finally we were getting cooperation from an aroused sportsman. "Tell me about it."

"Well," he began, "I was fishing off a dock down on the lake and after I had caught my limit, I watched two other fishermen. One of them had caught his limit of trout and then he handed the same rod to his buddy and he too caught his limit. Now there were two limits of trout caught with that same rod, and that's illegal!" As I explained to the fisherman that this did not constitute a violation of the fish laws I couldn't help notice John, a veteran of over thirty years in fish law enforcement, sitting there shaking his head slowly from side to side. Later, as we left, he said, "You meet them all, don't you!"
-- District Fish Warden James F. Yoder.
March 1968.

No Violation

YORK COUNTY - One day last October Deputy Raymond Schroll and I heard shooting about 7:10 p.m. Sunset had been at 6:45 p.m. so we investigated. I found a hunter who said he had been hunting doves, but didn't know it was after sunset. When I told him about the penalty, he said he would pay the fine, whatever the amount, because he should have known better. When asked to unload his gun, he sadly admitted running out of shells at 6 p.m. He couldn't leave because he was waiting for a brother. When I told him there would be no fine since he hadn't shot after 6 p.m., he insisted that he would have been shooting if he hadn't run out of shells. I told him violators paid fines only for what they did.
-- District Game Protector G. J. Martin, York.
April 1968.

Aw, Come On, Fellows

VENANGO COUNTY - During a sportsmen's club meeting this past fall two items were very seriously discussed by the members. Contacted about the items, all I could offer was, "No comment." One was the possibility of the Game Commission crossing wild turkeys with an ostrich to produce a larger turkey. The other possibility was a special deer season in Pennsylvania where spears only could be used.
--District Game Protector L. Yocum, Oil City.
May 1968.

Real Sacrifice

Interviewing persons for employment on the Food and Cover Corps is very interesting. One young applicant with shoulder-length hair pleaded his cause by saying, "If you hire me, I'll even have my hair cut... if it's necessary."
-- Land Manager P. A. Hilbert, Cleona.
June 1968.

Pistol Packer

BUTLER & LAWRENCE COUNTIES - While on a fishing trip a local angler stopped to have a cold drink in a tavern and overheard the following story. One fisherman said he had seen a two-foot trout in the stream and had tried everything, but could not catch it. Getting angry he said he pulled his pistol and shot it. The fellow he was talking to said "Do you know who I am? I'm the Fish Warden." The fisherman telling the story said the pistol packing fisherman quickly changed his story with a: "Do you know who I am? I'm the biggest liar in Pennsylvania."
-- District Fish Warden Eugene Scobel.
July 1968.

Turned Off

MONTGOMERY COUNTY - This incident was relayed to me by Fish Warden Rotchford: It seems he was checking fishermen along Unami Creek near Sumneytown one day, when all of a sudden this "hippie" came running down through the woods to him. He immediately asked Officer Rotchford whether he enforced the Pollution Laws. To this, Rotchford replied, "Yes." The stranger then asked if he enforced the Air Pollution Laws, and at this point Warden Rotchford questioned him further. It seems that two fellows had been in the area minutes earlier, hunting crows with an electronic call. The hippie claimed this noise was polluting the air and should be stopped. Needless to say, Officer Rotchford immediately "tuned him out."
-- District Game Protector R. G. Clouser, Lansdale.
August 1968.

Frustrating for Whom?

CRAWFORD COUNTY - While tearing out a dam on a beaver damage complaint, Deputy Gray looked up the channel to see the beaver already headed in his direction with a freshly cut limb in his mouth, ready to start plugging the hole.
-- District Game Protector J. Miller, Meadville.
September 1968.

Deodorant for Bridegroom

MONTGOMERY COUNTY - Deputy Dave Wentling found a small skunk and wanted to keep it as a pet so he decided to undertake the job of descenting it himself. The operation was successful, but left a lingering remembrance on Deputy Wentling. I'm quite sure Dave's bride of two weeks isn't crazy about his new type of deodorant!
-- District Game Protector R. G. Clouser, Lansdale.
October 1968.

151

Hide 'n' Seek

ROSS LEFFLER SCHOOL - While on my land management assignment for two weeks, Bill Fulmer, Land Manager, provided a little humor to our everyday routine. He was chasing a mouse across the barn floor, when it suddenly disappeared. After searching for several minutes, we gave up the chase. Five minutes later Mr. Fulmer began jumping around and out came the mouse from his pant leg. This episode taught me never to misjudge a mouse.
-- Trainee F. D. King.
November 1968.

Calling John Behel

CENTRE COUNTY - Recently I received a phone call from a young man who stated he would be 12 years old next year and that he planned to go hunting. I told him about the new law that would require him to have a hunter safety course before he could buy a license. After I had finished explaining the law to him, he stated he would have no trouble passing the test since he had been reading about gun safety for years. The conversation finally led to my asking him to name some of the safety rules when handling guns. He thought for a minute, then said, "Don't load your gun in the house or barn. Use only a .302 caliber or a 15-gauge for hunting. Always hunt with one friend, so if he shoots you he can help you home." After I got back on my feet I asked if he could think of any more safety rules and he stated that there were others but none of them were important. I suggested that he show up at the next hunter safety course to learn some of those "less important rules."
-- District Game Protector D. Sloan, Bellefonte.
December 1968.

We Know It Takes All Kinds, But-

LACKAWANNA COUNTY - While on patrol of Game Lands 135, Trainee Jerry Zeidler and I came into contact with quite an interesting character. He was clad in hunting attire, carried binoculars, etc., but had no firearm. This individual had been perched in a tree for some time, just looking around. He told us that if he hunts for small game and doesn't have a good year, it makes him so upset and nervous that he can't hunt for deer. So he comes out into the woods and sits up in a tree every day, looks around for two or three hours, then he goes home!
-- District Game Protector T. C. Wylie, Moscow.
January 1969.

Where the Guys Are

YORK COUNTY - I recently was told of a pretty young woman overheard in the beauty shop asking to have her hairdo set so it would last for two weeks. She blushingly said she was going to the mountains to cook for a deer camp for the season. Sorry, fellows, but which camp it was, I wasn't told.
-- District Game Protector R. L. Yeakel, Red Lion.
February 1969.

Protected Plug

CAMBRIA COUNTY - It seems Bob Shook was fishing Duman Dam recently and not doing so well with the particular plug he was using. He reeled in the line, and put on a new plug. On the first cast, a nice bass hit, but Mr. Shook didn't hook it. As he was about to make the second cast, his partner remarked that it was a rather strange looking plug. Mr. Shook looked at the plug, then rather sheepishly removed the plastic hook guard.
--Waterways Partolman Anthony Murawski.
March 1969.

Six-String Shooter

CLEARFIELD COUNTY - This story was told to me recently but the incident happened during the 1967 buck season before the new law on shooting from near highways was enacted. A man from Philipsburg, who is employed as a music teacher in State College, is a guitar enthusiast and carries one in the back seat of his car at all times. He is also an avid deer hunter, and it wasn't unusual that his rifle was in the back seat too as he drove to work through some prime hunting territory early one December morning. As the car descended a slight grade, the driver saw a buck with a beautiful rack crossing the road ahead. In a matter of seconds, the driver stopped the vehicle, grabbed for his rifle, jumped from the car, and stood by the roadside, searching intently for an opening to shoot. However, no shot rang out as the deer ran into view - but merely a melodic chord from the guitar he clutched in his hands.
-- District Game Protector J. R. Furlong, Ramey.
April 1969.

153

Good Intentions

CLEARFIELD COUNTY - I've heard of many different types of winter feeding programs for wildlife, but I think my three daughters have gone overboard a little. Found behind our house: three apples, four walnuts, a handful of peanuts, two slabs of cornmeal mush, at least a pound of bird seed and half a bowl of soggy sugar-frosted flakes.
-- District Game Protector G. J. Zeidler, Rockton.
May 1969.

How It Goes

JUNIATA COUNTY - The day started out with a search for illegal trout with a Waterways Patrolman. Then a highway-killed deer which required a 25-mile round trip. Then a farmer complaint, another contact on the Safety Zone Program, another highway kill 20 miles away, followed at suppertime by another highway kill. Then a lecture to a PTA meeting, and, as I walked in the door, three phone calls. Finally, about 11 p.m. a fourth deer to go for and dispose of. And the next morning the first person I talked to said, "Boy, you Game Protectors sure have it made at this time of the year with nothing to do."
-- District Game Protector R. P. Shaffer, Mifflintown.
June 1969.

Just Another Critic

BERKS COUNTY - While talking to a farmer in my district the other day, he related the following incident: He and his wife were watching television when they heard a curious barking outside their living room window. Sneaking to the window and peering outside, they noticed a large gray fox sitting on a stone wall staring in the window, apparently watching television.
-- District Game Protector J. K. Weaver, Kutztown.
July 1969.

Big Game Catch

ALLEGHENY COUNTY - On the 1969 opening day of trout season I was on a special assignment on the Yellow Creek area of Bedford County. District Game Protector Thomas and I were told this story: A young boy was fishing below the Fly Fishing Area at the mouth of Maple Creek when be thought he had a snag. After giving his rod a sharp heave-ho and the line gave a little, he was finally able to retrieve his line, although his rod was bent almost double. When the boy finally landed his catch he was amazed to find the head and antlers of a four point buck and a six point buck held together with a piece of wire. G.P. Thomas and I got a real laugh at our problem. Would the boy need a fishing license or a hunting license and also should he try for a Junior Citation or the Triple Trophy?
-- Waterways Patrolman James R. Smith.
August 1969.

Next Time Try "Monitor"

BLAIR COUNTY - It has been interesting to hear the different positive cures for rabbit damage to home gardens. One gardener thought he had a sure thing. He placed a small transistor radio in his garden and turned it to a rock and roll station (he said rabbits like classical music). The radio worked fine until the station went off the air, then the rabbits moved in and chewed up the leather case and part of the radio.
-- District Game Protector J. A. Lukas, Hollidaysburg.
September 1969.

Road Fishing

LACKAWANNA COUNTY - While on patrol of the East Branch of the Tunkhannock Creek, accompanied by Game Protector Altmiller, we came across a car with the trunk opened. The weather was very poor with rain coming down like cats and dogs. As we were passing the car which was parked by a bridge abutment, we saw rods sticking out of the trunk. Game Protector Altmiller backed the car up so we could investigate. We found two men in the trunk fishing contentedly. We checked their licenses, which were in fine order. As we drove away Game Protector Altmiller said he saw a lot of road hunting in his days, but this is the first time he ever saw anybody ROAD FISHING!
-- Waterways Patrolman Robert E. Fasching.
October 1969.

Deadly Digit

BRADFORD COUNTY - One evening at dusk, John Parsell, a local sportsman, and I had just finished tearing out a beaver dam when two mallard ducks flew overhead. John instinctively pointed his hand like a gun and said, "Bang." At that precise moment, one duck folded up and fell to the ground. John had the most surprised look and I in turn began to question him on the number of shot he was using in his finger. On a closer check we found the duck had flown into a wire.
-- District Game Protector W. Bower, Troy.
November 1969.

What's Next?

BLAIR COUNTY - As I was driving on a back country road one afternoon recently, I saw what appeared to be a woman hunting woodchucks. She was sitting in a field a short distance from the road with her back toward me. Her hair was neatly combed and reached below her shoulders. A rifle lay across her lap, but she did not have a hunting license visible. I stopped my car and walked out to her. As I approached, the hunter did not turn, so I said, "Excuse me, ma'am, I'd like to see your license." The hunter turned around and growled, "I ain't no woman!" It took me a little while to recover, because along with the long hair he had a mustache and beard. It was a little hard to advise a man to display his hunting license while laughing at him - but I managed.
-- District Game Protector J. A. Lukas, Hollidaysburg.
December 1969.

156

Chapter 5
1970 - 1979

During the seventies, the Fish and Game Commissions initiated numerous programs for children interested in the outdoors. Field officers often visited classrooms at elementary, junior-high and senior-high schools to teach the students about conservation. Almost invariably, these days ended with hundreds of questions from the curious young minds. Some priceless queries resulted from these sessions, and some interesting responses, as well (from the children and from the Warden).

Discerning Damsel

FULTON COUNTY - CIA Joe Chick and I were covering the elementary schools in the county with a Wildlife Conservation Program. Our theme was the life of the wild goose. Following the film, I asked if anyone could guess why geese fly in a V formation. One little girl thought that perhaps the one right in front might not smell very good.
-- District Game Protector C. E. Jarrett, McConnellsburg.
January 1970.

Seems Obvious to Us, Too

CLARION COUNTY - November proved to be the worst month of the year for road-killed deer in Clarion County. A small boy who lives up the street from my headquarters observed many of these being hauled on the back of my state car. One week in Sunday School class his teacher asked if any of the boys or girls had anything interesting to tell. The little neighbor boy said, "Yes, I do. Our neighbor collects dead animals."
-- District Game Protector L. L. Harshbarger, Knox.
February 1970.

A Thinker

CENTRE COUNTY - A hunter on State Game Lands 33 wasn't taking any chances of his buck sneaking through without being seen. He used his binoculars to catch any movement ahead of him and a rear view mirror to catch any movement to his rear.
-- District Game Protector M. Grabany, Philipsburg.
March 1970.

159

Familiar Face

DAUPHIN COUNTY - While working at our live fish display at the Gratz Fair, I was watching people admiring the fish, when a very excited lady hurried over to me. She asked if the fish (particularly the big northern pike) were the same ones that had been on display at the Port Royal Fair. I told her I didn't think so, but she insisted that they were. When I asked her why she believed this, she said, "The pike recognized me! Every time I looked at him, he looked at me!"
-- Waterways Patrolman John E. Stephanski.
March 1970.

Hope He Got Fleas

DAUPHIN COUNTY - The ingenuity of some Game Law violators never ceases to amaze me. Just recently my deputies and I had been trying to execute a warrant of arrest on a fellow who had been eluding us for about a week. One evening I was informed he was at his residence, and Deputy George Wert and I rushed over there. We couldn't find him. We were about finished checking out the violator's basement when Deputy Wert observed a pet dog disappear into a wood pile. His curiosity aroused, he started moving wood slabs and uncovered what looked like the entrance to an oversized dog house. He shined his light in the opening and, lo and behold, there was a human's ear. After much twisting and turning, our elusive friend wriggled out through the small opening. He then informed us that he had been hiding there on two of our previous visits to his home.
-- District Game Protector S. L. Opet, Millersburg.
April 1970.

Well, That's Something

BEDFORD COUNTY - While on patrol I was talking with a man who had just finished checking his muskrat traps. He told me he wasn't having much success due to the high water level of the streams. Many of his sets were destroyed by the high water. Finally he came to a set that had been sprung. His catch? One of his own traps from upstream that had been carried away by the high water.
-- District Game Protector G. B. Thomas, Woodbury.
May 1970.

Shoulda Gone Huntin'

MONTGOMERY COUNTY - Two friends of Bob Redd of Norristown were fishing in the dam above Schwenksville on Perkiomen Creek. One hooked a big muskie and the other was taking movies. The fisherman can be seen fighting the fish and looking over his shoulder to make certain his buddy is capturing all of the action. After a considerable battle, the film is black because, with a fish that size, it took both men to get the fish into the boat from which they were fishing. The next scene shows the proud smiling fisherman holding a large muskie for the viewers to see. Then you notice waterspots on the film and next a lot of bubbles. During the fierce battle, both men forgot about the dam. You're right - boat, both men, two large open tackle boxes, fishing poles and one large muskie went over the dam. I wonder, did the fish get away?
-- District Game Protector H. T. Nolf, Telford.
June 1970.

161

Well, You Can Ask

LUZERNE COUNTY - While on my way to pick up a road-killed deer, I thought I heard a woman scream. I turned the car around and investigated, but saw no one. A few days later I was told that a praying, letter-awaiting mother had mistaken my car and green uniform for that of an Army officer bringing terrible news about her son in Vietnam. My appearance has surprised and shaken up a few game violators in the past and I never gave it a thought. But now I may have a valid reason for requesting the Executive Director to issue me a bright-red sports car and a Mountie-type uniform.
-- District Game Protector T. Vesloski, Plains.
August 1970.

Self Made "Laws"

LUZERNE COUNTY - It is surprising to find the number of people who make up their "own" laws. And, in some cases, this might help some fish. Two Wilkes-Barre fishermen - Mr. Peter Misunas and Willard Lewis - have been catching some Co-Ho through the ice at Harvey's Lake the last two seasons, and the one method used was the old standard of jigging with meal worms, mousies, etc., on a #16 hook. Mr. Misunas was having some luck one day catching Co-Ho, perch, etc., when a nearby angler became curious as to the method being used. Mr. Misunas explained what he was using and the angler told him that was "illegal." When Mr. Misunas asked why, the angler explained that #16 hooks were illegal as fish could not see them!
-- Waterways Patrolman Edward D. Manhart.
September 1970.

Makes an Easy Decision

HUNTINGDON COUNTY - Apparently the spring turkey season has opened new horizons to Pennsylvania sportsmen. In the past they were faced with the dilemma of choosing a hunting or fishing vacation. Now many of them plan a May vacation and combine early morning turkey hunting with late afternoon and evening trout fishing. It seems to me this kind of holiday is hard to beat.
-- CIA H. W. Bower, Huntingdon.
September 1970.

Fish Thing

BEAVER COUNTY - One fall day I stopped at a local drug store to buy a few items. The young lady at the counter had never seen me wearing my reefer coat and trooper hat. She exclaimed, "Oh! I didn't know you were a policeman." "I'm not," I replied and pointed to the insignia on my left shoulder. "You're a fish thing," she exclaimed.
-- Waterways Patrolman Donald Parrish
October 1970.

162

Meet Mr. Clean

ROSS LEFFLER SCHOOL OF CONSERVATION - How many showers have you had today? This trainee had a few on August 19: 6:30 a .m. No. 1 - in the shower after physical exercises; 10:00 a.m., No. 2 - drenched in a downpour on a tree study hike; 10:30 a.m., No. 3 - in the shower after peeling off dripping clothes; 11:30 am., No. 4 - while fighting a fire in a Game Lands building; 12:00 noon, No. 5 - in shower after fire fighting completed; 2:30 p.m., No. 6 - caught in another shower on afternoon tree identification; 10:00 p.m., No. 7 - in the shower at the end of the day.
-- Trainee James F. Ramsey.
November 1970.

Attention, Mr. 216-00-4567

WAYNE COUNTY - Remember when your name was Jones? I would have liked to attend your 221 (sportsmen meeting) but I was tied up on an 05-502 (beaver damage investigation) and an 05-503 (law enforcement investigation). This necessitated filing an OA-191 report coded with the numbers 64000-11-23-91-70-2-12-04-107-50100-335-00; also a PGC 19 form and form PSAB-5 (Rev-7-60). I look forward to meeting you sometime within the next ten years of remaining service, providing I can fathom these codes, which will probably change weekly, and someone releases me from this printing piano. Computingly yours, 206-14-3700.
-- District Game Protector F. G. Weigelt, Galilee.
December 1970.

Rheumatism Remedy

POTTER COUNTY - Pete Impson told me that he and his wife decided they would try the Leetonia section of Tioga County for a brook trout fishing trip. When they got to the stream, Pete's wife started to fish. She had only gone a short ways when she let the hollers out and ran up the steep bank. Pete investigated and found that she had just stepped on a big black rattlesnake. Pete said, "You know the wife is bothered with rheumatism and arthritis and I didn't think she could move so fast but you know she wasn't bothered a bit for a couple of weeks with her ailments. Now that she is starting to stiffen up again, I think it's about time I took her down for another treatment. It was the best medicine she had ever taken!"
-- Waterways Patrolman Kenneth Aley.
January 1971.

A Real Swinger

CAMBRIA COUNTY - Many types of hunting garb are observed, but during the past bow and arrow season, a landowner reports seeing a hunter clad in Bermuda shorts.
-- District Game Protector L. D. Mostoller, Johnstown.
January 1971.

This We'd Have to See!

LANCASTER COUNTY - No doubt all Game Protectors are told how a hunter killed a piece of game by mistake and then reported it or was apprehended for killing illegal game. During October I received a call to investigate a mistaken kill: a 9-point buck deer allegedly was killed in mistake for a gray squirrel.
-- District Game Protector W. E. Woodring, Ephrata.
February 1971.

Shoulda Gone Fishin'

ERIE COUNTY - I have listened to a lot of "believe it or not" stories and this one comes directly from Waterways Patrolman James Carter. During the past archery season, Jim located a deer trail coming through a dense thorn thicket. Beyond the thicket he saw several deer feeding in a clover field. Jim knelt in front of the passageway the deer had through the thicket and nocked an arrow. Hunters on the other side of the field alarmed the deer and two small ones headed Jim's way. One darted through the hole in the thicket and ran into Jim's arrow, still on the bowstring, and then knocked Jim over. He managed to recover his position just in time to be run over by the second deer.
-- District Game Protector E. D. Simpson, Union City.
March 1971.

Must Be Nuts

ELK COUNTY - Last December 26, Frank Hughes and Jim Fannin of Ridgeway went to the Kinzua tailrace about 4:00 A.M. to fish. The wind and snow were blowing with the temperature hovering about 10 degrees and they were fishing by lantern as it was still dark. Someone hollered to them from up in the woods and asked if they were doing any good. Frank answered "no" and then asked the fellow if he was going to give it a try The man replied he was going hunting instead. Frank's answer to the fellow? - "Anybody who goes hunting in this kind of weather must be nuts." Needless to say the fellow continued on without any comments.
-- Waterways Patrolman Bernard Ambrose.
April 1971.

No Fishing Rod

ERIE COUNTY - Last Spring, Special Waterways Patrolman Zane Roberts and Bill Ager and I stopped for coffee near Corry. Seeing our uniforms, the waitress started talking about her husband's fishing trips. She said he often dug some worms and went fishing but never caught any fish. Mr. Roberts asked what kind of rod did he use. Her answer? - "he never takes one of those with him!"
-- Waterways Patrolman James R. Carter.
May 1971.

How It Goes

VENANGO COUNTY - At the Cleveland Sports Show in March, I was talking to an Ohio man who loves to hunt in Pennsylvania, his wife who doesn't like hunting at all, and their teenaged daughter. I asked the daughter if she hunts and she said she did at one time but not anymore. I asked why she stopped and she said she got too big for daddy's shoulders.

-- District Game Protector L. C. Yocum, Oil City.
June 1971.

That's Another Question

McKEAN COUNTY - While on patrol on Combs Creek, Deputy Hasper and I came upon two young boys fishing in an area closed to fishing. When the boys were approached one said, "Is this posted?" We replied yes. Deputy Rasper asked the boys if they went to school. The answer was yes. He then asked if they knew how to read, and again the answer was yes. He asked the one boy to step around the tree and read the sign (which read "Fishing Prohibited"). The boy told us it said "Fishing Not Permitted." I told the boys they could fish right above where the signs began, and the one lad asked, "Is that where they stock all the little ones?"

-- District Game Protector J. E. Rankin, Port Allegany.
July 1971.

The Word Is ...

BUTLER COUNTY - Recently I took the Bruin Elementary fifth graders on a nature hike and field trip to a local beaver dam. The topic of conversation moved from one thing to another and finally came to the different classifications of trees. When asked what word beginning with "C" would classify most trees which stay green all year and which bear seeds in cones, someone quickly replied "Coniferous." I then asked "What word beginning with "D" would describe the type of trees which lost their leaves, expecting an answer of "Deciduous." A boy standing near me raised his hand. "Do you know the word?" I asked. "Dead," he replied without batting an eye.
-- District Game Protector N. Weston, Boyers.
August 1971.

And What Did You Say?

ERIE COUNTY - Following a conservation lecture at an elementary school, I received many questions regarding wildlife. Some were quite thoughtful and others were humorous. For example, "Mr. Game Protector, how do you tell the difference between boy frogs and girl frogs?"
-- District Game Protector A. C. Martin, Erie.
September 1971.

Hot Seat

YORK COUNTY - According to District Game Protector G. John Martin, his brother David of Lancaster is an avid trout fisherman. While teaching his young son the finer arts of trout fishing on a recent outing, David climbed out on a log to catch a large trout which he was sure was lurking back under the bank. In trying to get just the right drift on the bait, the uncanny angler bent over a little too far -and backed into an electric fence. Result - one very wet father, a good laugh for the son, and a lucky trout!
-- Waterways Patrolman William F. Hartle.
September 1971.

Emergency Treatment Works

CRAWFORD COUNTY - Deputy Dunham and I found a young nearly dead beaver in a trap. We took it to Dr. Rees in Titusville. He called the hospital emergency room and told them he was sending a 2-month-old patient up there and to inject a prescription in its hip, which upon arrival they did. The beaver was kept warm with a hair dryer and towel; in 3 hours he recovered, and 4 hours later he was eating. I retained the beaver overnight and released him at Blair Bridge, where Officer Haines had previously released his mother.
-- District Game Protector W. E. Lee, Titusville.
October 1971.

Better Safe Than-

CLEARFIELD COUNTY - Alan Shaffer, of DuBois, tells of a friend who, while on a hike in the woods, discovered what he thought to be an unexploded guided missile. The friend notified police officials. In short order, a convoy of Army personnel, including several bomb specialists, converged on the area, found and "dismantled" a... (Would you believe?) wood duck nesting box! In defense of the friend, I am told the nest was the metallic cone type and was hanging upside down. Anyone can make a mistake, right?
-- District Game Protector G. J. Zeidler, Rockton.
November 1971.

Always the Way

PERRY COUNTY - Received a report concerning a woman who had her kitchen invaded by a woodchuck. Where was her husband at the time? You guessed it - woodchuck hunting.

-- District Game Protector L. L. Everett, Newport.

December 1971.

Roar, Chipmunk, Roar ...

CENTRE COUNTY - A tiny chipmunk took some of the play away from Penn State's football victory over Texas Christian on Saturday, October 23. The cavorting rodent near the south goal line kept those in view of his action in stitches. Once the game had to be held up to permit him to scamper away. Even an official got into the spirit of the occasion by signaling a touchdown as the chipmunk crossed the goal line.

-- District Game Protector J. L. Wiker, Pennsylvania Furnace.

January 1972.

Music Hath Charms?

HUNTINGDON COUNTY - While on foot patrol near the crest of Stone Mountain, Deputy Ray Crownover observed a brightly clad hunter take a stand approximately 60 yards below him. Shortly thereafter the sound of country music broke the stillness causing Ray to think that perhaps the previous several weeks of sleepless night work was getting to him. Sure enough after glassing the hunter with binoculars, Ray spotted a transistor radio. Remaining motionless for a period of time, Deputy Crownover saw three antlerless deer approach between him and the other hunter, cock their ears and move to within 30 yards of the music source, survey the situation for several minutes and then move quietly on. Needless to say, the "Grand Ole Opry" hunter never sighted the deer or Ray.

-- District Game Protector R. D. Furry, Huntingdon.

February 1972.

Shoulda Stayed in Bed

CUMBERLAND COUNTY - The first hunter I approached during the recent deer season, I addressed as "Sir" but he turned out to be a 72-year-young female hunter attired in red hunting clothing with her silvery locks tucked up under a cap. Apologizing for my mistake, I proceeded down the road where I observed a long golden-haired individual combing her curly locks and addressed her as "Ma'am." This turned out to be a 19-year-old male sitting in a vehicle waiting for his companion to return. Some days you can't win.

-- District Game Protector E. F. Utech, Carlisle.

March 1972.

Mad Dogs - Beware!

ELK COUNTY - While on duty at Erie, Officer Brown and I were assigned a section of the Lake Erie shoreline to search for a lost fisherman and boat. Our shift started at twelve midnight on a cold, snowy and blustery night. Officer Brown told me that we would have to be careful of dogs, and since we were on foot patrol and the terrain of the lakeshore made it necessary on some occassions to walk through residential areas, two of the biggest and meanest dogs came after us. Officer Brown was just saying something about the dogs being friendly as I jumped down over a thirty foot cliff. Guess who jumped after me? Officer Brown passed me up sliding down the cliff in hot pursuit!
-- Waterways Patrolman Bernard D. Ambrose.
March 1972.

Partners

CUMBERLAND COUNTY - Now I know why beagles chase rabbits! One of our local sportsmen was running his beagle at the Shippensburg Fish and Game Club's dog training area. It jumped a rabbit and the chase was going fine until the rabbit stopped. The sportsman ran to get the rabbit before his dog, because he didn't want the dog to kill it. But the dog beat him to the rabbit. However, when the sportsman saw what happened next, he couldn't quite believe it. His dog ran up to the rabbit and started licking it. Do you suppose the dog just wanted to be friends?
-- District Game Protector J. Beard, Shippensburg.
April 1972.

Hang in There, Gary

DAUPHIN COUNTY - The 1971-72 hunting season was my first as a Game Protector and I believe that my family was thoroughly initiated into the life, what with the countless telephone calls - many received in the wee hours of the night - using my children's swing set to hang deer on before distribution to needy families, warming up dinner because I was always late, etc. But what really topped off the season was the night I boiled a bear head in the kitchen. And I only have 34 years to go for retirement!
-- District Game Protector G. W. Packard, Millersburg.
May 1972.

Pumpkins or Punkins?

MONTGOMERY COUNTY - While cleaning my office, my wife came across some rifled slugs which interested my five-year-old daughter. "What are those?" she asked. My wife said, "Punkin balls." "Oh, I know!" my daughter said. "You use those to shoot punkins."
-- District Game Protector B. J. Schmader, Collegeville.
June 1972.

172

Now You Know

SCHUYLKILL COUNTY - During a speech about young wildlife to a group of Cub Scouts and their parents, I, mentioned that the young red fox pup I was holding was a female. Without a moment's hesitation, one youngster raised his hand and asked the inevitable question - how can you tell a boy fox from a girl fox? Immediately, another excited youngster raised his hand, exclaiming, "I know, I know." With some apprehension, I called on him to explain. He stood up and in a very confident manner said, "Well, you watch them for awhile, and if it has puppies, it's a girl."
-- District Game Protector S. L. Opet, Tamaqua.
July 1972.

Money to Shoot

LANCASTER COUNTY - Shooting clay birds can become expensive if you follow these rules: 1. Place $85 in the barrel of your shotgun. 2. Forget it is there. 3. Shoot at a clay bird. 4. Pick up the green confetti. 5. Collect $65 from the bank for matching serial numbers you found.
-- District Game Protector R. E. Gosnell, Millersville.
August 1972.

Loud Disappointment

ERIE COUNTY - While on patrol I heard several loud shots, so I left my vehicle and proceeded on foot through a marsh in the direction of the shots. After wading through knee-deep water and getting covered with mud and insects, I broke out into a field and found the shooter - a propane cannon for scaring birds.
-- District Game Protector A. Martin, Erie.
September 1972.

What Did She Say?

One of our Food and Cover Corps employees recently found his cooperative efforts embarrassing. He picked up a road-killed deer while returning his girlfriend to her residence from a date. A goodnight kiss was abruptly interrupted by an alert Pennsylvania State Policeman interested in enforcing the Game Law concerning the unlawful possession of a deer in close season. The red-faced man proved that he was "only doing his duty."

-- Conservation Information Assistant R. D. Parlaman, Franklin.
October 1972.

The Longest Night

BRADFORD COUNTY - Five Rome area lads had a camping experience they won't soon forget. They had retired for the night when they were disturbed by a strange sound. A flashlight revealed an animal getting into their food supplies. One of the boys yelled, "It's a bobcat!" and seconds later five boys were perched in the top branches of a nearby tree. I understand the boys found it to be a very long night before the sun came up and they came down.

-- District Game Protector A. D. Rockwell, Sayre.
November 1972.

174

HS Savoir-Faire

BUTLER COUNTY - Tim Hughes, a local Hunter Safety instructor, was teaching a class of 90 youngsters safe gun handling procedures. They also learned another lesson in composure. While demonstrating the proper way to cross a fence, Jim found his pants could not stand the strain and the seams gave way. Jim sent his son for his jacket and, not turning his back on the audience, nonchalantly tied the jacket around the waist and continued with his lecture.

-- District Game Protector W. N. Weston, Boyers.
December 1972.

Now We Know

CLARION COUNTY - A few weeks ago a self-proclaimed "deer expert" approached Deputy Logue with this statement: "The reason we don't have any deer left is that these guys come out spotting every night with those 2000 candle power watt spotlights and as soon as the light hits them, the deer start jumping up and down and quivering and die of a heart attack right there on the spot."

-- District Game Protector J. G. Bowers, Knox.
January 1973.

Out of the Mouths of Babes

LACKAWANNA COUNTY - Deputy Bud Moore's daughter has been doing some psychological counseling as a part of her work-study program. She recently asked a third-grade girl if she knew what season was coming, expecting the child to say fall, winter, Thanksgiving or Halloween. The child's prompt reply was "Hunting season, and I hate it." His daughter asked why. The reply: "When Daddy shoots out the window the noise makes me so mad and nervous that I feel like pushing Daddy, gun, and all right out of the car!"

-- District Game Protector T. C. Wylie, Moscow.
February 1973.

How Many What?

LEHIGH COUNTY - Every Game Protector gets his share of telephone calls. Some are in search of information, some have information to give, some have specific problems, and then there are just some. Such as the gentleman who wanted to know if it was all right to shoot mistletoe out of the trees before Christmas; the sincere lady who requested odor charts of our game species the day before small game season opened (she felt it would help her husband who was going hunting for the first time and was not too familiar with our game birds and animals); and, most unusual of all, the man who wanted to know how many aliens he could have if he bought an alien hunting license!
-- District Game Protector J. R. Fagan, Allentown.
March 1973.

Of Course

FOREST COUNTY - Prior to beaver season, several Game Protectors got into a discussion about beaver and their size and weight. After each man took his turn telling of the largest beaver he had ever seen, Duane Gross, Land Manager in the Marienville area, told about the beaver in Buzzard Swamp that measures 8 inches - that's between the eyes of course.
-- District Game Protector E. L. Taylor, Tionesta.
April 1973.

The One That Got Away

SNYDER COUNTY - A well known hunter from the Troxelville area told me he was hunting rabbits with his favorite beagle and had a chase going. The rabbit came running by but Ed only crippled it, and it continued on and made a dive for a hole. The dog then grabbed the rabbit and according to Ed the rabbit dragged the dog into the hole! And that's not all. A minute later this expensive beagle was heard tonguing and when the two animals came bolting out of the brush, the rabbit was chasing the dog!
-- District Game Protector J. P. Shook, McClure.
May 1973.

"Polecat" Diet

CLARION COUNTY - My first experience at removing a skunk from a box trap came recently. The skunk was caught in a wooden trap in a warehouse in Clarion. I remembered my training of only a month past and crept up to the trap slowly, covering it with a bag. I then picked up the trap and gently carried it out to the woods. The skunk was removed and I was really glad of the job I had done. The skunk had sprayed the box but not me. However, I got the scent on my hands and boots. Alas!-an apparent victory turned into defeat. However, I did discover a new way to diet, as you sure can't eat with that smell on your hands!
-- District Game Protector G. J. Couillard, Clarion.
June 1973.

Last Resort

MONTGOMERY COUNTY - "Charlie," an injured screech owl which lived with us awhile, got loose and was found by my three young daughters hiding in the fireplace. A little apprehensive about just reaching in and grabbing him, they tried several approaches of their own, including drawing, coloring and cutting out a life-size mouse to use as a lure. When that didn't work, they shone a flashlight on him so he would think it was daytime and thus go to sleep so the girls could grab him. That didn't work either. Finally, they did what most people do first - called the Game Protector.

-- District Game Protector B. J. Schmader, Collegeville.
July 1973.

Little Bit of Knowledge

BLAIR COUNTY - My wife was in the hospital during spring gobbler season and her mother was staying at our home at the time. I had written down some of the answers to the most commonly asked questions, such as shot sizes, shooting hours, etc. One call was in reference to the legal shot size. My mother-in-law informed the gentleman that nothing larger than No. 2 shot could be used. He said he guessed his No. 4 shot could not be used then. She agreed and, satisfied with this, the gentleman thanked her and hung up.

-- District Game Protector H. L. Harshaw, Hollidaysburg.
August 1973.

Just Moved Right In

MERCER COUNTY - The ways in which wildlife adapts to man's world never cease to amaze me. The most recent was a female raccoon that took up residence in a chimney of a Sandy Lake home. This wasn't bad enough, but she had to go one step further and give birth to her young in the pipe that runs from the furnace to the chimney. Thanks to the conservation-minded home owner, she is being permitted to raise her family in the chimney.

-- District Game Protector B. K. Ray, Sheakleyville.

September 1973.

Andy's Way

GREENE COUNTY - While investigating a beaver damage complaint, the lady who owned the property showed me all the damage the animals had done and insisted they had to go. That evening I contacted Deputy Andy Ewart to make plans to live trap the beaver. He told me he would go out and check the damage and talk with the lady. I don't know what Andy told her, but I hear he was sitting on top of the beaver lodge and when the lady asked what he was doing he said he was just listening to the babies cry. (I guess they just found out they were going to lose their home.) The lady then listened to the young beavers also, and after a long talk with Andy she decided that they could stay for the rest of the summer. My question is, "Was it the young beaver or Andy's way with the ladies that caused the change of heart?"

-- District Game Protector W. A. McGinness, Waynesburg.

October 1973.

Where Was the Coffee?

BEDFORD COUNTY - There are many things a Game Protector has to be on the lookout for when he is working at night for jacklighters. One night not long ago something happened that we weren't quite prepared for. We hid the car and moved to a good observation point, leaving the car doors open so we could hear the radio better. We returned some time later to find two cats helping themselves to our donuts.

-- District Game Protector B. L. Warner, Bedford.

November 1973.

Touchy

CLARION AND JEFFERSON COUNTIES - If anyone noticed a state vehicle weave back and forth and suddenly swerve to the side of the highway, here is the explanation. After checking on a sale of timber from State Game Lands, I returned to my vehicle and started driving down the road. After three sharp pains in the seat, I realized I was sitting on a large bee while wearing my thin summer trousers!

-- Land Manager L. L. Harshbarger, Knox.

December 1973.

That's Doing it the Hard Way!

CLEARFIELD COUNTY - While stocking Trout Run in Clearfield County last April 7th, there were a few unusual difficulties encountered. The four wheel drive vehicles had just crossed a very deep ditch on an old tram road when they came across a large poplar tree in the road. This caused two problems: (1) no one had a saw or axe, and (2) they could neither back up nor turn around! After some careful thought and study, I believe a fellow by the name of William Lanager saved the day by finding a claw hammer. Not only was that tree cut in two but four other poplar trees were done in by that claw hammer before they could find a place to turn around. Now this story should be reliable because there were three Deputy Waterways Patrolmen and a Deputy Game Protector and a District Game Protector on this trip.
-- Waterways Patrolman Edward W. Brown
December 1973.

The Game and Fish Officer's Lament

WYOMING COUNTY

If the game and fish officer asks to see your license, he's insulting.

If he takes your word for having one, he's corrupt.

If he arrests a violator, he's showing how rough he can be.

If he gives the culprit another chance, he's showing favoritism.

If he labors day and night to enforce the law, he's a tyrant.

If he relaxes at all, he's a shirker and a crook.

If he talks fish and game conservation, he's a tyrant.

If he keeps quiet, he's not interested in his work.

If he accepts suggestions or advice, he's incompetent.

If he works out problems for himself, he's a know-all.

If he acts like a gentleman, he's too easy.

If he acts firm, he's unfair and a rascal.

How can you win?

-- District Game Protector A. J. Kriefski, Tunkhannock.
January 1974.

Hey, There!

FOREST & WARREN COUNTIES - A hunter was lost in the Buzzard Swamp area and started firing signal shots for help. Sure enough, he got an answering signal. After more shooting and walking he got to the fellow who was shooting in return, only to have him say, "I'm sure glad you found me!" Both were soon found.
-- Land Manager D. W. Gross, Marienville.
February 1974.

Bad Advertising

ERIE/WARREN COUNTIES - While on patrol I found a tired hunter walking up a very steep hill. I stopped and checked his license and asked if he had seen many deer. "I have been up and down this hill three times today," he replied, "and I haven't seen a deer. I don't have much faith in these deer crossing signs that you guys put up for the hunters."
-- District Game Protector G. E. Gibson, Corry.
March 1974.

Close to Home

ADAMS COUNTY - One evening while my wife and I were in the kitchen, we heard our 4-year-old son and 6-year-old daughter making noises in the living room. We went in and found all the lights were turned out and the children going around the room with a small pen light. They said they were playing "jacklighter" and were trying to spotlight a deer. I wonder if any other officers have had any poaching problems in their living rooms?

-- District Game Protector G. W. Becker, Gettysburg.
April 1974.

Wait A Minute

CLARION/JEFFERSON COUNTIES - One of my sons read a book about beavers. The story explained how a beaver is sometimes killed when he cuts a large tree and it falls on top of him. My son then asked me why Game Commission employees don't go out along the streams and pick up the suicide beavers.

-- Land Manager L. L. Harshbarger, Knox.
May 1974.

Watch It, Granny

CLEARFIELD COUNTY - While giving a program on mammals of Pennsylvania to a group of kindergarten students, I asked the children some questions. Displaying the pelt of a grey fox, I asked, "What do you think foxes eat?" Out of the midst of the group came the answer - what else - "Grandmothers!"

-- District Game Protector C. L. Keller, Clearfield.
June 1974.

Gobblin' Peepers

POTTER COUNTY - At Lyman Run Creek on the opening day of trout season, State Trooper Jim Potiseek watched a fellow walking toward the water. Every time a frog hollered the fellow dropped to his knees and started looking around cautiously. After this happened three times, Jim walked up to the man to find out what was wrong. The fellow said he couldn't quite see those turkeys, but that they must be right over that little knoll. Jim didn't have the heart to tell the fellow that it was only the frogs croaking, so he just agreed and went on.
-- District Game Protector R. G. Clouser, Galeton.
July 1974.

The Book Said So

BUTLER COUNTY - One of our spring gobbler hunters told me he had read a book on Indian lore that described how the early Indians captured the ingredients for turkey stew. When a brave discovered a flock of turkeys, especially young ones, he would scatter the flock and try to get some to fly into trees. Then with the turkeys peering down from the branches at him, the Indian would run around and around the tree until the turkeys got dizzy and fell to the ground. At least that's the way the book told the story. The spring gobbler hunter tried to apply the same method to fledgling crows fresh from the nest. After a marathon run around the tree, with the young crows watching intently, all our modern-day Indian got was exhausted and dizzy.
-- District Game Protector W. N. Weston, Boyers.
August 1974.

Shore Patrol

CUMBERLAND COUNTY - One morning while I was on vacation at the seashore, the jellyfish were washing up on the beach, much to the dismay of the bathers. One large dead jellyfish came to rest on the shoreline and attracted a large crowd. I was standing there in my bathing suit with the crowd looking at the creature when a lady looked at me and said, "You can't just leave it on the beach, you have to do something with it." So I ended up burying it in the sand. Later my wife remarked that even on vacation you can't get away from wildlife. Even in my bathing suit I must have that "Game Protector look."
-- District Game Protector J P. Filkosky, Mechanicsburg.
September 1974.

Oh Boy!

ALLEGHENY COUNTY - While fishing for walleyes one day, I noticed a fisherman with a very nice stringer of them. He was using a gold-sided rapala and I asked if he was putting pork rind on it. He replied, "Oh, no, I sing my little song while I do my trolling and it works fairly well." When asked to hear his song, out went the plug, and as he began to troll, he sang, "Fishy, fishy, in the brook, put your mouth on my hook." Suddenly, there it was, about an 18" walleye! "You see how easy it is?" he asked. "Well, that's my limit, see you around," and away he went, whistling his little tune. It made me sort of mad, not because of the nice fish he had, but because I didn't bring a tape recorder with me. I had just let the number one tune get away from me!
-- Deputy Waterways Patrolman Gerald Greiner.
September 1974.

And You Think You Have Problems

CUMBERLAND COUNTY - I got a call from a woman who was being kept awake at night by several owls hooting and screeching in a tree near her home. I suggested that she go out when the owls started to make their nightly noises and disturb them. Probably after being disturbed several times they would move to another area farther from her house. The lady explained that she couldn't do this, as the area around the tree was full of copperhead snakes.

-- District Game Protector J. P. Filkosky, Mechanicsburg.
October 1974.

Hairy Problem Solved

LUZERNE COUNTY - One day while checking on my day-old chick raisers and getting information on how the pheasants were developing, I saw a farmer working in his vegetable garden. I walked over to the garden and noticed several small piles of human hair on the garden's borders. The farmer said he had gone to several barber shops and beauty parlors, gathered human hair clippings, and placed them around his garden to keep away the deer. One evening he noticed two big does going toward the garden. When they came to the edge they stopped, stretched out their necks, sniffed the air, and turned and ran into the woods. Later in the day I stopped in Dallas for a haircut, and the barber told me he keeps a box full of hair clippings for one of his customers for the same reason.

-- District Game Protector E. R. Gdosky, Dallas.
November 1974.

Walk on Water?

CLARION COUNTY - One evening a skunk saw an open door at the William Best residence in Williamsburg and walked in to investigate. He was frightened by Mrs. Best's screaming and ran into a laundry room, taking refuge behind several baskets of freshly laundered clothes. They asked the local Game Protector if he would solve the problem. (He wasn't too sure he could, but decided to slowly remove the baskets of clothing.) As he removed the basket the skunk was hiding behind, anticipating the worst, the skunk surprised him by nonchalantly walking out of the room, through the kitchen and out the door, proving again there's nothing the Game Protectors can't do.

-- District Game Protector G. Couillard, Clarion.
December 1974.

The Ruby Slippers
DAUPHIN COUNTY - One morning, I got up earlier than usual to complete some officework before going to the Game Commission's Harrisburg office to pick up some supplies. I recently had a birthday and donned a pair of bedroom slippers (bright red) which my wife had given me. I arrived in Harrisburg, parked my car and headed toward the South Office building. Much to my chagrin, I realized too late that I was still wearing the slippers. I now define "eternity" as the amount of time it takes a Game Protector to walk 75 yards back to his car in downtown Harrisburg, in full uniform, wearing a pair of red bedroom slippers.
-- District Game Protector J. E. Schweitzer, Hummelstown.
January 1975.

Father's Great Long whiskers
BEDFORD COUNTY - Each fall, you see many more men wearing beards in preparation for deer season. Deputy Bob Burkett told me about a man in the vicinity of Hyndman who probably found himself wishing he had never started one. During small game season he missed a squirrel which ran up a nearby tree. Following the path of the squirrel with his shotgun and trying to pump another shell into the chamber, the hunter got his beard caught in the action of the gun and had to get help to have it removed.
-- District Game Protector B. L. Warner, Bedford.
February 1975.

"What's Your Name, Son?"

LAWRENCE COUNTY - A while back I gave a program to a group of elementary school students. After I talked to the kids about hunting seasons and bag limits, one little boy proudly exclaimed that his daddy knows a man who shot a cow and it wasn't even cow season.

-- District Game Protector W. D. Shultz, New Castle.

March 1975.

He'll Be Sorry!

LUZERNE COUNTY - Not too long ago, while I was at the Northeast Headquarters building, I was approached by a man who wanted to know how he could go about getting a job like I had. When I asked him just what he thought I did on my job, he replied, "Oh, you know, just walking around the woods, looking things over." After giving this man a very brief rundown of the responsibilities of a Waterways Patrolman, he informed me that maybe he'd better stay on relief!

-- Waterways Patrolman Claude M. Neifert.

April 1975.

Trap Now, Pay Later

ERIE & WARREN COUNTIES - One of my deputies arrested a man for trapping without a hunting license. The man said he was just trying this trapping business out for a couple of days, and if he did good at it he was going to buy a license.

-- District Game Protector G. E. Gibson, Corry.

April 1975.

Wet Wake-Up

CRAWFORD COUNTY - On night patrol this year, Land Manager Miller and Deputy Randall scored a first. They sunk a car. The two found a vehicle blocking one lane of the highway and were unable to awaken the driver, so returned to their vehicle to check the registration via radio. Deputy Randall got the first three numbers, but was unable to get the balance before the car drove off into five or six feet of water. Since snorkels are not issued, the rest of the registration number could not be checked. The shock of the water finally revived the driver, and he got to safety.
-- District Game Protector H. L. Harshaw, Conneaut Lake.
May 1975.

Not in the Bird Book

PERRY COUNTY - One evening earlier this month, Waterways Patrolman Ben Leamer came to my home prior to attending a meeting. As we left the house, we were looking at the beautiful sunset when a large "bird" caught my eye. I asked, "Is it a hawk or a buzzard?" Ben informed me that it was a "bat kite" the neighbor kids were flying.
-- District Game Protector L. Everett, Newport.
June 1975.

The Fun Part of the Job

MERCER COUNTY - People never run out of tales to tell their friendly Game Protector. For instance, this month I heard stories of a 250-year-old parrot that spoke three languages; a full-blooded Indian grandmother who shot a rabbit with a bow and arrow as it ate her peas; more information on taming a great horned owl than I ever cared to know about; a man with a basket of trout on the first day of the season; and numerous accounts of a past spring gobbler season. Very interesting...

-- District Game Protector B. K. Ray, Greenville.
July 1975.

Reluctant Cook

ERIE COUNTY - State Trooper Carlson and his hunting party arrived at their camp after a three-hour drive, eager for their spring turkey hunt. When unpacking their gear, one member of the group was quite disappointed to find that he'd forgotten his 16-ga. ammunition. Since no one else had any 16-ga. shells, he spent his visit at camp as a very frustrated cook. To add insult to injury, when the hunter arrived home he found a box of 16-ga. shotgun shells, packed separately, sitting in back of the car's front seat.

-- District Game Protector A. C. Martin, Erie.
August 1975.

Potato Pickers

BEDFORD COUNTY - Over the years men have trained animals to do much of their work. I was talking to a farmer the other day, and he suggested that raccoons could possibly be trained to pick potatoes. Apparently, coons dig the potatoes out of the ground but don't like them, so they won't eat them.
-- District Game Protector B. L. Warner, Bedford.
September 1975.

Cancelled Duck Stamping

BEDFORD COUNTY - While picking up my mail at the post office one day, I overheard a gentleman saying that he was not going to buy a duck stamp this year. He said he's been trying for many years and has yet to catch one to put it on.
-- District Game Protector B. L. Warner, Bedford.
October 1975.

The Big Game

TRAINING SCHOOL - Game Protectors and uniformed Game Commission personnel are often mistaken for being anything from the dog catcher to the meter reader. Recently, one of the visiting instructors at the school said two young ladies asked him if he was in charge of the Pennsylvania Lottery. It seems they thought the word "Game" in the Game Commission referred to a different type of game.
-- Trainee D. E. Marks.
November 1975.

Frozen Goodies

CLEARFIELD COUNTY - Much to Mrs. Z's dismay, our freezer usually contains more wildlife specimens than food for the table. It's not unusual for the lady of the house to fetch what she believes to be a package of ground beef and instead come up with a frozen muskrat or woodchuck which has been promised to a school.
-- District Game Protector G. J. Zeidler, Rockton.
December 1975.

Born Loser

While heading to the Walnut Creek Access Area, Assistant Supervisor Hollen and I chanced to notice a Sunday hunter. We apprehended him and began to explain that Waterways Patrolmen are ex-officio Game Protectors also. Before we could finish explaining, the defendant said, "Yeah, I know. The Game Warden arrested me Wednesday for not having life preservers."
-- Area Waterways Patrolman Robert Lynn Steiner, Northwest Region.
January 1976.

Shucks, It's Expired

TRAINING SCHOOL - It was interesting when a DGP and Trainee were called into an area already under surveillance by two irate farmers and one State Trooper. It was more interesting when the violator was apprehended for shooting a dove before noon opening, shooting a hen pheasant out of season, committing a safety zone violation, trespassing and hunting without a current license. It was even more interesting when we had to go to the Dublin State Police barracks to find an interpreter to talk to the violator, who didn't speak English. But when he produced a 1969 hunting license from a European country, I knew we had us a Field Note!
--Trainee R. G. MacWilliams.
February 1976.

Ask... Just Ask

COLUMBIA & MONTOUR COUNTIES - I was fishing for salmon from one of the concrete jetties at Lake Erie when I was joined by another angler. After a half hour of fruitless casting and conversation, I learned the man was a minister. In view of the futility we were experiencing, I told him jokingly to use his influence with the Almighty to help us get some fish. He turned his face skyward and, going along with the scene, said, *"Lord, if it be not beneath Thy notice, I'd sure like to catch a salmon."*

The next cast, he hooked a huge salmon that departed on its way to New York with a loud crack as the line parted. He looked at me then turned his face to Heaven again and with a very hurt tone of voice said, *"Lord, I don't mean to question Your understanding, but really, catching also implies landing!"*
-- Deputy Waterways Patrolman Bill Huffnagle.
February 1977.

A Rash Decision

DAUPHIN COUNTY - This past season brought a new law enforcement tool to Dauphin County. After Land Manager Ken Zinn disposed of a deer, he spent the next day at the hospital trying to get rid of a rash. Returning to duty, Ken handled a deer hide and the rash broke out again. When away from any hide, the rash went away. Now, instead of training a dog to smell out illegal venison, we are going to use Zinn for searching out suspected poachers' residences. If Ken breaks out, we'll know we've struck pay dirt.
-- District Game Protector G. W. Packard, Millersburg.
March 1976.

A Red-Bristled Push Broom

BRADFORD COUNTY - Deputy George Barrowcliff got a telephone call to remove a strange animal from a cellar. George arrived, was directed downstairs and was shown a box which the animal had supposedly gotten into. It was dark in the box and he couldn't see anything. He took a stick, and approached the box while the houseowner kept a safe distance. When George looked in, there it was! A push broom lying there with the bristles up. What a weird, frightful creature.

-- District Game Protector A. D. Rockwell, Sayre.

April 1976.

Cozy!

WASHINGTON COUNTY - A recent caller asked if it was legal to take his dog with him while crow hunting. Out of curiosity I asked what kind of dog he had. "A collie," he replied. My next question was "What does he do, retrieve the crows?" The caller replied, "No, I use him to keep warm. We snuggle up together while waiting for the crows to come in."

-- District Game Protector J. M. Kazakavage, Washington.

May 1976.

4/1/76

JUNIATA COUNTY - A local radio announcement said: "Seven fresh water dolphins have escaped from a marine aquarium in the Philadelphia area and have been seen swimming up the Susquehanna River. They have split up at the junction of the Susquehanna and the Juniata. Two went on up the Susquehanna and five are coming up the Juniata. Be on the lookout for same. Locally we had people standing on bridges, cars parked on outlooks and access areas, kids running around, binoculars in evidence, and everyone talking about dolphins. Then toward midday people began realizing what the day and date was. Nice way to celebrate April Fools Day! The red flush to their faces was not sunburn.
-- District Game Protector R. P. Shaffer, Mifflintown.
June 1976.

Bushytailed Bubblegummer

HUNTINGDON COUNTY - Larry Spielman of Chambersburg, a member of the Green Acres Hunting Camp located in the vicinity of Broadtop, reported to me that a gray squirrel stole his bubble gum. He'd settled down comfortably to call turkeys, and had removed his bubble gum from his mouth and placed it on a log in front of him, within arm's reach. Shortly thereafter, a squirrel came along, jumped up onto the log, and started edging closer and closer to the gum, nervously flicking its tail. Finally, it grabbed the wad, ran off about fifty feet, hopped up onto a stump and started chewing.
-- District Game Protector D. J. Adams, Saltillo.
August 1976.

194

Exit, Stage Right

RLSC - While jogging on one of the State Game Lands roads near the Training School, I noticed two large porcupines comfortably perched about five feet up a small striped maple. Neither seemed concerned about my presence, so I ran quickly back to the school to alert several classmates interested in wildlife photography. When we returned there was still one quill-pig up the tree. He seemed about as bothered by the clicking cameras as a fish might be with water. He cooperated admirably - until I jokingly put a comb on his back as if to comb his quills. That proved to be too much for him and he decided to exit while his dignity was still intact.
-- Trainee M. W. Schmit.
September 1976.

Roadhog

MONROE COUNTY - Elwood Fenner, of Stroudsburg, has had his share of problems with groundhogs over the years at his Cherry Valley farm. But recently, when he returned to his tractor after lunch to continue mowing, he found a large woodchuck standing on the seat looking things over. Putting up with the critters is one thing - but to have one try to hijack your tractor is the last straw!
-- DGP Dave Overcash, E. Stroudsburg.
October 1976.

195

Ouch!

POTTER COUNTY - Recently we had some neighbors in our home showing them the renovations we made to the house. Their young son Michael was impressed with my office and the mounted specimens. As they returned home, the father told Michael that I was a game warden and if he went out and shot deer illegally, I would pinch him. Michael didn't say a word for a while. Finally he looked up and asked his dad, "Where does he pinch you?"
-- DGP Ron Clouser, Galeton.
November 1976.

Everybody Out!

BRADFORD COUNTY - DGP Ed Gallew was having problems with several bears coming into a cornfield in the New Albany area. He and Deputy Harold Haverly set a trap and the first night caught a young male bear. They tranquilized the bear, removed it from the trap, weighed and tagged it and took other vital information. Not wanting to remove the trap and take it to the release site, Ed and Harold put the drugged bear in the back of their Jeep station wagon. On the way to the release point, they kept checking the bear to make sure that he was still under the drug. While crossing SGL 36 and getting close to the release point, Mr. Bear stood up, looked at Ed and Harold, gave a grunt and jumped out the back window. What a picture that would have made: the bear jumping out the back and Ed and Harold jumping out the front - SIMULTANEOUSLY!
-- DGP Bill Bower, Troy.
December 1976.

196

Not Even Close

BEAVER COUNTY - During the National Hunting and Fishing Day celebration, District Game Protector George Szilvasi and I were working our consolidated display at the Beaver Valley Mall when a six-year-old boy approached to admire some of the furs George had placed on the table. With a very confident smile on his face, the lad picked up a mink pelt and proudly announced, "This is a musky, isn't it?"

-- Waterways Patrolman Don Parrish

December 1976.

Glug, Glug, Glug

BLAIR COUNTY - While on night patrol, Deputy Focht and Special Waterways Patrolman Corl radioed for assistance as follows: "Could you assist us, we are taking on water." A slight delay then, "Could you hurry, we already have six inches of water in the cab!" Upon arrival the call was found to be correct. One chain and one Matador rescued one four-wheel-drive. Oh, for a camera and a flash! Now, the Special Waterways Patrolman might be able to convince some people that he was checking for fishermen, but the driver has little excuse for driving into three feet of water.

-- DGP Larry Harshaw, Hollidaysburg.

January 1977.

Talent

During waterfowl season, DGP Sneath and Deputy Homer Hart were patrolling in a canoe. As they approached a couple of duck hunters, Hart in the bow and Sneath in the stern with pipe clenched between his teeth, the boat got tangled in some marsh grass. They both pushed from the same side of the canoe, and the inevitable happened. As Sneath came bobbing to the surface, one of the hunters said, "Look at that guy! His pipe is still lit!"

-- Land Manager John Miller, Jr., Meadville.

February 1977.

197

Cold and Deep

ELK COUNTY - The daily accumulation of snow reached above the knees of most hunters and made the extended season difficult. I watched two young hunters taking turns carrying their small beagle while hunting on Haney Hill.
-- DGP Harold Harshbarger, Kersey.
March 1977.

Tackle Twist

LEHIGH COUNTY - Deputy Ernie Massini and I were talking to a musky fisherman along the Lehigh River, when out of the corner of my eye I saw a can fly through the air and land in the water. He hurried to the spot from whence the can had emerged to try and spot the litterbug. By that time, no can was visible on the water, and the brushy shoreline prevented us from seeing who threw it. I said to Ernie, "I wasn't seeing things. I'm sure I saw a can fly."

Ernie said, "Yeah, I guess you did. There it goes again!" Sure enough, we both watched a small can sail from the shoreline and into the water. It lay still for a second then wiggled a little bit, then started for the shoreline. As it swam its way to shore, and to its owner, we realized that we were seeing our first Budweiser beer can lure in action! This novelty lure is sold in many tackle shops, and looks exactly like a beer can, only with hooks. If a fish likes the brand, I suppose it can be effective.
-- Waterways Patrolman Fred Mussel.
March 1977.

They're There!

YORK COUNTY - While working at the Game Commission's booth at the Farm Show, a lad of about 18 started to complain to me that the Commission had spoiled deer hunting and that we had no more deer, because he had not seen many. He had expounded for about five minutes when an elderly Amish gentleman who was listening offered him some sound advice. "Sonny, what you should do is get up early, eat a good breakfast with a hot cup of black coffee, get out of your car and walk back into the woods two ridges from the road. Then you will see deer. "
-- DGP Bob Yeakel, Red Lion.
April 1977.

198

This is a Stink-Up

CAMBRIA COUNTY - Recently I had a bank holdup in my district. The bandit managed to keep the customers and bank personnel at bay for about an hour. Seems a skunk decided that inside would be cozier than outside, so it nonchalantly dug a hole and found itself a home in the bank. From time to time, it would wander in and out and around the parking lot, causing mayhem. Arriving at the bank, I found the parking area empty and bank personnel on top of counters and up against the walls. I quickly remembered what I had learned in school and yelled to the skunk to come out with its paws up. This it did, and I quickly placed it in cuffs and sped off.

-- DGP Dan Marks, Johnstown.

May 1977.

Owl of Dismay

ERIE COUNTY - This winter I received a snowy owl which had been accidentally killed. I wrapped it in aluminum foil and placed it in the freezer until I could take it to the Division Office. Recently, my wife called home from the office and told our oldest daughter, Becky, to go to the freezer and take out a loaf of Italian bread which was wrapped in aluminum and to warm it in the oven to have with our spaghetti dinner. After the bag had been in the oven about 15 minutes, Becky thought she would open the bread and butter it while it was still hot. Her response to the kidding by her brother and sister that night: "Well, how would you like to open up a loaf of bread and see two big eyes staring up at you?"

-- DGP Andy Martin, Erie.

June 1977.

No Cause for Complaint

LEHIGH COUNTY - I recently received a call from a local veterinarian. A friend of his who is quite particular about her lawn had found some small round "pellets" in her grass. Fearing someone was trying to poison her lawn, she collected a few and gave them to him for identification. Upon seeing the "poison pellets" he gave me a call to see what species of wildlife was the culprit. You probably guessed it by now. Instead of having her lawn poisoned, this woman was getting a little free fertilizer from a neighborhood cottontail.

-- DGP W. Q. Stump, Germansville.

July 1977

Emergency

MIFFLIN COUNTY - Two young lads were waiting for the school bus as I stopped to pick up a highway killed deer nearby. I opened my trunk and got my deer rack out. As I was loading the deer on the rack, the boys walked over. After a slight pause one of them asked, "Ya gonna call Rampart?" I got the connection when I realized he saw the phone-type portable radio in my trunk. I said, "Nah, gonna give it 5cc D5W and transport immediately." As I pulled away I think they were still trying to figure out whether I was "Gage" or "DeSoto".
-- DGP Tim Marks, Belleville.
August 1977.

?-?-?-?-?

MERCER COUNTY - While patrolling the Shenango Wildlife area, a young lady asked if I had seen any "herrings." "You know, the ones with the long necks," she added at my puzzled look. "Oh, you mean great blue herons. There are a lot of them in this area," I replied. "Good," she said. "They're extinct, so that's why we come up here to see them. "
-- DGP Frank S. Zalik, Mercer.
September 1977.

201

Weasel On The Loose

SCHUYLKILL COUNTY - During our rabbit trap-and-transfer program, Skip Ahrensfield and his son Brad, from the Landingville Hunting and Conservation Club, were transferring a weasel that had been caught in a box trap. The trap got open somehow and the weasel got loose in the car. For a moment, it was sitting on Brad's lap! Skip slammed on the brakes and he and Brad jumped out. But not the weasel. The little critter ran under the back seat and into the trunk. As Skip and Brad pursued, the weasel simply moved back into the car, then into the trunk, then into the car. Not till the trunk lid was left open overnight did their furry friend finally depart.
-- DGP Rod Dilling, Auburn.
October 1977.

Unusual

CUMBERLAND COUNTY - Recently a local snake hunter told me that he had found a nest of "buzzards" in a rock cliff in the south mountains. After giving this find considerable thought, I decided to investigate. The walk and climb was considerable, but the site was finally found with the help of another local youth and a schoolteacher. Our efforts were well repaid. This proved to be the fourth nesting site yet discovered in Pennsylvania of the black vulture. Despite the stench of the nest area, we managed to quell our rebellious stomachs long enough to approach their rocky labyrinth for a few pictures.
-- DGP E. F. Utech, Boiling Springs.
November 1977.

Too Shallow

ADAMS & YORK COUNTIES - While having a discussion with several fellows at a sportsmen's club meeting of the McSherrytown's Fish and Game Protective Association, the discussion itself was about the use of turtle hooks, the legal size, etc. One sportsman asked what he should do when he finds opossums on his turtle hooks! Maybe he'll try setting them a little deeper in the water.
-- Waterways Patrolman Warren W. Singer Jr.
November 1977.

Noble Intentions, But...

POTTER COUNTY - Sometimes things just aren't what they appear to be! As a good example, late one night I got a phone call that a "spotlighter" had located a black bear that had just been shot. Since it was in DGP Lynn Keller's district, I called him and then accompanied him to the scene. A friend of the caller had been watching the area, but hadn't gone near the body so he wouldn't disturb any evidence. The bear turned out to be a large piece of black plastic covering a mountain spring. After explaining the difference between black bears and black plastic, we left.
-- DGP Ron Clouser, Galeton.
December 1977.

Elementary, Watson

ROSS LEFFLER SCHOOL OF CONSERVATION - Everyone here constantly tries to sharpen his outdoor skills. One trainee found some droppings he could not identify. He called an experienced trapper over and by the process of elimination they ruled out raccoon, opossum, skunk and fox, but were still puzzled. It took an experienced tobacco chewer to tell them what it was!
-- Trainee Don Smith.
January 1978.

Just Being Friendly

RLSC - While on my field training assignment in Clarion County with DGP Bowers, I have had some amusing experiences. One occurred while we were on night patrol in an area where some shots were fired after dark. Minutes after hearing the shots, we stopped a car coming along the only road from that area. Upon approaching the vehicle, I saw that it contained two visibly shaken occupants - a teenaged boy and girl. When questioned, the young man said he'd been only about a half mile up the road. I asked what he was doing in the area - parking? He hesitantly replied, "Oh, no, Officer! We weren't parking, we were just kissing a little."
-- Trainee C. H. May.
February 1978.

Pennsylvania Pied Piper?

MCKEAN COUNTY - While on jacklight patrol last fall, Trainee Gary Smith an I received a radio call from a deputy. He was sitting in an old railroad fill when he heard a strange wailing sound. He walked up the fill to see if he could determine where it was coming from. Finding nothing there, he started down the road in his auto. Suddenly his lights revealed something strange moving. There came a man playing bagpipes. It was 10:45 p. m. and raining hard, and the man went right by the deputy as if he were not even there, never missing a beat. The nearest house was approximately one-half mile away.
-- DGP Jim Rankin, Port Allegany.
March 1978.

Was He Greased?

I knew my field training assignments would cover a wide variety of law enforcement situations, public relations, and the rest of a Game Protector's duties. I never thought, however, that I would assist DGP Dan Jenkins pursue a piglet through a dense forest in Cambria County with a flashlight in the middle of the night.

-- Trainee R. C. Snouffer.

April 1978.

Smile, You're On...

LANCASTER COUNTY - For some time, I had suspected a young woman, who was always with the same group of young men, of fishing without a license. One dark night I spotted their vehicle and quietly approached while they were all gathered around a gas lantern. They were talking very excitedly about a very large catfish, and were preparing to take a picture of the girl holding it. When the flash went off *I was standing behind the girl in the darkness.* As they still had not noticed me, I quietly left. I'm betting that after those pictures were developed, the girl went out and bought a license.

-- Waterways Patrolman Kerry L. Messerle.

May 1978.

What???

LEBANON COUNTY - Returning home one evening recently, I switched on my Code-A-Phone to get the day's messages and heard a conversation between two women with Pennsylvania Dutch accents that went something like this:

"Hello, hello."

"What's going on?"

"I don't know. He talks so fast, I could not answer him still. He just hung up."

"Who does he think he is?"

"I'm already tired. This number I'm going to call again."

"No, call the police."

I was disappointed that I never had the pleasure of knowing what that call was all about.

-- DGP Ron Sutherland, Campbelltown.

June 1978.

Wouldn't Work

LANCASTER COUNTY - Deputy Game Protector Donald Ruth and I were patrolling a stream that had just been stocked that afternoon. Officer Ruth apprehended a violator who had over-the-limit of trout. As he took the information and seized the fish he heard the usual plea of, "Let me put some back." What was so unusual in this instance was that the defendant's fish had the entrails and heads removed.!

-- Waterways Patrolman Kerry Messerle.

July 1978.

206

Doin' the Bunny Hop

SCHUYLKILL COUNTY - During the deep snow I took care of a rabbit complaint just outside of town. One cold morning I picked up a rabbit that had entered the trap overnight. Placing the bunny in a woven plastic feed bag for transfer out of town to a more remote area, I tied the bag shut and set it on the sidewalk while I reset the trap. The bag took off across the yard in three feet of snow with one DGP in hot pursuit. After a thirty-yard chase I caught the bag and put it in the trunk. When I got to a release area and opened the trunk, the bag leaped out and I just barely caught it before it took off again. Maybe I need a heavier, darker bag?

-- DGP Rod Dilling, Auburn.

July 1978.

Ooops!

FOREST COUNTY - Upon checking out the Cooks Forest State Park's fishing pond for youngsters and disabled persons, I found a young lady about five years old fishing very seriously along the shoreline. I watched her attempt to throw her fishing line out into the water. Moments later I heard her exclaim, "Ooops!" She had flung pole, line, bait and everything into the water... I retrieved the pole, to find a very grateful young lady standing at the edge of the pond.

-- DGP Alfred N. Pedder, Marienville.

August 1978.

An' That's the Truth!

CLINTON COUNTY - As I was getting out of my state vehicle in Renovo, a boy about five years old approached me. He looked at the Game Commission emblem on the door - a decal of a white-tailed deer head - and then tugged at my shirt to get my attention. Then with all the innocence and trust of a young boy he whispered, "If you kill one of them when you're not supposed to, the woods cop will arrest you.
-- DGP John Wasserman, Renovo.
September 1978.

Ulp!

CAMBRIA COUNTY - Charles Harpster of Ebensburg got a double surprise recently while fishing Raystown Lake. He was lucky enough to land a large bass and placed it in the live catch of the boat. Shortly after being placed there, the bass coughed up a whole bat. This caused much guessing among the trio of fishermen as to how it got there. One possible answer: maybe the bass and the bat went for an insect near the surface of the water and both got more than they bargained for.
-- DGP Daniel W. Jenkins, Patton.
October 1978.

208

Silent Partners

ERIE & WARREN COUNTIES - The owner of a local sporting goods store was working in the store when he noticed a red squirrel hopping down the main street. When it reached the display window of the store, it stopped and looked at two mounted squirrels in the window, its head tilted questioningly. The squirrel proceeded to enter the store through the front door, which was open. It jumped up on the window ledge and approached the two mounted squirrels. After chattering at them for a short time with no reaction, it jumped off the ledge and exited through the door. Probably thought those guys weren't very friendly.
-- DGP George E. Gibson, Corry.
November 1978.

Scared Eggs?

BUTLER COUNTY - A local woman was having difficulty with something eating her ducks. The culprit, a great horned owl, was removed from the area. Not an unusual complaint, and yet part of my ensuing conversation with the woman left me scratching my head. She commented that not only did the owl kill the mother duck, but also frightened the eggs, and in her opinion, the Game Commission should be liable to pay damages. Now, if the PGC could be held liable (which it couldn't) it shouldn't be too difficult to determine the value of the hen duck, but for the frightened eggs, we might need the services of a sharp big-city lawyer.
-- DGP Ned Weston, Boyers.
December 1978.

That's the Spirit!

DAUPHIN COUNTY - While I was getting my hair cut this summer, I noticed a young lady walking down the street wearing fluorescent orange shorts. I commented to the barber that she should wear them hunting. He replied, "She does!" End of conversation.
-- DGP Gary W. Packard, Millersburg.
January 1979.

Mistaken Identity

CAMERON COUNTY - While patrolling the Dents Run area I passed Deputy Game Protector John Dzemyan and stopped to talk. Earlier in the day I had passed a patch of blueberries which were too nice to pass up so I picked about four quarts and carried them in a plastic pail. I held the pail up to the car window and John's wife, Carol, quipped, "Are you collecting *those*?" We were puzzled at the terminology Carol used, so John mentioned they were blueberries. To this, Carol replied, "Oh, I thought they were deer droppings and I couldn't think why you would want to collect deer droppings."
-- Waterways Patrolman Stanley G. Hastings.
January 1979.

Hot Item

BRADFORD COUNTY - Deputy George Barrowcliff was watching a field where deer were feeding when a car pulled in and turned its lights out. He'd received complaints of night shooting in that field, so he cautiously approached the car and turned his flashlight on the occupant as he knocked on the driver's door. The startled occupant was smoking and, seeing the uniformed officer, proceeded to swallow his cigarette without bothering to put it out. It turned out he was swallowing evidence; the car reeked of pot fumes. Wonder if he got heartburn from that lighted cigarette!
-- DGP A. Dean Rockwell, Sayre.
February 1979.

But Don't Self-Destruct

ALLEGHENY COUNTY - A young man from McKeesport, who was hunting for the first time, shot and killed a buck in Somerset County. He had never gutted a deer but had a plastic diagram in his pocket which showed how it should be done. He pinned this to the chest of the deer and proceeded to follow the instructions. Another hunter came along and asked what the plastic was for and the fellow told him. The other hunter asked, "So now they even come with a complete set of instructions?"
-- DGP S. E. Lockerman, Pittsburgh.
March 1979.

An Easy Miss
LUZERNE COUNTY - Adam "Brownie" Knelly was hunting pheasants on State Game Lands 187 and approached two hunters sitting under a tree. He told them a pheasant was perched in the tree above them. One hunter said, "What are you, some kind of wise guy?" They looked up just in time to see the pheasant take off and fly away. Both hunters missed it cleanly.
-- DGP Bob Nolf, Conyngham.
April 1979.

Ye of Little Faith
MIFFLIN COUNTY - Being an active deputy doesn't leave a fellow much time to hunt. Deputy Rich Eby, however, was fortunate enough to bag a deer this past season. Upon returning home he was greeted by his two young children, who asked if he had any luck. Telling them that he did, and seeing their somewhat doubtful expressions, he prompted them to look in the back of his pickup. As they approached the truck his boy was heard whispering to his older sister, "I'll bet he just picked up another roadkill!"
-- DGP Tim Marks, Belleville.
May 1979.

One of These Days

FULTON COUNTY - The least appealing part of my job is the paperwork. Sometimes it shows in the monthly reports we all have to submit. The other day at the Division Office I saw one of the secretaries correcting a sloppy report. I commented that it would be a lot easier for the girls if some of the guys would be a little more careful with their paperwork. She agreed and went on working. I walked over and glanced at the name and guess whose report it was. You're right - mine!

-- DGP Mark Crowder, McConnellsburg.

June 1979.

Always Prepared

ADAMS COUNTY - *Nature of the complaint* - Three skunks have taken up residence in the crawl space beneath the kitchen. *Problem* - They stink! *Solution-* Take along Cub Scouts Jeff Ridinger and Patrick Heffner as part of the Adams County Civic Day Program. Let them investigate and determine the facts. *Action* - Jeff promptly investigates and locates the entry point, a small hole where a brick has fallen out of the house foundation. Patrick has an idea: use a big rubber band to shoot moth balls through the hole all the way back to the opposite corner where the skunks are residing. Being the best paperwad shooter in his class, he proves to be deadly accurate. The skunks, unable to stand the odor of the moth balls, finally leave. The home owner is happy, the Game Protector has learned something, and the Scouts have done their good deed.

-- DGP Larry Haynes, Gettysburg.

August 1979.

"Smile..."

LUZERNE COUNTY - While working at the Fish Commission's recent EXPO 79 which was presented at the Wyoming Valley Mall in Wilkes-Barre, we had a small, very realistic looking rubber snake rigged up on a display table with other mounted snakes, so that when a spectator got a little too close, we could make it jump with the aid of a piece of almost invisible monofilament fishing line. One persistent gentleman kept poking his finger toward the snake, only to take a jump backwards everytime the snake "struck out." He kept telling me that he knew we must be playing a trick on him, and that he thought we made the snake strike "with the aid of a magnet."

Taking off my dark glasses, I asked the gentleman to take a good look at me to see if he recognized me. He remarked that I "sort of looked familiar" to him. I then replied, "I am Allen Funt," then pointed to a picture on the wall behind me and stated, "You are on Candid Camera."

To this, the man let out a yelp, "You got to be kidding!" Then after taking a good hard look at the picture on the wall he started to walk down the corridor, laughing and yelling back to me , "I knew you guys would get me some day."

Somewhere in Luzerne County today there is a man telling his friends about the time he got "caught on Candid Camera."
-- Waterways Patrolman Claude M. Neifert.
August 1979.

A Ladder, Maybe?

BRADFORD COUNTY - Now I have heard them all! While stocking fish in the Schrader on SGL 12 and 36, Special Waterways Patrolman Mac Davenport was talking to a local sportsman who was helping. They were near a beaver dam and also under a tree a porcuine had been working on. The man looked up at the tree and commented to Mac, "I just don't know how these beaver climb so high to eat the bark like that!"
-- DGP Edward Gallew, Wyalusing.
September 1979.

Please Don't Eat the Warden

BRADFORD COUNTY - Bob White of Snedekerville complained that a beaver was flooding his fields. This is not unusual, but Bob said the beaver was using railroad ties. Sure enough, the industrious critter had somehow managed to get five abandoned ties into the dam. Standing hip deep in water and trying to remove the bulky ties, I imagined that this must be a BIG beaver. As the background music from "Jaws" ran through my mind, a floating branch hit my leg. An instant later I was standing on the bank... laughing?
-- DGP William A. Bower, Troy.
October 1979.

Calling Marlin Perkins!

LYCOMING COUNTY - Live-trapping beavers can be a very disturbing process. Everything has to function perfectly because if you miss the beaver one time, your chances of getting him into the cage trap again have been greatly reduced. On the first night of an attempt to trap a nuisance beaver, one side of the trap didn't spring. On the second night, I found the trap to be the center portion of the beaver dam, the beaver had used it to plug the hole I made in the dam. It took me an hour to remove the trap and reset it. The following week the trap didn't go off after the trigger had been sprung. On the third week, I thought I had my quarry as I found the trap sprung and intact. My catch turned out to be a 15-inch largemouth bass. I'll keep trying. Who knows what I'll catch next... maybe even a beaver.

-- DGP Dennis Dusza, South Williamsport.
November 1979.

Uh-oh!

BERKS COUNTY - While checking dove hunters near Lake Ontelaunee, I inspected a limit of doves piled on the ground between two hunters. On the bottom of the pile was a bird described by the lucky hunter as being a "red breasted dove." His luck changed rapidly, as the bird in question turned out to be an immature robin - protected by state and federal law.

-- DGP Clayton G. VanBuskirk, Kutztown.
December 1979.

Chapter 6
1980 - 1993

In this chapter, we encounter field notes which reflect today's high paced lifestyle. Many advances in technology took place during this timeframe, but the life of a conservation officer never seemed to get any easier as a result. In fact, new equipment and techniques in law-enforcement sometimes produced hilarious results.

Most of the WCO's who contributed the notes we see here are still currently in service with the Fish and Game Commissions. Their notes are indicitive of their high-speed authors. A fun spirit of competition arose and CO's frequently used the *Field Notes* and *Notes From the Stream* forums to play practical jokes on one another.

216

Who Needs a Dog?

WESTMORELAND COUNTY - Waterways Patrolman Barry Pollock made perhaps the best shot of the dove season recently. As he stood in the edge between a cornfield and a winter wheatfield, four doves approached him head-on. Someone shot and two of the doves veered away, the two remaining ones continuing straight ahead. Picking out a single target, Barry shot. The dove folded up, but its momentum continued to carry it forward. Pollock reached up, caught the bird and deposited it in his game bag.
-- DGP Barry K. Moore, Saltsburg.
January 1980.

"Dumbest?" No Way!

WARREN COUNTY - After writing up a nonresident hunter during the archery season for a violation, he had the nerve to tell me that this country has got to have "the dumbest lawmen in the world." I had to ask why. This is what he said, "None of you know what you are supposed to be doing." In Wyoming, the county sheriff arrested him for a game law violation. On Kinzua Dam, a Game Warden arrested him for a fishing without a license. Now, a Fish Commission man was arresting him for a game law violation.

I told him that somehow it looked like the laws *were getting enforced.* After paying a fine to Game Protector G. W. Waldman of McKean County, he got back his equipment. Maybe someday he will give up violating the laws!
-- Deputy Waterways Patrolman Owen F. Quarles.
February 1980.

217

Up, Up and Away

JEFFERSON COUNTY - Fox hunters beware, says a hunter of the Emerickville area of Jefferson County. A local hunter was using a squealing rabbit tape on his electronic fox call one night, and noticed the sounds from the speaker seemed to be fading. When the hunter turned on his light, he could see a great horned owl attempting to fly away with his speaker.
-- DGP Willis A. Sneath, Brockway.
February 1980.

Maybe It Was THX 1138

PERRY COUNTY - It was just one of those horrible days that come along every now and then. The phone kept ringing, the radio was squeaking and squawking with both the Game Commission and the skip from California, the kids were yelling and fighting and dinner was burning when the phone rang again. My wife answered the phone by saying "434X bye." I'm sure the caller is still wondering what's going on.
-- DGP LeRoy Everett, Newport.
March 1980.

Landing Leaves?

ELK COUNTY - While on routine patrol along Route 5 in Erie, I observed an elderly gentleman using a large diameter landing net to scoop up the excess leaves in his front yard.
-- Waterways Patrolman Bernie Ambrose.
April 1980.

Booster

LEHIGH COUNTY - In October, I received a call from a concerned woman in Allentown who had a hummingbird (which is protected under state and federal law). The bird had flown into her patio window and she had been keeping it until it was ready to fly again. According to her "bird book," the migration period for these birds is during September and it was now early October. Since the Allentown-Easton-Bethlehem Airport was so close and since many airplanes fly south from there every week, she was wondering if there might be someone on one of the planes who could carry the bird south and give it a chance to catch up with the rest of the migration.
-- DGP W. Q. Stump, Germansville.
April 1980.

218

Somebody's Not Listening
BLAIR COUNTY - At a recent meeting I had been asked how many bear were harvested in the state during the one-day season. As I replied that 736 legal bears had been taken, an elderly lady put up her hand. I asked her what she would like to know. Her question, and I quote: "Are there any bears in Pennsylvania?"
-- DGP Larry Harshaw, Hollidaysburg.
May 1980.

Century of Protection
DAUPHIN COUNTY - This country is entering its second century of law enforcement in the out-of-doors. New Hampshire and California had the first game wardens in 1878. Thirty-one states had wardens by the turn of the century. All states today regulate hunting and fishing in various degrees. A bit of trivia you can use when the conversation gets dull.
-- DGP Gary W. Packard, Millersburg.
June 1980.

We're All Human
Recently a disgruntled individual came into the Southwest Division Office in Ligonier and complained about the manner in which a certain Game Protector's wife spoke to him when he phoned for information. He was advised that the game protector had three small children and maybe his wife was just having a bad day. He replied, "Then the game protector should divorce her and marry someone who would answer the phone nicer." I believe in dedication, But enough is enough. Just how unreasonable can people be?
-- CIA John Badger, Ligonier.
July 1980.

No Flounder?
LEBANON & DAUPHIN COUNTIES - I had an interesting conversation with an older fellow while stocking Stover's Dam today. We were stocking trophy size palomino trout when he said that he wished the Fish Commission would stock lobsters. Tongue-in-cheek, I told him that I would get right on it. Hearing this, the old man said he would also like some scallops!
-- Waterways Patrolman Bill Snyder.
July 1980.

Take the Easy Way

GREENE COUNTY - Why is it that the simplest solutions to problems are usually the last ones considered? Deputy Jim Cooke received a call from a woman who was in a panic about a bat in the house. She wanted help immediately and hung up before Jim could say anything else. By the time Jim arrived, the woman's husband had taken things into his own hands. He climbed to the top of a six-foot ladder, swatted at the bat with a broom, missed it and crashed to the floor, injuring himself. When Jim arrived and heard what had happened, he asked where the bat was. The woman replied that after her husband fell, she opened the door and shooed the bat outside.
-- DGP Stephen A. Kleiner, Waynesburg.
August 1980.

That'll Teach 'Em All

BUTLER COUNTY - A certain Game Protector (no name mentioned but he has the northern half of the county) related a strange story to me. It seems he knows of a woodchuck killing a honeybee. Perhaps the strangest part of the story is that the Game Protector was holding the woodchuck in his hand at the time. As he tells it, the bee suddenly went to work on the back of his neck. Reacting out of instinct, the Game Protector swung the hand with the woodchuck in it, clubbing the bee. End result: one dead bee, one astonished woodchuck, and one swollen neck.
-- DGP Larry Heade, Butler.
September 1980.

Dessert?

BUTLER COUNTY - Maybe Deputy John Regal has answered too many beaver complaints. After he and I answered the latest one near Clintonville, we stopped for a sandwich on the way home. When the hamburgers arrived, I noticed they had large wooden toothpicks holding them together. Apparently John did not notice this, as when halfway through his sandwich, he had also consumed about half of the wooden toothpick. Perhaps I should pull him off beaver complaints awhile, as he seems to be picking up some of their eating habits.
-- DGP Ned Weston, West Sunbury.
October 1980.

First Liar

CRAWFORD COUNTY - While working on experimental methods of trapping nuisance animals with Wildlife Conservation Specialist Jack Weaver, Pete Askins of Woodstream, and my two neighboring officers, Will Wingo and Wayne Lugaila, we exchanged countless "tall stories." By the end of the week, Wayne had all the honors with a muskie which he saw eat a muskrat and a bullfrog with a cedar waxwing in its stomach. Until our last stop that is... As we were setting a trap under an old aspen tree for a problem woodchuck, the elderly lady who lived nearby told us, "You may not believe this, but that tree blew down in a bad storm a few years back, and as sure as I'm standing here, another storm came along and blew it right back up." None of us could top that one.
-- DGP Robert L. Lumadue, Saegertown.
November 1980.

Endangered Species?

COLUMBIA COUNTY - Bigfoot mania has hit this area following several reported sightings of this legendary beast. One sporting club has even erected a "Bigfoot crossing" sign alongside a road in an area where the creature supposedly was seen. Just the other night I checked four men who were armed and looking for Sasquatch! If this kind of enthusiasm continues, I soon expect to see a hairy, smelly, man-like creature at my door, seeking protection.
-- DGP Charles Arcovitch, Orangeville.
December 1980.

No Open Season

TIOGA COUNTY - Youngsters are known for asking the darndest questions. In a recent Hunter Education course, while discussing the Game Law, I mentioned that it is illegal to shoot at random. One student raised his hand and asked, "What does a random look like?"
-- DGP Steve Gehringer, Covington.
January 1981.

What a Service

BEDFORD COUNTY - Deputy John Corle was on foot patrol in the Blue Knob area when a hunter called him over. The hunter told John he had shot a turkey and he supposed John would want him to tag it. John said that was correct and asked where the turkey was. The man pointed straight up. Forty feet overhead, hung up in a tree, was one dead turkey. John shinnied up the tree, retrieved the bird and watched as the hunter filled out his tag.

-- DGP Steve Schweitzer, New Enterprise.

February 1981.

Know It All

CRAWFORD COUNTY - This must have been my month for strange telephone calls. In one evening received three calls in a row that went a little out of my line. The first wanted to know how to dispose of "an old, dead lion," the second wanted to know who could perform an autopsy on a muskrat, and the third wanted to know where he could get some maple sugar. The second and third calls weren't hard, but the first one had me stumped. (P.S. I checked, the moon was full!)

-- DGP William C. Wingo, Centerville.

March 1981.

Deodorant Yet

BUCKS COUNTY - Some time ago a woman from the lower end of the county called to tell me that a groundhog had died in her backyard. She wanted to know when she could expect me to remove it, and since it smelled so badly, would I bring some deodorant to spray around the area.

-- DGP E. F. Bond, Fountainville.

April 1981.

Cold Country

BRADFORD COUNTY - Low water and cold temperatures created problems for wildlife as well as people this past winter. A number of beaver dams were abandoned because the water was completely frozen to the bottom of the dam. In the middle of January a muskrat was found wandering on the Sayre High School grounds. Because everything was frozen over, I ended up with a boarder until weather conditions improved and I could find open water to release it in.
-- DGP A. Dean Rockwell, Sayre.
May 1981.

It's True, So Help Me

After 25 years in this business, I felt I had done it all, but there is always something new. A man recently asked me to verify that he had hit a deer with his auto. He had missed work the day he hit the deer and his boss was reluctant to accept it as a valid reason. Upon checking the auto and verifying the damage was done by a deer, I wrote "an excuse" for the man's absence from work.
-- CIA John Badger, Ligonier.
June 1981.

Just Wait

CRAWFORD COUNTY - Recently, we arrested an individual for illegal beaver trapping. During the investigation he revealed he was going to Alaska soon. He was found guilty at a hearing before the district justice and the following day this ad appeared in the classified section of the newspaper: "To the Crawford County Game Protector: I'm Gone! Bye, Bye!" and his name. A warrant has been issued for non-payment, but "the boss" said NO on my request for travel to Alaska to pick him up.
-- DGP Dave Myers, Linesville.
July 1981.

Progress

SNYDER COUNTY - When I teach hunter safety, I like to spend some time explaining the SPORT Program to the students. I think I might have reached one little boy with the message. During the break, he came up to me and said, "When I get home, I'm going to tell my dad not to outlaw anymore!"
-- DGP John Roller, Beavertown.
August 1981.

Snoozing

ERIE COUNTY - While on patrol on State Game Land 218, I saw a woodchuck hanging over a low limb on a tree very close to the road. Believing some unthinking chuck hunter had displayed his trophy, I stopped my car, put on a rubber glove, approached the "carcass" and prepared to dispose of it properly. I grabbed the chuck, but very quickly ungrabbed him when the startled animal awoke. He turned, but didn't leave the limb. I backed away from him and as I drove off he appeared to resume his sleep, in spite of the uninvited intrusion.
-- DGP Andy Martin, Erie.
September 1981.

Experienced

ELK COUNTY - I stopped at the Fred Meier residence in Toby Valley to check out a bear that had been hanging around the house only to learn that Mrs. Meier had already taken care of the problem by taking her broom to the bear a couple of times. I did wonder after I had left if she might have been practicing on Fred over the years.
-- DGP Harold Harshbarger, Kersey.
October 1981.

The Mouse that Roared

BERKS COUNTY - At 5 o'clock one morning, Deputy Bill Buckley of Malvern received a request from the Malvern Police Department to help investigate a report of a large animal in a private residence. Bill's initial inspection of the home revealed nothing, so he went to the backyard to look around. It was then that the lady of the house let out a scream that could have awakened the dead. It seems that the large animal was actually a small mouse that had gotten into her trash can and was chewing on aluminum foil. The can must have magnified the noise several times.
-- DGP Michael W. Schmitt, Birdsboro.
November 1981.

Dreamer

RLSC - Here at the Training School we have assignments we are to perform every morning, but we have a red squirrel that's trying to help us out. When we hang the mops out to dry he likes to chew them up. Maybe if he gets to them all we won't have to mop floors anymore.
-- Trainee Dale E. Hockenberry.
December 1981.

225

Controlled

CRAWFORD COUNTY - After Jussi Kopra, 17, an exchange student from Finland, successfully completed our Hunter Education course, I asked him about hunting in Finland. "We have very different hunting traditions there," he said. "For example, only a few select hunters are able to hunt for elk in Finland. Finnish sportsmen must first pass very stringent and expensive courses on hunting, firearms and game management. And if a hunter is fortunate enough to be selected for a license, he must then be accompanied by a government game manager who not only acts as his guide but even tells him which animal he must shoot at."
-- DGP Dave Myers, Linesville.
January 1982.

Yes, Yes, Yes

LUZERNE COUNTY - As a game protector, I receive many unusual calls. Last month I received three very unusual calls, namely: "I hit a deer with my truck, the horns are lodged in my radiator and I brought the deer home by placing it on the hood of my truck. Can I saw off the horns and remove the deer from the hood of my vehicle, without getting in any kind of trouble?" A lady employed at a local supermarket called about a wild mallard she had hit on her way to work. It was still alive, but lodged in her grille. She wanted me to come to the market parking lot and release the duck. And then a man called to ask if he could be arrested while hunting in a farmer's field with one of the farmer's watermelons in his game bag.
-- DGP Edward R. Gdosky, Dallas.
February 1982.

Tired Reindeer?

CAMBRIA COUNTY - During October, DGP Dan Marks and I held a Halloween party for our deputies and their wives. I still have to wonder, though, what passing motorists thought when they saw Mr. and Mrs. Santa Claus (actually Deputy Richard Ramsey and his wife Loretta) picking up a roadkilled deer on Route 219 north of Ebensburg.
-- DGP Denver A. McDowell, Carrolltown.
March 1982.

Not That Easy

TRAINING SCHOOL - The Game Commission's liberalized policy which allows the public to pick up roadkilled deer has made it easy to use these deer which might otherwise be wasted. But the man who called DGP Scott's office to order a 20-pound venison roast for a Christmas party thought it was even easier than it is.
-- Trainee Donald R. Schauer.
April 1982.

Occupations?

COLUMBIA COUNTY - While reviewing hunting license applications, I realized how many types of occupations there are in today's society. I came across a few that were quite unusual. One applicant was a "slave," another was a 24-year-old brain surgeon, and then there was a professional playboy. If this last fellow did not get a deer, I'll bet I can tell you why.
-- DGP Charles J. Arcovitch, Benton.
May 1982.

Mush, Sadie!

ARMSTRONG COUNTY - It seems that when I go to pick up an illegally killed or roadkilled deer, the location of the deer is such that it requires removal to another area. And all too often, it seems that the deer is enormous and the drag is uphill. The other day I harnessed my black lab, Sadie, to a large doe and the two of us really made a team as we dragged the deer out in record time. It worked so well that when I get to be an older officer, I may keep two or three labs around and have them do all of the dragging. Now, if only I could teach Sadie to type!
-- DGP Al Scott, Rural Valley.
June 1982.

227

"Hey, PGC!"

CAMBRIA COUNTY - I had just finished a phone conversation with a man who felt there weren't any deer left in the county and that the Game Commission better do something about it when I received a call from a farmer, telling me he had just counted 39 deer in his fields. He then proceeded to tell me there were too many deer in the county and that the Game Commission better do something about it. As they say, "You can't please all of them all of the time, half of them half of the time, and some of them anytime."

-- DGP Dan Marks, Sidman.

July 1982.

Something Costs Too Much

CAMBRIA COUNTY - A woman came up to me recently and started to complain about the high cost of Pennsylvania's fishing license. After she realized I worked for the Game Commission, she started on the high cost of the hunting license. After I explained to her how low our fishing and hunting license fees are compared to other states, she could see she was getting nowhere. Finally, she exclaimed, "Well, I think we are spending too much on the space shuttle, don't you?"

-- DGP R. A. Lizzio, Johnstown.

August 1982.

New Bird Feed?

BUCKS COUNTY - I recently learned a new way to use roadkilled deer. A caller asked what I do with roadkills. When I explained that we make use of all of the deer that we can, he asked if I could drop one off sometime to feed his buzzards. When I was telling my husband about the call, he began to laugh hysterically because all he could picture was a giant bird feeder with a deer stuck in it.

-- DGP Cheryl A. Trewella, Quakertown.

September 1982.

How's That Again?

WESTMORELAND COUNTY - A neighboring officer, Charlie May, recently asked if I would like to help him in the trap and transfer of a nuisance beaver. Charlie figured that since I don't have too many beaver in my district I may never have a chance to live trap one and that I should see how an experienced game protector does it. Upon my arrival, I found Charlie and a brand new Hancock Live Trap (the instructions were still wired on the trap). For those of you who do not know, this trap is made of heavy gauge wire and is designed to work like a giant clam that holds the beaver until it is moved and released. We selected a likely looking spot, set the trap on dry ground and Charlie scooted out on a log over about four feet of water. He then wired the trap to the log and reached down to release the safety catch. Well, you guessed it. The trap went off and Charlie was caught from the waist up.
-- DGP R. Matt Hough, Greensburg.
October 1982.

Dedicated

NORTHUMBERLAND COUNTY - Deputies Balavage and Cooper were watching some occupants in a vehicle who were suspected of littering. The deputies were parked about 60 yards behind the vehicle, but the driver must have gotten a little nervous because he moved about 100 yards farther down the road. Suspecting that they might frighten off the suspects if they drove closer, the deputies pushed their vehicle to within 20 yards of the suspects' vehicle and in no time had two litter violations. They were second violations and carried a double penalty.
-- DGP J. M. Kazakavage, Sunbury.
November 1982.

Flying Low

BRADFORD COUNTY - In my 15 years as a game protector, I've had deer hit by cars, trains, trucks, motorcycles, bicycles and, yes, even a jogger. But to top it all off, the other day I read in the newspaper about a deer that was hit by an airplane.
-- DGP William A. Bower, Troy.
December 1982.

Logical

BEDFORD COUNTY - During a hunter education class at the Northern Bedford County High School, I was discussing the difference between male and female pheasants. When I explained that males are more colorful and handsome than females, a girl's voice from the back of the room piped up, "That's why we shoot them!"
-- DGP Steve Schweitzer, New Enterprise.
January 1983.

Now He Knows

DAUPHIN COUNTY - While registering students for the hunter education course he was teaching, Instructor Mel Gochenaur found one of the students did not know his birthdate. No amount of memory searching helped, so Mel told the youngster to ask his parents and let him know on the last night of the class. On that night, when Mel asked if he had found out what day he had been born on, the boy proudly replied that they had to go back through the years, one by one, until they made sure of the day.

"I was born on a Wednesday," he said.
-- DGP Skip Littwin, Hummelstown.
February 1983.

Faster Than a Speeding Bullet

CLINTON COUNTY - This story keeps coming back to me so I thought I would share it with our readers. Several years ago I checked some hunters near Renovo as they were on their way home. Later that day, when they were in the Philadelphia area, my twin brother, Bill, checked them also. They were shocked that I had traveled over such a distance so quickly, and it was not until a year later that they found out that there are two of us!
-- DGP John Wasserman, Renovo.
March 1983.

Caught Napping

WESTMORELAND COUNTY - A hunter watched with amazement as a black bear spent twenty minutes nosing around another hunter on State Game Lands 42 near New Florence on the first day of the antlered deer season. After the bear left, he went over to talk to the other hunter about a sighting they would both remember for years. To his surprise, he found the other hunter had not seen the bear at all, but was sound asleep.
-- DGP B. K. Moore, Saltsburg.
April 1983.

Quiet Cruising

WESTMORELAND COUNTY - I've heard of game protectors going to many extremes to apprehend deliberate violators of the Game Law, but during deer season this year, Deputy Paul Puglia and I were accused of patrolling on 10 speeds. Now, if we could just figure out where to mount the red light and radio!
-- DGP R. Matthew Hough, Greensburg.
May 1983.

Thanks, Pig

CRAWFORD COUNTY - While patrolling with Deputies Gene Soltesz and Rob Hitchcock recently, the three of us began quizzing one another on general wildlife knowledge, habits and identification. As both men had just taken the civil service test for the district game protector position, and had been spending countless hours studying, they were, to put it mildly, "up" on their wildlife. In fact, matters were quickly beginning to get out of hand as the two began firing questions on some very fine points. I could just see their heads swelling as the experts increased their barrage of questioning in a game of "stump the leader." I was quickly fading far behind until the "Green Guardian Angel" who watches over all game protectors made me turn onto a secluded dirt road and past a remote cornfield. There stood a 400-pound pitch-black boar. Both deputies immediately yelled "Bear!" It was one of those times where a flood of events occurs in the blink of an eye. The vehicle lurched to a stop, papers and equipment slid to the floor, the passenger window was frantically cranked down, and one very startled pig looked up from an otherwise relaxing meal of corn stubbles. After regaining their composure, the two deputies were once again able to get the very recently too-tight Stetson hats back on their heads and I continued on into the sunset with my deputy force once again under control.
-- DGP Robert L. Lumadue, Saegertown.
June 1983.

All in the Mind

POTTER COUNTY - When Del Kerr, managing editor of the *Potter Enterprise*, read my field note about how hunters consistently overestimate the weights of the animals they harvest, he told me about an incident that happened a number of years ago, during a local big bear contest. On one occasion, three big husky bear hunters from Lancaster County came in with a bear, and it took all three men to drag it to the scales. When they found out what it actually weighed, however, it took only one man to drag it back out.
-- DGP Ron Clouser, Galeton.
July 1983.

Off Limits

CRAWFORD COUNTY - This is reputed to be the only county in the state to have as many roadkilled fish as roadkilled deer. With the abundant wetlands, heavy rains and beaver problems to boot, aquatic life can easily get misdirected at times and end up in some unlikely places. I recently went out on a beaver complaint in Cambridge Springs and, upon arriving at the distraught landowner's residence, saw two 20-inch carp swimming around in the man's tomato and cucumber patch.
-- DGP Robert L. Lumadue, Saegertown.
August 1983.

Getting Rich

CLARION COUNTY - Deputy Tom Curry has discovered a new bait for live trapping beavers. Tom places a soft drink bottle next to the pan of the set trap. The beavers move the bottle around to help block the flow of water through the trap and are captured when they trip the pan. Tom has successfully used this technique on two occasions while using no other bait or guide sticks. It has crossed our minds, however, that the beavers may only be removing the bottles to turn in for the refund deposit.
-- DGP Keith E. Harbaugh, St. Petersburg.
September 1983.

State Record Classification

LANCASTER COUNTY - I recently received a phone call from a youngster who said, "Could I have an application for a state record?" I asked him what it was for, and he replied, "I caught a 13-inch nightcrawler!"
-- Waterways Patrolman Kim Pritts.
September 1983.

Never Know

MONTGOMERY COUNTY - Working in a suburban district, I receive a great variety of phone calls. Often, someone will call and say he is having a problem with one type of wildlife, but when I get there it turns out to be something completely different. For example, there was the badger that turned out to be a groundhog, the red fox that was really a raccoon, and the eagle that was really a turkey vulture. It certainly makes things interesting to go on a call wondering what I'll really find.
-- DGP D. M. Killough, Zieglersville.
October 1983.

233

They All Ran

WAYNE COUNTY - When Deputy Dick Costa went to retrieve a live trap he noticed the door was closed, so he carefully lifted up the blanket covering the trap and discovered that it contained a skunk. Skunks being very docile animals, Dick knew there was no danger to himself or to the small crowd of bystanders who had gathered, so he picked up the blanket-covered trap and started to carry it away. Much to the surprise of the deputy and the bystanders, however, a second skunk which had evidently curled up for a nap inside the blanket, came rolling out on the ground at his feet. The second skunk merely righted itself and waddled away. When Richard turned to explain this occurrence to the audience, he found they had disappeared.

-- DGP Donald R. Schauer, Honesdale.

November 1983.

No Fish Dealings

LAWRENCE COUNTY - Unusual telephone calls quickly become routine in this job but the call I recently received was the strangest by far. It seems a local man had purchased three piranhas and fed them some smelt which were purchased at a local supermarket. The piranhas died after eating the smelt so he wanted assistance from me in recovering the cost of his fish. I was very sympathetic to his plight but, as in all fish-related calls, I had to refer him to Joe Houck, the local waterways patrolman.

-- DGP Gene W. Beaumont, New Castle.

December 1983.

Name Game

LUZERNE COUNTY - Who did a local television station in my area send to cover the opening day of trout season last year? Two guys named Gill and Finn, of course.

-- Waterways Patrolman Robert Steiner.

January 1984.

The Last Word

WAYNE COUNTY - Since game protectors sometimes find it difficult to be two or more places at the same time, we were each provided with a telephone answering device to take calls while we are in the field. These devices have enabled us to better serve the general public, but not everybody can be pleased. One recent caller was surprised when the recorder answered his call, but instead of leaving a message or a phone number so his call could be returned, he left a three-minute recording of an argument with his wife - they were discussing whether or not he should talk to the recorder.

-- DGP Donald R. Schauer, Honesdale.

February 1984.

Twenty Hours and A Couple Minutes

MCKEAN COUNTY - A grouse hunter told me that in four days of hunting grouse he had put in over twenty hard hours of walking and failed to flush even one grouse. He went on to say he was giving up on grouse and going to hunt the swamps for woodcock and ducks. At that moment, I pointed to a grouse that had just flushed and was flying across the road in front of us. As I left, the hunter quietly said something about grouse hunting for a couple more minutes.

-- DGP John Dzemyan, Smethport.

March 1984.

It's Jack Webb!

DAUPHIN COUNTY - As happens many times, a telephone caller listened to my answering machine but hung up without leaving a message. In one instance my phone rang just as I got to my office. I answered the phone, identified myself and was then told by a somewhat taken-aback woman that I wasn't the taped message she had heard just a few minutes earlier. Pleased that some people could tell the difference between the real me and the Memorex version, I asked the lady how I could help her. She said she had just called back so her son could listen to my answering machine. She thought it sounded just like "Dragnet." Maybe I should change my recorded message to one asking the caller to leave his name, telephone number and "just the facts."

-- DGP Skip Littwin, Hummelstown.

April 1984.

Industrious

This past winter, after observing a red squirrel storing pine cones in one of my feeders, I decided to see how many he would collect in a period of time if I removed them. But when I began removing the pine cones, he began to replace them with rabbit "marbles." Counting pine cones is one thing, but I have no intention of counting rabbit marbles - Field Note or not! By the way, he gathered 294 pine cones in a four-day period - and a whole bunch of rabbit "marbles."
-- LMO Barry K. Ray, Sr., Rockwood.
May 1984.

She's Right

BUTLER COUNTY - I recently received a complaint from a lady concerning skunks. I agreed to lend her a trap and asked for directions to her home. She told me how to get there, indicating her house was on the right-hand side of the road, the fifth one after a stop sign. I said I'd be coming from the opposite direction, so her house would be on the left. She said no, that I should go to the stop sign, turn around and go back, and I would then find that her house was on the right.
-- DGP Larry P. Heade, Butler.
June 1984.

Sore All Over

CENTRE COUNTY - Overheard at a recent deputy game protector self-defense training conference: "On the way home, I'm going to stop off and pick up a six-pack... of Ben-Gay!"
-- DGP George Mock, Coburn.
July 1984.

Scary Critter

FOREST COUNTY - A young lad approached me while I was checking fishermen along Spring Creek and proceeded to tell me of fishing below the swimming hole and getting a bite. When he pulled the critter in, he dropped his pole and ran like crazy. When I asked him why, he said he had caught an alligator. When I asked his father about what had happened, he - while trying to keep a straight face - explained how his 11-year-old son had caught a "waterdog."
-- DGP Alfred N. Pedder, Marienville.
August 1984.

Unique

WAYNE COUNTY - Game protector's wives tolerate a lot of inconvenience and neglect but they also receive unusual benefits. Who else could get a 500-pound bear for a Mother's Day present?
-- DGP Donald R. Schauer, Honesdale.
September 1984.

Title?

PERRY COUNTY - Like good Boy Scouts, deputy game protectors should be prepared. Over the years I have heard of officers forgetting their handguns, ammo, permit books or other items when called out at night to dispose of a deer. But how about the guy who makes two trips back to his house to pick up something he forgot, only to run out of gas and have to bum a ride home? Some nights it just doesn't pay to get out of bed. Right, Bruce?
-- DGP Leroy Everett, Newport.
October 1984.

Smelly Business

MIFFLIN COUNTY - During the July hot spell my neighboring officer, John Roller, was stopped along a roadway, picking up a roadkilled deer, which obviously had been dead for several days. Just as he was loading it on his deer rack, a youngster rode up on his bicycle and asked John if he liked being a game protector. John gave him the only logical answer at the time -"Not today kid, not today!"
-- DGP Tim Marks, Milroy.
November 1984.

Enough of That

COLUMBIA COUNTY - A peeping raccoon? I was skeptical at first, but I became a believer when Barbara Parsell of Orangeville showed me raccoon tracks leading from an opened breezeway window up onto the roof and then to a bedroom window where the raccoon apparently did his peeping. I loaned Barbara a trap and she caught the culprit the next night. His punishment - confinement to life at hard labor, gathering food on a remote section of SGL 13.
-- DGP Charles J. Arcovitch, Benton.
December 1984.

237

So There!
PERRY COUNTY - While my daughter was babysitting for the neighbor's 4-year-old, the little girl asked, "What does your daddy do?" Theresa went into a long description of the duties of a Game Protector. When she finished, the little girl gave her a wide-eyed stare and replied, "Well, my daddy works!"
-- DGP LeRoy Everett, Newport.
January 1985.

Where's the What?
While working in Union County on the first day of small game season, Waterways Patrolman Guy Bowersox apprehended two men with untagged turkeys. I arrived on the scene and, after they settled on field acknowledgements, one defendant insisted I watch him affix the tag to his turkey. After tagging the bird he asked if it was a hen or a gobbler. When I said gobbler, he looked puzzled, picked up the head, pointed under the beak and asked, "Where's the beard?" I'm still not sure I convinced him that the small tuft on the bird's chest was called a beard.
-- LMO Ken Zinn, Jersey Shore.
February 1985.

Satisfied
FAYETTE COUNTY - On the evening of the second day of buck season, I stopped in at home for about half an hour to check on phone calls and get a bite to eat. While there, my five-year-old daughter, Sheila, pulled my wife aside and asked, "Does Dad ever sleep?" Two days later I slept late *just* to satisfy her curiosity.
-- DGP Don Smith, Uniontown.
March 1985.

Continuing Ed

CENTRE COUNTY - We're continually learning something new. DGP Joe Wiker and I recently learned some new things while trying to get a bullet from a .30-06 for ballistic tests. To do this we filled a garbage can with water and then placed the can in a stream to prevent the sides of the can from blowing out. I then got on a footbridge five feet above the water and fired down into the water-filled can. From this experience Officer Wiker learned that they lied to him in the service when they told him that bullets would travel only five or six inches in water before losing all their energy - we had a neat hole in the bottom of the can to prove it. And I learned that five feet above the water is not far enough to avoid getting drenched from the splash of such a bullet.
-- DGP George Mock, Coburn.
April 1985.

Honest Mistake

GREENE COUNTY - During the past muzzleloader season, Deputy Doug Kerr noticed a "deer" hanging behind a residence. He made a routine check and then returned with a red face, mumbling something about "skinned hogs don't have to be tagged." Just for the record, Doug - we've all made the same mistake.
-- DGP Robert P. Shaffer, Carmichaels.
May 1985.

Still a Bargain

MIFFLIN COUNTY - While working at Harrisburg's Eastern Outdoor Sport Show, I was pleasantly surprised to hear many favorable comments concerning the proposed license increases. Occasionally, however, somebody would express their dissatisfaction about having to pay $15 for a year's worth of hunting. But they invariably fell silent when it was pointed out they had just paid $5 to enter the show which entitled them to walk around on concrete for a couple of hours.
-- DGP Timothy Marks, Milroy.
June 1985.

Just Like Dad

VENANGO COUNTY - Some time ago, my three-year-old daughter Amy went with me to pick up a roadkilled deer. I was surprised to find her interested in the whole operation - including our trip to the deer pit. I didn't realize just how impressed she was, however until recently. She was picking up her stuffed animals from the floor and putting them in her wagon, and her grandmother asked what she was doing. Amy replied, "Picking up roadkills."
-- DGP Len Hribar, Oil City.
July 1985.

Deputy Operators

ADAMS COUNTY - One morning a month or so ago a problem developed in the phone lines here. My line and that of an elderly lady in a local nursing home became crossed. Consequently, she began receiving my calls. Needless to say, both she and the callers were quite surprised. For about four hours that morning she received calls about rabid raccoons, sick skunks, skunks in basements, questions about the Game Law, and who knows what else. In the meantime, for a change, my phone was pleasantly quiet except for a couple of calls from her daughter who was understandably confused when I answered. I thought the arrangement worked quite well. Maybe this will lead to a new force of volunteers to assist the Game Commission.
-- DGP Larry Haynes, Gettysburg.
August 1985.

He's Not Mine!

LUZERNE COUNTY - This months Bleep, Bloop and Blunder Award goes to the police officer who volunteered to the county communications operator: "I know where Nolfie lives. I'll get him up." He did, at 2 o'clock in the morning, to report a bear eating garbage in Weatherly Borough, Carbon County!
-- DGP Robert W. Nolf, Conyngham.
September 1985.

Stuck

YORK COUNTY - In gobbler season, Dashel, a friend of mine, and I located a bird at dusk. The following morning found us in the woods by 4 o'clock. An hour's hike got us to the turkey's area. Dashel found a place to sit, and I moved about 50 yards away and lay down. The woods were abnormally dry and noisy, and during the next half-hour I couldn't understand why he hadn't started calling. Finally, the calling began, and for 20 minutes we had two birds responding. Suddenly, Dashel stood up and walked down to me, pulling at the seat of his pants the whole time. I asked what his problem was. "I thought I sat on an ant hill," he said, "only to find out later it was a dead porcupine."
-- DGP G. J. Martin, Spring Grove.
October 1985.

And the Rattles

LUZERNE COUNTY - Prior to picking up a new state vehicle in Harrisburg, I had to clean out the trunk of my old one. In it I found several items I had long considered lost - a fluorescent orange hat, a dog leash, a snare, a waterfowl I.D. book, some hand cleaner, and a deer's jawbone. Now I know what that funny smell was last summer.
-- DGP Edward J. Zindell, Wilkes-Barre.
November 1985.

Crash, Splash

I wonder when Federal Aid Supervisor Harry Richards, of the Southwest Regional Office, realized he was having one of those days. Was it when a motorist ran into the back of his state vehicle? Or was it later, when he had to hit the brakes fast and dumped a milkshake over the dash? Such occurrences would dampen anybody's day, but they were probably especially hard on Harry. He's our regional automotive officer.

-- LMO R. B. Belding, Waynesburg.

December 1985.

So There

TRAINING SCHOOL - During a recent open house here, Trainee Jim Trombetto showed his three-year-old son some damage a bear had done to a tree. After returning to the school, Jim 's son approached Supervisor Dick Furry and told him to spank that bear and tell him not to do it again.

-- Trainee Peter E Aiken.

January 1986.

What's a Few Letters?

ARMSTRONG COUNTY - A caller recently requested an application for a "perpetrator's permit." This really threw me because in law enforcement jargon, perpetrators are the guys we try to catch - and few of them call to request a permit. We finally agreed that what he wanted was a propagator's permit, which is a far more common request.

-- DGP Al Scott, Rural Valley.

February 1986.

One of the Good Times

FULTON COUNTY - I had a student officer assigned to me, and it was great. When the phone rang, he answered it. When reports were due, he did them. And when people got nasty, I referred them to him. It's too bad he had to leave so soon. Karen says I became almost human again.

-- DGP Mark Crowder, McConnellsburg.

March 1986.

Where Was Little John?

POTTER COUNTY - During the past archery season a successful archer dragged his buck to the Lewis Motel along Route 6. Mr. Lewis and the hunter started talking and the conversation led to the hunter's name, which was Robin Hood. Robin quickly produced his license as proof. Sure enough, Robin Hood killed a deer with a bow and arrow in "God's Country."

-- DGP Ron Clouser, Galeton.

April 1986.

Jaws

LANCASTER COUNTY - While investigating a report of a fish kill, I discovered that someone had dumped the remains of several saltwater fish into a stream after filleting them. It reminded me of a similar situation encountered by one of my deputies. He was a little nervous for his first pollution investigation, but as he approached the stream, he became even more disturbed. The first fish he found was a four-foot shark!
-- WCO Kim D. Pritts.
April 1986.

To Be Continued

ALLEGHENY COUNTY - Being in an urban area I've gained a lot of experience with nuisance squirrels, raccoons, rabbits, deer, skunks and groundhogs. But in December I added a new species to my nuisance list - a wild turkey. A person here was raising a couple of domestic turkeys for Thanksgiving, and a lonesome wild turkey repeatedly came into their yard and "kidnapped" the tame birds, forcing the owners to keep going out into the woods to rescue them. You're probably wondering if I was successful in capturing this nuisance turkey. Well, stay tuned for Part II, entitled "A Comedy of Errors!"
-- DGP D. E. Hockenberry, Pittsburgh.
May 1986.

Part II - A Comedy of Errors

ALLEGHENY COUNTY - In a Field Note last month I told how a wild gobbler was added to the list of nuisance wildlife I've had to deal with in this urban district. This bird was in the habit of coercing domestic turkeys into the wilds with him. My first idea was to tranquilize him. I hit the bird on my fifth shot, but the dart was apparently faulty as no drug entered the bird. My second idea was to net him, but although the net is nearly invisible, he had no trouble seeing and avoiding it. My third idea was to net him when he entered the pen of domestic birds. The next day the owners phoned to say the old boy was trapped, but by the time I arrived he had escaped under the pen. The bird was captured again the following day, after the bottom of the pen had been secured, so I finally got my hands on him. I carefully wrapped him in a blanket to keep him immobile. But as I was leaving, my bundle exploded and the gobbler flew away. Final score: turkey - 4, game protector - 0.
-- DGP Dale Hockenberry, Pittsburgh.
June 1986.

Cold Feet

BRADFORD COUNTY - Deputy Charlie Fox and I attended a weekend meeting at Milford last winter to plan our hunter education camps. The Milford facility is solar heated, and half of it is built into a bank to conserve heat. Our room was on the second floor, but a door opened to the ground level in back. In the middle of the night Charlie got up to go to the bathroom, but got the doors mixed up. He opened the outside door and stepped out into the snow. When his bare feet hit the snow... well, now I know what is meant by a "blood curdling" scream.

-- DGP William A. Bower, Troy.

June 1986.

Unique

WESTMORELAND COUNTY - I received a call from a woman who had a unique problem. She said there was a skunk with antlers in the wall of her house. Upon investigation, I found that a skunk had found a set of discarded antlers and was trying to drag them through an opening in the side of the house. I was relieved to learn it was neither an abnormal skunk nor a smelly black and white deer.

-- DGP Dennis L. Neideigh, Greensburg.

July 1986.

Well Fed

MONTGOMERY COUNTY - A woman phoned Deputy Ed Glover in March about a young groundhog wandering around. Knowing that was no time to find a young groundhog, Ed wasn't surprised to learn the animal was a full grown muskrat. But he was surprised to find it seated in front of a food tray the woman had provided. The banquet included a peanut butter and jelly sandwich, two carrots, a wedge of cabbage, and assorted broccoli and cauliflower. Ed thanked the woman for her concern and transferred the muskrat to a nearby marsh, for more traditional dining.
-- DGP D. M. Killough, Perkiomenville.
August 1986.

Plant 'Em Where?

ADAMS COUNTY - Each year I help with a Cub Scouts program called Civic Day, by sharing my activities with two scouts. This is always a lot of fun. This year the day was beautiful and I took the boys on a tour through a local Game Lands. At a pond the boys asked if they could take a few cattails home, and I let each pick two. We then headed for Gettysburg. On the way, one of the boys accidentally bumped the long, dry flower spike, and it burst open, releasing what seemed like millions of tiny seeds, each attached to a fuzzy parachute. The other boy then examined his and it popped open, too. I'm sure we looked like one big frizzy snowball rolling into town. I'm still removing them from my vehicle, my clothing, my hair and my teeth.
-- DGP L. D. Haynes, Gettysburg.
September 1986.

Honeymoon's Over

JEFFERSON COUNTY - Starting out totally unfamiliar with the Game Commission, my new bride has been coping well. Cindy has learned to put up with deer jawbones and litter (needed as evidence) in the basement, packages containing everything from songbirds to bear bait in the freezer and two fawns in the living room until they could be delivered to Penn State. She did draw the line, however, when I stopped our personal car to pick up a roadkilled coyote. She understood the need for study specimens and my willingness to help out, but she refused to travel over 80 miles with a smelly carcass in the trunk. I couldn't change her mind and ended up reporting it to a local deputy. We then drove home in silence. We were married less than a month at the time, and this was our first fight - one we will probably never forget.
-- DGP Don Chaybin, Brookville.
October 1986.

Ear Piercing

BUTLER COUNTY - Among the June Field Notes was one about a Bradford County deputy who let out a "blood curdling" scream after stepping barefoot into the snow. I feel I have a deputy who may be able to outscream him. This deputy - who shall remain nameless - was recently asked to crawl into a culvert where a beaver was hiding. I was to bag the critter when he came out. However, when the beaver looked out my end of the pipe, it turned and ran back. The deputy ended up needing ten stitches. Standing at the other end of the pipe, I immediately realized I have an Olympic-class screamer on the force. We did capture and release the beaver. I don't think it was harmed, but I did hear that 12 days later it was still holding its ears.
-- DGP Ned Weston, West Sunbury.
November 1986.

A Frog and a Bobber

FAYETTE COUNTY - A bass fisherman relayed the following information to me: One night last August, he was using a frog for bait. He had been fishing for almost an hour and hadn't gotten one hit. When he turned his flashlight on his bobber, he discovered the problem - on top of the bobber sat the frog.
-- WCO James E. Ansell.
November 1986.

Jot 'Em Down

LYCOMING COUNTY - Whenever I get to the Field Note section of my monthly report, I recall how several times during the month I said to myself, "Now that would make a good Field Note." Well here I am again, but, as usual, I'm not sure what the instances were. Maybe it was the one about the guy who wanted to know if it was possible to get rabies from a human bite because he and his wife had just had a fight and she bit him.

-- DGP Dan Marks, Proctor

January 1987.

Overworked

ADAMS COUNTY - While out on night patrol, Deputies Curt Shilling and Al Shull stepped up onto a pile of stones to get a better view. Curt was startled by a noise below him, and when he looked down his Stetson fell off and landed on a cat. The surprised cat, still under Curt's hat, bounded off into the brush. When Al turned to look, all he saw was Curt's Stetson bouncing away through the field. All Al could think was that maybe they had been out too long and should think about heading home to get some much needed sleep.

-- DGP Mike Dubaich, Aspers.

February 1987.

Naturally

CENTRE COUNTY - Despite the wide media coverage and many programs by public agencies, there's still a lot of confusion about rabies. For example, the State College police department recently received a call from a woman who, in all seriousness, wanted to know how a dead squirrel behaves if it has rabies.

-- DGP Jack Weaver, Bellefonte.

March 1987.

Love-Bang!

CRAWFORD COUNTY - I was checking waterfowl hunters when I examined a hunter's shells to make sure he was using steel shot. When I opened the box I noticed that some of the shells were missing and that there was a note inside. It said, "I love you, Honey, and don't forget, shoot a big duck." I guess it's common for wives to leave notes in lunches husbands take to work, but after seeing all the good natured ribbing this fellow endured, I'm not sure notes should be sent afield.

-- DGP Dave Myers, Linesville.

April 1987.

Dangerous Combination

SUSQUEHANNA COUNTY - A friend of mine experienced the trauma of a hunting accident last year. He heard a shot, felt something explode against his side, and yelled, "I'm hit!" When he removed his hands to see how bad the wound was, he found nothing. Then he checked his pocket and found the remains of a butane lighter, a badly mangled handwarmer case, and what was left of a chicken salad sandwich. Fortunately, only his pride was hurt. I'm sure he'll never put a cigarette lighter and a handwarmer in the same pocket again.

-- DGP Charles J. Arcovitch, Kingsley.

May 1987.

Cordless

LUZERNE COUNTY - I was presenting a program on survival to a Cub scout pack and was trying to get the audience to name items which should be carried in a survival kit. After several items were mentioned, I asked them how they would get their clothes dry if they got wet and started to display the first signs of hypothermia. One youngster, in all seriousness, responded with, "Easy - just carry a blow dryer in your pack."
-- DGP Edward J. Zindell, Wilkes-Barre.
June 1987.

The Truth's Out

MCKEAN COUNTY - A certain deputy, who will remain anonymous, had been raving about how good his year-old beagle was last rabbit season. When I paid him a visit I noticed the dog and mentioned how nice it looked. Before the deputy had a chance to reply, his young son said, "He's nice, but afraid of rabbits. The other day there were five scampering around the yard and he wouldn't come out of his box."
-- DGP Jim Rankin, Port Allegany.
July 1987.

Covering All Bases

CRAWFORD COUNTY - At dinner one evening one of my deputies told us how devoted he is to his marriage and the outdoors. He said he rewrote his fiancee's wedding vows to read,"... for better or worse, in sickness and health, and during hunting and fishing seasons...."
-- DGP David Myers, Linesville.
August 1987.

248

Ole

ALLEGHENY COUNTY - Being in an urban district, I get a lot of phone calls. Calls about raccoons are most common, but deer run a close second. The calls about deer concern roadkills, crop damage, what to feed them, how to get rid of them, how to attract them, where to hunt them, when they mate, when they lose their antlers, and on and on. But the most unusual and amusing was from a lady who called and said she was in charge of the "Dance For Mexico" show in a folk festival, and she wanted a small deer head for a dancer to wear; one that wasn't too heavy.
-- WCO Dale E. Hockenberry, Pittsburgh.
September 1987.

Mix Up

SOMERSET COUNTY - When a gentleman called last spring requesting a permit to keep a roadkilled doe, I explained that in addition to giving me the head and hide, I also needed to know the sex of each of the two fawns she had been carrying. Even though I explained how to do it, he wasn't able to. So he brought the embryos to my headquarters. After a quick glance at the "embryos" I had to agree that I wasn't able to determine the sex of the two kidneys either.
-- WCO Clifford E. Guindon, Jr., Boswell.
October 1987.

Gets Job Done

INDIANA COUNTY - Last summer I had all sorts of bear complaints and absolutely no luck at trapping the nuisance critters. While lamenting about the situation to my wife, our five-year-old daughter proudly announced that she had just trapped and tagged her teddy bear. Sure enough, there it was, hair clips in its ears, weighing an estimated 16 ounces and ready to be released. (Pulling a tooth wasn't necessary; we knew the bear's age). Now all I have to find out is what she used for bait.
-- WCO Mel Schake, Indiana.
November 1987.

High Premiums

McKEAN COUNTY - My children and the neighboring kids are accustomed to me bringing home wildlife, some dead, some alive. In fact, when I'm leaving the house it's common for one of my kids to yell, "Bring home another deer; Dad, a live one." The other day I just happened to be leaving the house to investigate a bear report when a life insurance salesman came knocking at my door. You can imagine his surprise when my 4-year-old chimed in, "Hey, Dad, bring that bear home alive."
-- WCO John Dzemyan, Smethport.
December 1987.

Go For March

WESTMORELAND COUNTY - Some folks actually do plan early. A gentleman recently asked for the opening dates of the 1989 small game seasons. He was planning his wedding date and wanted no conflicts with the hunting seasons. As he stated, "Nobody would show up, and my bride would be upset."
-- WCO Dennis L. Neideigh, Greensburg.
January 1988.

Why Not?

A certain officer revealed to me that he wears pantyhose while fishing because they make it easy to get chest waders on and off. If anybody would like more information on the subject, Chuck usually takes his coffee break in Montrose.
-- LMO Chester J. Harris, Athens.
February 1988.

Knows Better Now

WASHINGTON COUNTY - Fourteen years ago, on the opening day of the first small game season after Frank and Kibby, Eldersville, got married, Frank decided to go hunting. Kibby, coming from a nonhunting family, didn't know much about the sport and didn't want Frank to go. He went anyway and bagged a large cottontail and a quail. After Frank cleaned his game he decided to save freezer space by placing the quail inside the rabbit. Several days later Frank came home to a very distraught wife; Kibby couldn't understand how he could have been so cruel as to shoot a rabbit that was about to have a baby.
-- WCO R. Matthew Hough, Washington.
March 1988.

Quick Cleaning

PERRY COUNTY - It's impossible to please everyone. I met two hunters who were happy with the pheasants they had taken, but they complained about the feathers being too hard to remove. When I told them we were trying to breed a pheasant with a zipper, they thought that was okay, but suggested that Velcro might be better.
-- WCO Jim Brown, Loysville.
April 1988.

Nick Rosato

The Box, Too?

PHILADELPHIA COUNTY - Like all wildlife conservation officers, I take littering seriously. One morning, at 2 o'clock, I watched an individual throw pieces of pizza at a deer standing alongside a road. When he finished, he threw down the empty box and drove off. I stopped him and charged him with littering. He requested a hearing in municipal court and was issued a citation. At the hearing he pleaded not guilty. His argument was that he felt deer liked pizza. After the laughter died down, the judge found the man guilty and ordered him to pay a fine.
-- WCO Richard J. Shire, Philadelphia.
May 1988.

Bring Plenty of Salt, Buddy

VENANGO COUNTY - A while back I decided to spend my day off with my 6-year-old daughter Amy. I offered to take her anywhere she wanted, thinking she would choose a movie, shopping or some other normal place. She chose, however, the deer pit. Well, that's where I took her and a friend, fully expecting the girls to be repulsed by the sight. But, to my amazement, they were actually very interested; they even helped me salt some hides. I'm certainly glad Amy has such an interest in my job, but I can't help but wonder what's going to happen when she starts dating and a young boy asks her where she would like to go.
-- WCO Leonard Hribar, Seneca.
June 1988.

Still a Good Idea

SUSQUEHANNA COUNTY - To my fellow officers I say thanks. Since my friend, Land Manager Chet Harris, wrote a Field Note about me wearing pantyhose under my fishing waders - to make them easier to get on and off - I've heen receiving strange looks and even stranger comments from people throughout the county. Furthermore, my pantyhose wardrobe has never been more complete or colorful, thanks to contributions from many GAME NEWS readers.

-- WCO Charles J. Arcovitch, Kingsley.

July 1988.

Use With Caution

PERRY COUNTY - My wife and her parents gave me a good bit of teasing when I modeled a pair of camouflage coveralls designed to look like tree bark, but my father-in-law did give me some good advice. "You look so much like a tree," he said, "that you better not stand still when any dogs are around."

-- WCO Jim Brown, Loysville.

August 1988.

Once Over

SOMERSET COUNTY - I must have slept in an awkward position because my back hurt, and traversing the mountain roads on the opening of small game season didn't help. While patrolling I encountered Doc Ridinger and his hunting companion, who stands well over six feet and weighs nearly 270 pounds. While we were talking I mentioned to Doc, who's a retired chiropractor, about my back. Doc said he'd be glad to help. He lowered the tailgate on his pickup and asked me to lie down - remember, I was in full uniform. So I was lying there, Doc was working over my back, the big guy was looking on, and a car full of people came by. I don't know what the occupants thought, whether I was getting what I "deserved," or whether the big guy was just too much to tangle with. Who knows? The car just slowed down momentarily and then sped away. Anyway, my back was much better and I finished the day in comfort.
-- WCO Daniel W. Jenkins, Somerset.
September 1988.

Well, It's Like This

BRADFORD COUNTY - There's a story going around about a lady who has a dog and her neighbor who has a pet rabbit. One day the dog's owner came home and found the dog in her yard along with the neighbor's rabbit, but the rabbit was dead. Terribly upset, the lady didn't know what to do. She took it in her house, washed and combed it, and then dried it with a hair dryer. Then she took it to her neighbor's and put it back in its pen, before the neighbor got home from work, fully expecting to tell her about it the next day. Later that evening, however, she noticed her neighbors outside, looking in the rabbit pen. She went over and very casually asked what was wrong. Her friend turned to her, with a very puzzled look on her face, and said they were trying to figure out how the rabbit got back in its cage because they had buried it the day before.
-- WCO Edward N. Gallew, Wyalusing.
October 1988.

Welcome Home

TRAINING SCHOOL - I was fortunate to have my wife's wholehearted support during my ten years as a deputy wildlife conservation officer, and such is still the case. I forgot, however, before reporting to the training school last June, to tell her to refer all Game Commission related calls to the new 800 number. Consequently, when I returned home after my first week, there was a surprise waiting for me. My truck was parked as far away from the house as possible, and it didn't take me long to discover why. My wife Diane had picked up a roadkill during the beginning of the week, and it was still on my deer rack. It's no wonder the neighbors were so glad to see me come home.
-- Trainee Douglas C. Carney.
November 1988.

Procrastinator

MCKEAN COUNTY - I received a report last July about a roadkilled deer at the end of a person's driveway. When I went to pick it up I couldn't find it, though, so I went up to the house to find out just where it was. The lady who answered the door said, "How could you miss it? It's been down at the end of my driveway since last December." Sure enough, under all the summer weeds, were a backbone, ribcage, a couple of leg bones and a patch of hide.
-- WCO John Dzemyan, Smethport.
December 1988.

What He Expected

CENTRE COUNTY - Don Cameron, State College, was having a woodchuck problem. One was in the habit of chewing the spark plug wires on Don's pickup. After getting a box trap he tried all the normal woodchuck fare - lettuce and carrots, for example - but he had no luck. Finally, in frustration, he threw in - you guessed it - several spark plug wires, and promptly caught the critter the next day.
-- WCO Jack Weaver, Bellefonte.
January 1989.

Valuable Learning Experience

TRAINING SCHOOL - I was on field assignment in northern Dauphin County when WCO Scott Bills took me to a farm to show me a barn owl. He told me to watch for the owl while he walked toward the silo. As Scott got close the beautiful bird flew out, just as he had predicted. Scott then called me over and said two more were inside. I peeked in the silo - at his suggestion - and was immediately "baptized" with owl droppings.
-- Trainee Donald R. Burchell.
February 1989.

Fast Learner
My neighbor, Bob Byers, has a lane about a half mile long up to his dairy farm. One evening his brother Tom was spotlighting deer along the lane when he saw a small buck. The deer began running across a pasture, but when it tried to jump a fence, its antlers got caught in the wire and it did a complete somersault. Bob saw the deer several times afterward and marveled at how it crossed the fence. Bob says the deer would make a couple false starts, take a running leap and clear the fence by about six feet, run a few yards, and then stop and look back at the fence as if to make sure he had cleared it.
-- LMO Jim Bowers, Knox.
March 1989.

Patient
JEFFERSON COUNTY - Deputies Gene DeFoor and Randy Coleman were patrolling in deer season when they noticed an elderly hunter holding onto a tree beside the road. When they stopped and asked him if everything was okay, the man said he was just waiting for his buddy to catch up. The deputies could see pretty far down the road and nobody was in sight, but the gentleman insisted that his friend would be along. "He's 80 years old now, and can't keep up with me. I'm only 78."
-- WCO Donald C. Chayhin, Brookville.
April 1989.

Ouch!
A small game hunter I encountered last November 26 was taking full advantage of the unusual warm spell. Along with his boots, gun, hunting coat and fluorescent orange hat, he was kicking through the brush, wearing a pair of Bermuda shorts.
-- LMO Barry S. Zaffuto, Ebensburg.
May 1989.

Super Jack
CENTRE COUNTY - After spending two hours above the suspended ceiling at the Bellefonte BiLo Store, working around duct work, pipes and I-beams, trying to capture a sharp-shinned hawk, I started to wonder when I'm going to be issued a cape.
-- WCO Jack Weaver, Bellefonte.
June 1989.

Missed the Point

My brother, Ralph Ray, and his friends Don Himler and Chuck Moffit, all of Latrobe, went hunting during the flintlock season. Chuck wounded a doe, but there was no snow, so the only trail was occasional drops of blood on leaves. Chuck, not being much of a tracker, left the trailing job to Ralph and Don. Chuck's job was to follow along and stay with the most recently found blood stain. After proceeding for a short way, Ralph turned and found Chuck just two steps behind. When asked what he was doing, Chuck replied, "You told me not to lose the trail and I didn't. I picked up the leaves with blood on them and have them all right here." Well, Chuck didn't lose the trail; in fact, he probably still has it.
-- LMO Barry K. Ray, Sr., Rockwood.
July 1989.

Easter Treats

CARBON COUNTY - Deputy John Skerchock investigated an incident in which a bear had lumbered on to the back porch of a Nesquehoning resident on Easter Eve, carefully removed the lid on a canister full of several dozen freshly made chocolate eggs, and then proceeded to eat every last one, right in front of the dismayed resident who had planned on giving them to her children the next morning. If there's any saving grace, the bear hasn't been seen since, possibly because of an upset stomach.
-- WCO Richard E. Karper, Weatherly.
August 1989.

Gaining Experience

LACKAWANNA COUNTY - While investigating the killing of a protected bird (a turkey vulture), the need to produce the carcass as evidence found me dangling upside down through the seat in an outhouse. Suspended in this most resourceful hiding place, I couldn't help but recall the words of my mentors during my recent course of instruction at the training school. Many new and unique experiences awaited us, they said. Little did I realize what they meant by perils of the job. Oh well, I guess it's all in a day's work for a wildlife conservation officer.
-- WCO Keith P. Snyder, Clarks Summit.
September 1989.

Convenient

I recently went with a friend of mine to look at a piece of property he was considering buying. With both of us interested in wildlife, we were glad to see plenty of animal sign on the property. Before we left we decided to inspect the old house. Upon entering we heard a loud noise in the kitchen and then discovered that a deer had just left through the back door. Like I told my friend, "You won't find deer hunting any closer to home than that."
-- LMO James Denniker, Sandy Lake.
October 1989.

Or Butter

I was attending a Project Wild Facilitators Workshop at Crooked Creek Environmental Learning Center when a teacher related to me an experience she had had while teaching one of the lessons. She was discussing animal coverings - feathers and fur, for example - and asked the group what fish are covered with. Immediately somebody replied, "bread crumbs"
-- IES Barry Moore, Saltsburg.
November 1989.

Hung Over

Pest control agent Walt Savitz, Northampton County, received a call at 5:15 one morning from a homeowner who had a sick raccoon on his porch. Walt was there in minutes, only to learn that the homeowners had hosted a large lawn party that evening, and that many half-filled glasses of wine and beer had been left scattered about. Well, the booze was all gone at this point, and Walt knew exactly where it had gone. Walt slipped a noose around the raccoon's neck without a struggle, and the animal politely walked along to the cage, got inside, and fell fast asleep - on its back with all four legs pointing straight up. As Walt tells the story, the poor raccoon had a hard time just lifting its head even after several hours sleep. The next day, when the callers asked what they owed him for his troubles, Walt replied, "Forget it. The laugh was worth the trip."
-- IES Mike Schmit, Southeast Region Office.
December 1989.

Bad Example

BEAVER COUNTY - After investigating a complaint about a beaver flooding a person's yard, I decided to remove the dam in hopes the beaver would move on. When I returned to do so I took along my golden retriever Max for some companionship. After breaking apart the dam a movement in the water caught my eye. It was the beaver, swimming towards the dam, carrying a large branch in its mouth. And following right behind was Max, also with a branch in his mouth. Believe me, that's the last time Max is going to help with any beaver problems.
-- WCO K. A. Falasco, Beaver Falls.
January 1990.

Tracking Expertise

ERIE COUNTY - One snowy, mid-December evening around 10:00 p.m., DWCO Russ Fisher came to my house and said that Trout Run had just been hit by poachers and that it may be a good idea to check out the tracks before the forecast snowstorm arrived that night. By flashlight I surveyed a familiar scene: blood-covered snow, a discarded beer can, and a drag trail made by a large quantity of recently bludgeoned trout. I continued on to the poacher's point of escape, approximately 300 yards downstream from where it began, and waited for Russ to retrieve our vehicle.

On his return I told him that it was a good thing that he came and got me since my "expertise" in tracking enabled me to ascertain that this suspect was 5-feet, 8-inches tall, 160 pounds, had hazel eyes and blond hair. While he was puzzling over this information, I went on to tell him the suspect's name and address. With a grin, I then showed him the blood-stained fishing license that had been knocked off while loading the getaway vehicle. We told the suspect that one of the fish had informed us of his involvement, at which point he confessed his violations. We were sure that the license was knocked off by a trout in a final act of defiance.
-- WCO John W. Bowser.
February 1990.

Expensive Banding

BUTLER COUNTY - The cost of raising and stocking pheasants fluctuates somewhat, depending on feed costs and weather, for example, but normally comes to about $10 per bird ultimately harvested by a hunter. One particular bird stocked by Deputy Harold Kennedy, however, ended up costing considerably more. It seems that as Harold was holding up a bird for release, it got its foot caught on Harold's wedding band and pulled it off when it flew away.
-- WCO D. E. Hockenberry, East Butler.
February 1990.

Taking No Chances

POTTER COUNTY - One day a while back a foreman left a new Food and Cover Corps employee alone to pick up stones from a food plot. When he returned the new Corps member was nowhere in sight. As the foreman stood there, looking around, an apple fell on his truck. He looked up and there, perched high up in the apple tree, was the missing man. He said that when he went to a hedgerow and threw in a load of stones he happened to hit a bear. The bruin let out a loud woof, sending the man scurrying for the nearest tree.

-- WCO Ronald C. Clouser, Galeton.

March 1990.

Good Decoys

MIFFLIN COUNTY - I recently heard from my brother about a fellow named Kenny who regularly goes to his camp near Pymatuning. Kenny also has a pontoon boat up there and, like many people, he enjoys riding around the lake and feeding the ducks. Late last fall he took some friends along, for one last boat ride of the year. Armed with several loaves of bread, Kenny located a flock, carefully maneuvered into position, and then they proceeded to throw pieces of bread toward the ducks. Surprisingly they got no response. That is until after about 20 minutes a hunter finally stood up and yelled for Kenny to get away from his decoys.

-- WCO T. A. Marks, Milroy

April 1990.

Chewy

BEDFORD COUNTY - While on night patrol, Deputies George Conner and Clyde Spade were eating their snacks, and each began complaining about his wife's cooking. They chewed and chewed and complained and complained until George finally turned on the interior light. Clyde had somehow gotten the end of his tie in his sandwich, and George was chewing on the chin strap of his Stetson. Honest, guys, I won't tell your wives.
--WCO D.B. Koppenhaver, Everett.
May 1990.

Just Hopping By

LYCOMING COUNTY - For years wildlife conservation officers received some very unusual phone calls. Now, with the 800 numbers in place, our regional operators are getting the strange reports. Recently, at the start of his shift, operator Ken Krah received a call from a person who said he had just seen a kangaroo hopping along Route 44 near a local tavern. Ken's comment summed it up, "What a way to start the day."
-- WCO R.L. Stout, Jersey Shore.
July 1990.

Better Safe Than Sorry

BRADFORD COUNTY - One evening about 11 p.m. I received a call about a roadkilled bear. The caller said the bear was in the middle of the road where it could easily cause an accident. When I arrived all I found was clothing strewed all over the highway and, in the middle of the road, a big teddy bear. Figuring I was bearing the brunt of a bad practical joke, I immediately set about to make the last laugh mine; it's illegal to give false information to an officer. I picked up the teddy bear and then telephoned the caller as soon as I got home. In talking to the man, who was very sincere, it became apparent that what he had seen was the black bag, which he thought was a bear. By the time I arrived, somebody had hit the bag, spreading the clothes and teddy bear that were inside all along the road.
-- WCO William A. Bower, Troy.
August 1990.

Not Normally

CLEARFIELD COUNTY - I was presenting a program about my job to Cub Scout Pack 21, DuBois, and was showing the youngsters some of my equipment. I held up a potato rake I use to remove nuisance beaver dams, and asked them to guess what I used it for. After several incorrect answers, one scout blurted out, "You use it to grab onto car bumpers when bad guys try to drive away from you."
--WCO Colleen M. Shannon, Luthersburg.
September 1990.

Wise Quacks

BERKS COUNTY - I was at the Blandon Senior Citizens Center, discussing the roadkilled deer problem and the need to reduce the deer herd, when one gentleman jokingly suggested that we also should reduce the mallard population. He said he had just hit a mallard with his car and that it caused $70 in damages. Then, adding insult to injuries, the feathered critter uttered a few wise quacks about the man's driving ability as it waddled away.
-- WCO Alan C. Scott, Cressona.
October 1990.

Vivid Imaginations

CAMBRIA COUNTY - My two sons, Steven, 6, and Scott, 4, have always been interested in nuisance bears I've brought home, and they're quite familiar with how I tranquilize a bear and then weigh, tag and tattoo it and remove a tooth for aging. So when I returned home one day last summer I shouldn't have been surprised to find that the boys had hooked their wagon up to their electric Big Wheels, and that on the wagon was my portable kennel. Inside the kennel was Snoopy, the boys' new beagle pup. Next to the Big Wheels was their doctor's bag, a tool box, and a rope for weighing Snoopy. The boys also had a toy syringe taped to a toy broom handle, and they were carefully trying to tranquilize Snoopy. Needless to say, Snoopy was glad to see me, especially because I arrived before the boys got around to weighing him or pulling his tooth.
-- WCO Douglas C. Carney, Johnstown.
November 1990.

Just Kidding

MIFFLIN COUNTY - Deputy Dick Grassmyer's wife, Carole, developed a great "attention getter" for our display at the county 4-H fair. It was a box about a foot high, with a wire mesh cover, and a sign that read, "Caution, Baby Rattler." Just about everybody peeked in, hoping to see a baby snake, but were amused to find a toy rattle for infants.
-- WCO T.A. Marks, Milroy.
December 1990.

261

Aloha, Pig

ADAMS COUNTY - I just can't seem to get away from roadkilled animals, especially deer which are a continual problem in the Gettysburg area. My deputies and I have dealt with thousands of them. On a recent trip to Hawaii, one of the first things I saw was - wouldn't you know it - a roadkill. While driving between two large volcanoes, my wife and I came upon a roadkilled wild pig. It felt good to pass by without feeling responsible for picking it up.
--WCO L.D. Haynes, Gettysburg.
January 1991.

And Then...

CLINTON COUNTY - New methods of controlling nuisance animals are always welcome. When a feral rooster wandered into my neighborhood, it decided to take up residence in a spruce near my house. Every morning about four o'clock it began crowing, and after a week of little sleep I was getting desperate. Then I got a call from a Westport resident who'd caught a bobcat in his box trap. Seems the cat had been killing his chickens...
-- WCO John Wasserman, Renovo.
February 1991.

No, Sir

During small game season, some hunters found a license and gave it to me, and I returned it to the owner. The owner was 87 years old, and during our conversation I asked him how long he was going to continue to hunt. "Why?" he asked. "Is there an age limit?"
-- FAS P. A. Hilbert, Cleona.
March 1991

262

No Charge, Either

Lots of folks don't appreciate the diverse abilities possessed by members of our deputy force. A pet turkey owned by Ted and Vickie Garfield, Farm-Game cooperators in Venango County, had dislocated his neck and was in great pain. The Garfields called a veterinarian, but he was unable to help. Not willing to give up, daughter Rebecca called Deputy James Lowros, a chiropractor. Dr. Lowros went to the farm and manipulated the turkey's neck. Within two days the bird was eating, gobbling and doing fine.
-- Special Operations Division Chief John A. Shutter, Jr.
April 1991.

Ho, Ho, Ho

CLEARFIELD COUNTY - On the last day of buck season, Deputy Russ Bell and I went to interview a suspect at his place of employment - Clearfield Mall. We waited to question him until his shift ended, and when we met him after work he was still dressed in his work clothes - a Santa outfit. No wonder I got only coal in my stocking this year.
-- WCO Colleen M. Shannon, Luthersburg.
May 1991.

On A Silver Platter

"If arrests ever came any easier" I told a group of fellow officers, "violators would he running up to my vehicle, asking to be arrested." That very night, while assisting WCO Doug Carney, I was investigating a report of shots being fired. I had stopped along the road to read the name on a mailbox when a man jumped inside my vehicle. It's impossible to describe the expression on his face when he saw my uniform. It seems the individual had been dropped off by his buddies to look for a deer they had shot at earlier that evening, and I had just happened to stop at their prearranged pickup point - where the suspect mistook me for his ride. His partners, likewise, were surprised when they arrived to retrieve their friend.
-- LMO Barry S. Zaffuto, Ebensburg.
June 1991.

Water Sports

CHESTER COUNTY - Early spring turned out to be a wet one for me. First, water poured over top of my waders as I tore out a beaver dam that was flooding a farmer's field. Next, while investigating river otter sightings on a local stream, my canoe got caught in some rocks and began taking on water; I ended up standing in five feet of 40-degree water. Then, trying to rescue an injured snow goose on Octoraro Lake, I decided to just wade right in and retrieve it. A WCO takes on many personas through the year, but I never knew that one of them was a fish.
-- WCO William C. Ragosta, Nottingham.
July 1991.

Lesson Learned

A proud grandfather told me about taking his grandson for a walk near his camp up in northcentral Pennsylvania. First they found a shed antler, and then grandfather pointed out an old buck rub. They continued their walk, and when they returned to the buck rub, the grandson backed against the tree and rubbed up and down. "What are you doing," the grandfather asked. "I'm rubbing my butt," the boy replied. "I said buck rub, not butt rub," the grandfather said, and then with the antler showed the boy how a buck rub is made.
-- Federal Aid Supervisor P. A. Hilbert, Cleona.
August 1991.

Left Holding the Bag

BRADFORD COUNTY - My deputies and I have dedicated a percentage of our law enforcement program to the apprehension of litterbugs. One of my deputies recently came across some garbage bags along Route 220. He couldn't find any usable evidence in the first bag and went through the rest without turning up any clues. Feeling disgruntled, he left - only to find more bags down the road. He enthusiastically sifted the bags for evidence. I wish I'd been there when he finally realized they were placed there on purpose by members of the Adopt-A-Highway program.
-- WCO Richard P. Larnerd, Warren Center.
September 1991.

Neat Trick

CHESTER COUNTY - You know you're bound to have a bad day serving arrest warrants when your own deputy arrives at your door, locked in his own handcuffs. I shouldn't mention names, to avoid embarrassment, but how did you get here, Jimmy?
-- WCO William C. Ragosta, Nottingham.
October 1991.

Bird's Eye View

LAWRENCE COUNTY - A young New Castle man got the opportunity to view wildlife from a slightly different perspective. While he was playing in his backyard, a screech owl alighted on the brim of his baseball cap. The owl abruptly lost its balance and hung upside down - right in front of the boy's face. I don't know which of the two was more surprised, but I imagine the owl got the ride of its life.
-- WCO Gene W. Beaumont, New Castle.
November 1991.

Bemoaning Bazooka

LANCASTER COUNTY - While on boat patrol on the Susquehanna River in the vicinity of the PP&L Brunner Island Power Plant, I noticed a 10-foot rowboat within 100 feet of an intake tower. Two huge signs caution boaters from approaching within 200 feet of the towers. When I approached the boat, I noticed that the operator was the same man who I arrested two years ago for the same violation in the same area. It is illegal to boat within 100 feet of water siphons or intake towers. I explained the dangers and risks involved, because not only was this man boating in a prohibited area, but his boat was anchored, too. After settling on a field acknowledgement, the man told me that 10 minutes before I arrived, he had opened up a piece of Bazooka bubblegum. He showed me the comic strip that was enclosed in the wrapper. It read: "If you don't play by the rules, don't complain when you lose!"
-- DWCO Dave Eichler.
November 1991.

Showing Him the Ropes

BRADFORD COUNTY - I was working with fellow officer Bill Bower when we made a vehicle stop. The driver paid no attention to the flashing red light, so Bill decided a short siren blast was in order. Imagine his surprise when he couldn't remember how to turn off the siren. He nearly kicked a hole in the floorboards as he pounded at the foot switch - which only turned the siren to an air horn. For some reason he began landing open-handed blows on the radio, and at that point the siren changed modes again - completely confusing him. Although doubled over with laughter; I managed to silence the device for him. It wouldn't have been so bad, except the incident occurred in downtown Towanda at noon. I'm sure this is one story you won't read in Bill's book.
-- WCO Richard P. Larnerd, Warren Center.
December 1991.

At Your Service

CLEARFIELD COUNTY - While teaching the game law portion of a hunter-ed class, I asked the students, "What should you do if you forget to take a pencil to complete your deer tag?" One student responded, "Call the game warden and ask him to bring one to you." I hope cellular phones don't become popular with hunters.
-- WCO Colleen Shannon, Luthersburg.
January 1992.

Having A Bad Day

An Orwigsburg resident had a full day on the opening of duck season. In heavy fog he paddled onto the Landingville dam and shot his limit. Then he capsized his canoe, losing his shotgun and birds in the process. He asked his rescuers if they could find his gun and ducks, which turned out to be a mistake. By the time I got there they were pulling his sunken craft from the water. I informed the soaked and shivering hunter that two of his ducks were illegal; one was a grebe - a protected species - and the other was a brant, which wasn't in season.
-- LMO Stephen L. Opet, Tamaqua.
February 1992.

Now They Know

DAUPHIN COUNTY - The employees of Metal Industries, Elizabethville, now have a good idea what it's like to handle decaying roadkilled deer. One of my deputies inadvertently parked his pickup, with a long-dead roadkill in the back, next to the firm's air intake fans.
-- WCO Scott R. Bills, Halifax.
March 1992.

No, I Wrestled It

Among other questions we ask hunters at the Trout Run bear check station is whether or not they were hunting as a group or out of a camp. In one instance, Ken Hess, director of the Bureau of Administration, was overheard asking, "Did you get that bear with a club?" The hunter, obviously astonished, replied, "Why no, sir. I shot it with my rifle."
-- I&E Director Lantz Hoffman, Harrisburg.
April 1992

Hold On, Sir

GREENE COUNTY - Last hunting season Trainee Bradley Myers was driving my state vehicle. As we zipped along on narrow, twisting and gravelly county roads, I checked my seat belt, braced my feet firmly against the firewall and gripped the door and dash so tight it's a wonder they didn't break. "Don't worry," Myers said. "I had a defensive precision driving class." I just wondered if the plastic cones used on the course were anything like the maple and cherry trees flashing by my window.
-- WCO R. S. Ansell, Rogersville.
May 1992.

Might Work

BEDFORD COUNTY - Farm-Game Manager Terry Hoenstine was talking to a cooperator when the man asked if the Commission had any signs that read "jump." Terry, of course, asked why he wanted such a sign. The landowner said he figured if he posted "jump" signs around his fence, the deer would jump over the fence instead of going through it.
-- WCO R. Jim Trombetto, New Enterprise.
June 1992.

From Outer Space

BEDFORD COUNTY - Last spring I read a local newspaper article concerning UFO sightings in the state. People reported finding mutilated white-tailed deer and cited this as evidence of extraterrestrial visitors. They found deer that had been "eviscerated and the lower jawbone neatly removed." I have an explanation. Each spring WCOs collect embryo data from roadkills, and they remove jawbones to age the animals. The information is necessary for the agency's deer management program. And, yes, the carcasses are eviscerated and jawbones removed by little green men and women.
-- WCO R. Jim Trombetto, New Enterprise.
July 1992.

But Hard To Carry Off

SUSQUEHANNA COUNTY - Dale Black of Hop Bottom learned an unexpected lesson about predator/prey relationships while spring gobbler hunting. He set up and began to call. Within seconds he heard flapping wings near his head and felt a rap on his skull. It seems a small hawk, drawn by the call and the movement, thought Dale might make a good meal.
-- WCO Chuck Arcovitch, Kingsley.
August 1992.

Fair Is Fair

POTTER COUNTY - As many times as I've come home soaking wet after a day of hunting, fishing, trapping or tearing out beaver dams and other such work, I've never gotten any sympathy from my wife. She figures I get what I deserve. So I don't understand why she's still upset with me for grabbing the video camera when she fell into an icy cold mountain stream. I guess she thought my first reaction would be to help her.
-- WCO W.C. Ragosta, Coudersport.
September 1992.

Uh Oh

BRADFORD COUNTY - While presenting a program on bird life to a woman's group, I began the lecture by imitating a great horned owl. Someone answered from the back of the room. I asked who'd done it, and a woman in the back raised her hand. "You're in trouble," I said. "I just gave the mating call and you answered." That broke up the group for about five minutes, after which 1 was able to continue my program.
-- WCO William Bower, Troy.
October 1992.

That's *Mr.* Crockett to You

MCKEAN COUNTY - A downstate fellow I know has been hunting here for years and has developed some admirable skills. Still, I'll always remember how one time he thought his dad said turkey tracks make little arrow shapes that point in the direction they're headed. Dad meant the opposite, of course. Of all the good stories I've heard over the years, few top the tale of how my friend and his partner backtracked turkeys for miles and miles in the snow.
-- WCO John P. Dzemyan, Smethport.
November 1992.

Hand 'Em Over

LUZERNE COUNTY - I was giving a bear program to a second grade class, telling them about the bear's natural history and habitat requirements. When I began to explain how bears can sometimes be costly to farmers and beekeepers, one student raised his hand. "I know," he said. "They take their wallets."
-- WCO Edward J. Zindell, Wilkes-Barre.
December 1992.

Could've Sworn It Was

LYCOMING COUNTY - Food & Cover employee Philip Landon and I sat quietly along the road, watching cars pass uncaringly by while 100 or so crated ringnecks in the back shuffled in their cages. After what seemed like hours, Phil finally said, "Guess we better call someone." "Yes," I said. "Are you sure the tank was full when you left this morning?"
-- WCO Terry D. Wills, Williamsport.
January 1993.

Take a Vacation

MONROE COUNTY - I realize my deputies squeeze as many hours as they can into conservation work. But when their report on a bear complaint reads that a sow and three cubs were playing on a swingset; one cub sitting on a swing and swatting at the sibling that was trying to push it, I think I'll have to order them to take a few days off.
-- WCO Thomas M. Smith, Bartonsville.
February 1993.

Help Wanted

NORTHUMBERLAND COUNTY - While patrolling during antlerless season, I saw a man dressed in full orange, a rifle slung over his shoulder, raking leaves on his front lawn. I stopped to talk to him, and he said he always sees deer while doing yard work. His wife wanted him to finish the yard before he went hunting so he decided to be prepared. Later that day 1 saw a deer hanging from an oak in his yard; the time on the tag indicated the man shot it shortly after I left. I'll bet if he advertises that job next season, he'll get a lot of takers.
-- WCO James M. Kazakavage, Sunbury.
March 1993.

269

Just One Favor

ELK COUNTY - We were working a deer decoy to catch roadhunters when one guy shot and knocked over the decoy. As we cited him, he asked the deputies if he could keep the deer. They explained that the decoy wasn't real, but the man still had one more request. Before he walked to his car to explain to his wife that he'd shot a decoy, he asked the deputies if they'd come to his rescue when she began beating on him.
-- WCO Dick Bodenhorn, Ridgway.
April 1993.

Dreaming of Horses

PHILADELPHIA COUNTY - Philadelphia police rely on me and my deputies to dispatch injured deer because department policy prohibits them from doing it. When a horse was hit by a car in the early morning hours, the police dispatcher called Deputy Stephen Landis, waking him from a sound sleep. Steve told the dispatcher the Commission doesn't handle domestic animals and went back to sleep. Later that morning, Steve began to wonder if he'd dreamed the whole incident, but a call to the police confirmed he hadn't.
-- WCO Richard J. Shire, Philadelphia.
May 1993.

File and Forget?

BEDFORD COUNTY - During hunting seasons, field work takes precedence over office duties. After an overdue office clean up session, I found a training school handout titled "Comprehensive Filing System for WCOs." I knew it was around here somewhere.
-- WCO Len Groshek, Everett.
June 1993.

Dead On

ALLEGHENY COUNTY - When I talk to Scout groups I usually take along several animal pelts. I use them while explaining how the animals live and where they can be found locally. The talk is usually followed by a question-and-answer sescion. At one of these, when I asked what all the animals had in common, one Scout quickly replied "They're dead."

-- WCO Richard T. Cramer, White Oak.
July 1993.

Ghostly Apparition

SCHUYLKILL COUNTY - Hearing a commotion outside his home late one night, Tom McGovern of Branch Township went to investigate. He could hardly believe his eyes when he saw what looked like a ghost running across the yard. The white object went up a tree and immediately fell back to the ground and lay motionless. Tom went over and found the "ghost" to be a white garbage bag filled with trash - and a frightened black bear perched above him in the tree.

-- WCO Stephen S. Hower, Pine Grove.
August 1993.

Norm!

ADAMS COUNTY - A male rubythroated hummingbird has been visiting my parents' feeder, and it's amazing how much he can drink. Once he was so full he nearly fell backwards off his perch. He's certainly the fattest hummingbird I've ever seen, and it wasn't hard to name him after the *Cheers* character.

-- WCO Larry Haynes, Gettysburg.
September 1993.

271

Eyeballing a Nap

TRAINING SCHOOL - After a long day of visiting taxidermists and other special permittees, we returned for our evening class. Halfway through, a classmate leaned over and asked if 1 had picked up any glass eyes during the day. I asked what he'd want with them, and he said he was having trouble staying awake. He wanted to stick them behind his glasses so he could take a nap.
-- Trainee Jeffrey G. Mock, Harrisburg.
October 1993.

How Dare She

I've been thinking a lot lately about my 34 years with the agency, reflecting on how things have changed mostly for the good. For instance, back in the "good old days" - before my phone number was unlisted - the telephone would ring off the hook night and day. In my second year on the job, my wife went to see her parents for a while, and I told a supervisor I could spend more time in the field while she was out. He promptly told me she shouldn't be visiting like that because there would be no one at home to answer the phone.
-- LMO Robert K. Muir, Kittanning.
November 1993.

At Least They Weren't Ticking

LYCOMING COUNTY - One day last fall I got a call about an animal trapped in a window well. I arrived to find not one but five skunks caught deep in the bowels of an old celler window well. After nearly half an hour of painstakingly careful work, I had all five out and loaded into my vehicle. In the process I learned to respect the guys who dismantle bombs for a living.
-- WCO Terry D. Wills, Williamsport.
December 1993.